Cox's Rural Rides

36 tours in the south-east

Tim Cox

TWO WHEELS

First published in 1994 by

Two Wheels - an imprint of
Two Heads Publishing
12A Franklyn Suite
The Priory
Haywards Heath
West Sussex
RH16 3LB

A catalogue record for this book is available from the
British Library.

Every effort has been made to ensure the accuracy of
information in this book. Details such as Rights of Way,
tracks, roads, places to see and refreshment stops may
be subject to change and the authors and publishers
cannot accept liability for any errors or omissions.

ISBN   1-898933-05-7

Cover Design by David Spencer.
Maps by Patrick Lee.
Photographs by Tim Cox.
Printed & bound by Caldra House Ltd., Hove, Sussex.

PREFACE

In the 1820's William Cobbett traversed large tracts of England on horseback. He had been a farmer, was a social reformer, and was passionately interested in the land. He saw not only the crops but the abject poverty amongst those bound up in agriculture. He wrote about where he had been, what he had seen, and eventually this was published as 'Rural Rides'.

Perhaps adopting more or less the same title for this book might seem a little pretentious since this is a guide book and not a commentary on agriculture or the social plight of country folk. However, in so many of the places I visited, Cobbett had been there before. His name was constantly appearing as my researches progressed. Another similarity is that we both wanted to delve into the depths of the countryside. Cobbett wished to avoid the Turnpike Roads, which could be likened to the motorways of the time and in my own rides I sought the small twisting narrow lanes. He used horseback, ideally suited to the obscure ways he found. I rode my bicycle to journey round the small roads, the old roads - the 'Rural Rides'.

I have lived in the London area for over 20 years but am a country person at heart having moved up from rural Devon. My knowledge of the south-east before then was largely based on preconceptions, largely derived from the Shell county posters that decorated the walls of my Junior School classrooms. So I saw the wooded hills of Surrey, the oast houses of Kent, the South Downs of Sussex in these colourful collages.

Already a keen cyclist, my first outings in the area were with my local Cyclists Touring Club section. There can be no better way of getting to know an area. I got to know more from Youth Hostel weekends, train-assisted rides, and excursions into the country to satisfy my natural curiosity about places. This book is a compilation of what I consider to be the best with a few new helpings added here and there, laced with history and, perhaps, a small dose of William Cobbett.

Contrary to widely held views, outstanding countryside can still be found in the South East. From the Hampshire Downs, the White Cliffs of Dover, the Thames Valley, the Weald of Kent and Sussex. Woodlands, downland, coast - an enormous variety. See it in spring when the blossom appears in the Kent orchards and the woods awash in seas of bluebells; in the rich green foliage of summer, the time of droning bees and fluttering butterflies; in autumn awash with gold; and in winter landscapes held together by the bare bones of the trees.

Through exploring and writing about cycling in the country I want to encourage people to visit it to appreciate what is still there. Not in the car but by bicycle. To learn the art of travelling slowly down the little roads, to see what is there, and appreciate what has been. To know how vital it is to preserve our heritage from the strangulation of future demands. William Blake wrote 'Jerusalem' from Glastonbury Tor as a hymn against what he saw going on around him at the time. Would he have done the same gazing down upon the Channel Tunnel workings from the North Downs above Newington - 'And did those feet in ancient time. . . ?'

INTRODUCTION

The Rural Rides

This book is one of ideas of where to cycle. Routes are arranged mostly in clusters and can be linked together or ridden individually, either in part or whole. Grouped together they form a comprehensive cycling guide to some of the best scenery the south-east has to offer.

The majority of the rides start and finish at the same place, a railway station, easy to find on the map and accessible to those with or without cars. There are four linear routes leading from the south coast ferry terminals (and the Channel Tunnel) to the outskirts of London. The rides concentrate on scenic alternatives to main roads.

Each ride is described in three sections. The introduction is the appetiser to give the route a flavour along with essential information such as the maps needed, start point, distance, train access, places to see and refreshment stops. Then follows the sketch map to give the shape and prominent features of the ride. Lastly there is the ride description itself. The left hand column is the distance in miles from the start. This is followed by detailed instructions of the route to take. The ride directions are interspersed with details of places to see, where to stop and fascinating local history. If you want to concentrate solely on the route itself, it is easy to skip the narrative and just follow the directions.

I have ridden every mile of these routes in both fair weather and foul, and I hope you will enjoy them as much as I have.

Maps

Definitions of what constitutes the south-east of England vary widely. This book takes in the traditional Home Counties that touch London, with the exception of Essex. Then are added parts of Hampshire, Berkshire, Oxfordshire, Buckinghamshire, Hertfordshire, and the Isle of Wight. William Cobbett had to ask people directions and, more often than not, got misleading answers. Nowadays we are fortunate in having a wide variety of maps available.

I used the 1:50,000 Ordnance Survey Landranger series and they are referred to as **OS LR,** followed by the sheet number, in the book. In the ride descriptions, the relevant map is mentioned whenever the route passes from one sheet to another.

If you are familiar with the area you wish to cycle in then you might only need the sketch map in the book. Bear in mind however that the sketch is not designed to be used as a map in its own right and I recommend that you mark the route onto an Ordnance Survey map before setting off. This will provide maximum detail in terms of route finding and will allow diversions and short-cuts to be undertaken with ease.

Of my collection of over 300 maps, a very large proportion are other peoples throw outs or have been picked up cheaply at jumble sales, secondhand bookshops and at library sales. Another alternative is to use a smaller scale map like the 1:200,000 A-Z Series and rely on the text of the book to fill in the details.

Maps do go out of date. Many of the road numbers given are taken from the London Home Counties A-Z map which, if anything, is too up to date, for while researching, some of the roads marked were still being built! For finding my way around towns I find the 'County Red Books' of Estate Publications to be very useful. They contain street plans of all the major towns and cities in a county, they are very compact, reasonably priced and show one-way systems - the arch enemy of cycle route planners!

Distance, hills and other things

Distances from the start point are given regularly throughout the ride description and also on the sketch map. The amount of off-road riding, if any, is mentioned in the introduction to the ride. I define off-road as any stretch of uncoloured road, on the map, in rural areas. This covers RUPP's, BOATS, bridleways and canal towpaths - long stretches of which can be surfaced.

The word 'hilly' is used a lot in my descriptions. I have also listed the number of 'hills' for each ride, on the reference table. To me, hills and beautiful scenery go hand in hand and this is particularly true in the south-east with its rolling countryside and the North and South Downs. What one cyclist calls a hill can be a mere incline to another! My definition of a steep hill is anything which causes me to crawl upwards in bottom gear or severe enough for me to resort to Shank's pony. Gradients are not the only factor in determining how hard a ride will be. Off-road riding plays a part and the weather is always a wild card. Cycling in a flat exposed area like Romney Marsh can be more tiring with a strong wind against you than a more sheltered ride in the hills.

Trains

Not having a car I had to use the train to take myself plus bicycle to wherever I wanted to go. Thirty eight separate journeys were involved and I experienced almost no trouble in getting to anywhere I wanted, courtesy of NetWork SouthEast. How that will fare in the future, with rail privatisation, it is difficult to say.

However there is a certain knack in travelling by train with a bicycle. For one thing be aware of exactly when you can take a bike on a train, especially mid-week when there are restrictions in force in the rush hour periods, where the general rule seems to be that you can only take a bicycle if going against the general flow. Guidance leaflets are issued but goal posts do get shifted quite suddenly. At weekends there are fewer travel restrictions but then there are engineering works. Sometimes this means a substitute bus service on which no cycles can be carried. Most NetWork SouthEast stations display such disruptions on a map, usually from Thursdays onwards. Forewarned is forearmed. The best advice I can give is to check with your local station before setting off.

Space levels vary considerably. On all the trains I have used, cycle carriage is free and does not need to be booked in advance. However space is limited on the diesel turbo units operating between London Marylebone and the Chilterns, Paddington along the Thames Corridor and on the suburban electric services operating from Waterloo, Victoria and other London stations. Often bicycles need to be leant in the space by the sliding doors and a weather eye kept on platforms to see that they are not hindering other passengers getting on or off.

Other trains, like those on the Thameslink service, have tip-up seats in the area near the front indicated by a Royal Mail sign, with just enough space for a bicycle to be inserted. However many, including the new electric trains on the Portsmouth and Southampton lines, still have proper guards vans. Since the guard is often in other parts of the train it is best to remove anything valuable, especially items like cycle computers which can easily be slipped into pockets. If you are in a group, remove protruding items like pannier bags to save space. Although most cyclists do not bother, attach a label to the bicycle. You might know where you are going but you can't expect the guard to do so. Don't lock your bicycle to anything though a bungy strap is useful to stop it falling over. Lastly, common courtesy towards rail staff does not go amiss.

If intending to do a lot of train travel it is worthwhile purchasing a NetWork Card. Applicable only to NetWork SouthEast it does give a 33% discount off standard day returns and singles. As well as yourself, up to three other adults can be taken at the same rate and there are substantial reductions for children. However they can only be used after 10.00 on weekdays through there are no restrictions at weekends or Bank Holidays. Hopefully something like this will continue after privatisation.

I found the ABC Rail Guide very useful for planning journeys. As well as giving a complete timetable for NetWork SouthEast it gives fares, and, as it comes out monthly, can be kept as up to date as you want. Rail services vary more and more from summer to winter, as I found out while researching this book, particularly with regard to Sundays.

In the introduction to each ride I also give alternative stations both for starting or finishing or as escape points if ravaged by fatigue or mechanical trouble. If you intend to use a car, you might well ask what use is this to me? As well as being prominent well defined places from which to start or finish a ride, many stations in the commuter belt have large car parks.

Places to see

When researching a book like this one quickly becomes aware that it is impossible to see everything. Churches, castles, farms, vineyards, museums all compete for attention. I have concentrated on places along the route rather than at the start or finish. If you started looking around Canterbury, for instance, you would not have time to do any cycling unless a few days were going to be spent in the area.

Tourist Information Centres are invaluable. Accommodation can be arranged, also a great variety of free leaflets are on hand advertising the various attractions of the locality. Location, addresses and telephone numbers can be found in the map and directory of Tourist Information Centres published by the Tourist Authority.

In the text I do try and give approximate opening times correct at the time of writing. Usually they do not vary a great deal from year to year. NT and EH means National Trust or English Heritage. Joining either of these organisations gives free admission to their properties, saving money if you intend to visit many, as well as free handbooks and magazines that give up to date information. Addresses may be found at the back of the book.

Refreshments

The refreshment places listed in the ride introductions are by no means an exhaustive list and are just places I spotted on my travels which are conveniently placed on the route. Some are only for visitors to various properties and may or may not offer sustenance separately (another advantage of NT or EH membership!). Pubs I have not generally included in the introduction but they are mentioned in the text as landmarks. There is just not enough room. Most pubs serve food and many are now open all day. It is for you to make a personal choice of where to stop. I have included railway station buffets as when researching the routes I often found them very convenient at the start or finish of a ride. Despite their bad image they are generally becoming very much better. Little Chefs, Happy Eaters and similar roadside establishments have long opening hours and can be an oasis to the hungry traveller when all else is shut. However when the weather is fine there is nothing like a picnic meal, preferably at a place with a fine view, and that is what I prefer.

YOU, YOUR BICYCLE & THE WHERE & HOW

One thing I am not going to do is tell you how to buy a bicycle. I assume you have done that already. Neither will I delve into the technicalities of repair and maintenance, for that is more than covered in other books. The techniques of riding are also covered elsewhere. Now you are just itching to get those wheels turning to explore the possibilities unearthed in this book. Since I have ridden every one of the miles described in the book, I will describe my own approach.

As to the bicycle I used. Well, no great shakes. What I call my 'bits and pieces' machine is an old Dawes Super Galaxy, resprayed and the only original part, except for the frame, is the right hand crank. All the rest comes from odds and ends accumulated over the years.

Tools

Sometimes things do go wrong and out comes my tool-kit kept in one of those cylindrical zip-up rolls that fit into a drinking bottle cage. Pride of place goes to the 'Cool-Tool', an ingenious arrangement of adjustable spanner, chain riveter/breaker, crank tightener, and two double headed allen keys, one of which has a Philip head screwdriver. There are additional attachments for the bottom-bracket lock ring and head-set. And it really does work, saving an enormous amount of space. Then there are three plastic tyre-leavers that clip neatly together. In the puncture repair outfit, along with the rubber solution and patches, are a few extras such as a spoke key and a nut and bolt to fit the mudguards and rear carrier on the bicycle. Last but not least is the Swiss Army Knife. Its scissors are good for cutting patches down to size, the straight bladed screwdriver for tightening non-Philips head screws, the tweezers for getting thorns out of my tyre, and even a tiny pen if summoned by a creative urge!

Elsewhere I carry one or two spare inner tubes, a roll of insulating tape to fasten things together or for sticking over small cuts inside the tyre, spare gear and brake cables, and an old piece of tyre in the event of a large hole in the outer cover. And I must not forget a piece of cloth.

Lights

Even if there is the remotest possibility of cycling after dark I take lights with me. Spare batteries go along as well. The front uses a halogen bulb which runs through the rechargables I use very quickly. Also I carry a spare bulb inside the handlebar wrapped up in a piece of paper.

Wet weather wear

If there are lots of black clouds on the weather forecast with the prospect of heavy showers, then my cape must come along. I admit they are old fashioned but it is the one single garment that can be put on and will keep the rest of the body dry, apart from the feet. Also it is useful for sitting on wet ground or for keeping most of the bicycle dry while you are sitting in a cafe wondering if that piece of blue sky is an illusion. Overshoes come along as well for keeping the feet dry and warm.

What else?

Along comes the camera, a simple but very tough Olympus Pen half frame that travels in a padded 'Camera-care' case. Maps are needed and so is my lunch. If it's cold I'll take a thermos flask, unbreakable of course.

Got everything? Money, NetWork Card. Oh the lock! It's a thick cable affair that stretches to over 6 feet when uncoiled with a powerful kick if allowed to spring back. Unfortunately in this world the size and weight of the lock goes up in proportion to price and quality of the bicycle!

How I carry things

Black cotton duck saddlebags as faded as mine now is are definitely non-starters in the ranks of trendy cycling accessories. However the fact that they are really waterproof counts for a lot in my opinion. In my experience I find that synthetic materials let in water through the joints as much as anywhere else.

On the front

The trip computer lives on the handlebars. All I really want is distance and speed so I opted for a fairly basic model as reliability is more important. Many short out in the damp so that you need a plastic bag plus an elastic band to keep those figures appearing. So much for modern technology!

There is the map-holder as well. Mine is home-made but there are others on the market. Especially when using more than one map I like to mark out the route before hand using a very soft pencil such as an 8B which can be obtained in art shops. Everything can be rubbed off without leaving any trace. Important if it's not your own map!

What to put on

Nothing to beat the proper cycling clothing. The racing jersey, with those pockets for stuffing with odds and ends and a jacket to keep the wind out. People call the one I wear 'a coat of many colours'. I take the view that if you invite comments then you are noticed and being noticed is the name of the game on todays roads. Experience has taught me that its better to take too much rather than too little. Extra clothes can always be carried and is more convenient than stuffing newspapers round yourself to keep warm!

With shoes, I go for convenience rather than style and I don't particularly want to wear a special pair of shoes to fit a pair of clipless pedals. So I use toe-clips and if my pair of cycling shoes are still drying off then a pair of trainers can be worn instead.

With a chill in the morning the track-mits will be put away and out will come the gloves. One arrangement that I have found satisfactory is a pair of woollen gloves underneath the tough variety used for gardening as brake and gear levers wear through the fingers very quickly.

Off-road

Even if there is a fair amount of off-road work to do, it is nothing my bicycle won't handle. The tyres I use are the Michelin World Tour or Continental Top Touring, 700 x 32, with a meaty tread. A wide mud-guard clearance is important as well as a low bottom gear. Obviously a mountain bicycle would be good for that type of riding. Really for me it's a question of one horse for many courses.

Can I or can't I

That stretch of track over the South Downs should be OK but is it a bridleway. I can also ride on BOATS (Byways Open to All Traffic) that replace RUPP's (Roads Used as Public Paths). With footpaths, well, the ground is more uncertain. Technically it is an offence to cycle on one but it really needs a prohibition notice enforced by a local by-law to be a criminal act. On the other hand the landowner could bring a civil action against me. With the canal towpaths in this guide there is again nothing to prohibit cycling.

However it is up to the me to exercise the utmost courtesy to all other users of tracks, paths and roads. The reckless few, charging along, scattering all and sundry do untold damage. Up go the 'No Cycling' signs and once up it's very difficult to legally take them down again. With footpaths it is important to use ones own discretion. On one that is very narrow it would be inconsiderate to cycle, while others turn out to be wide metalled roads along which cars may go. Obey signs that ban cycling, be reasonable if challenged and don't become belligerent. It just makes things very difficult for other cyclists.

Ready to go

Now, find my reflective belt and ankle bands and the little flashing 'cue-light' that I attach to my right arm to help in giving arm signals in the dark. And my helmet - well perhaps. I like the freedom to choose when or when not to wear one. It will not give me a cloak of invincibility, especially against a car or lorry. On tracks, roads covered with greasy mud, wet leaves, ice, well yes, it will afford a degree of protection if I fall off. On charity rides like the London to Brighton where there are thousands of inexperienced riders, a helmet is a very good idea. Cycling on busy roads is a matter of planing ahead, of co-existence not confrontation. In the majority of cases it is thoughtlessness and not deliberate action on the part of motorists that causes accidents. And the same can apply to cyclists as well.

THE RIDES

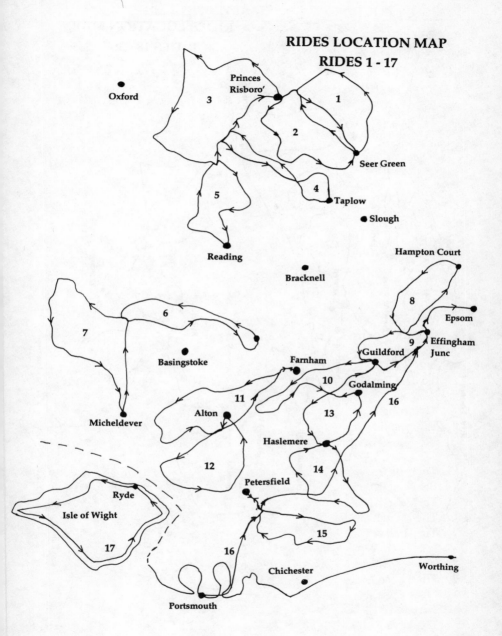

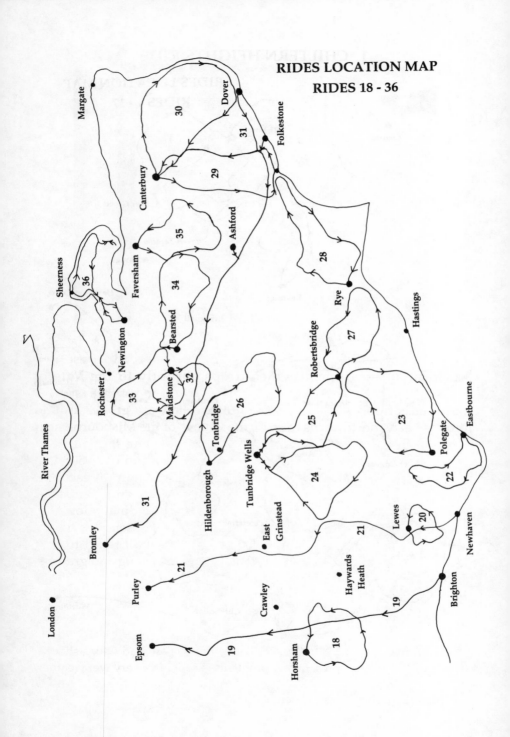

RIDES LOCATION MAP
RIDES 18 - 36

1 CHILTERN HEIGHTS RIDE

Chiltern is derived from the Saxon term for chalk and these hills form an escarpment which drops abruptly to the Vale of Aylesbury in the North West and gradually to the South East. This route starts from Seer Green and through the leafy groves around Jordans heads northwards to cross the valleys of the Misbourne near Chalfont St Giles, the Chess before Latimer and the Bulbourne at Berkhamsted. Afterwards there is a gradual climb to over 800 feet before descending the steep face of the hills past Ivinghoe Beacon.

The route follows the line of the hills through Tring and Wendover, before ascending to 852 feet at Coombe Hill. It is gradually downhill from here into the Misbourne valley to Little Missenden, before climbing into the hills again with a mainly downhill trend to Seer Green. This is a hilly route but the ascents tend to be long and gradual, the steepest being out of Little Missenden.

Maps	OS LR 165, 166, 175.
Distance	53.7 miles. Of these 4 miles is off road which should present few problems except after very wet weather.
Start/Finish	Seer Green Station.

Railway access

Seer Green is served by stopping service from London Marylebone, and occasionally from Paddington, to High Wycombe and beyond.

Berkhamsted and **Tring** are on the line from Euston.

Wendover can also be reached from Marylebone.

Princes Risborough could be used as an escape point.

Amersham, Chalfont & Latimer on Metropolital Line from Baker Street. Cycle carriage now free with London Transport.

Places to see

Quaker Meeting House & Mayflower Barn - Jordans.

John Milton's Cottage, Chiltern Open Air Museum - Chalfont St Giles.

Chenies Manor.

Village green - Latimer.

Castle EH - Berkhamsted.

Ashridge Estate & monument (NT).

Ivinghoe Beacon & Pitstone Windmill (NT).

Zoological Museum - Tring.

Coombe Hill (NT) - Wendover.

Church of St John the Baptist - Little Missenden.

Refreshments

Old Jordans Guest House - Jordans.

Tea room - on the green & at Chiltern Open Air Museum (for visitors), Chalfont St Giles.

Tea rooms - for visitors to Chenies Manor.

Tea kiosk - weekends only, by NT Info Centre on Ashridge Estate.

Tea rooms - Albury.

Nell Gwyne Cafe - not Sundays, Tring.

Landon Tea Rooms - popular with cyclists, Wendover.

Deep Mill Diner - on A413, near Little Missenden.

Good choice of pubs in all the main places visited on this route.

afterwards the castle (EH) was built and remained important until the 15th Century. Little of the building now remains though the earthworks are impressive. One oddity that you have passed is a totem pole, carved by a Kwakiath Indian from Vancouver Island for a local firm and erected in 1967. Good selection of pubs including old coaching inns like The Swan, The Bull, The Crown and, on weekdays, cafes.

16.0 RIGHT at crossroads by railway station and immediately LEFT into Bridgewater Road.

16.7 RIGHT into Bridleway just before T-Junction. Climb hill and at the top continue straight across onto unmetalled bridleway.

17.3 CONTINUE onto private road/bridleway and after Long Acre STRAIGHT ON through woods.

17.8 STRAIGHT ACROSS in front of Northchapel Farm and follow through more woodland. Keep to RIGHT and reach the B4506.

This stretch of bridleway is mostly quite rideable even after wet weather. It can be avoided, however, by following the main road through the town and taking a right turn to the B4506.

18.1 RIGHT and continue past entrance to Ashridge Estate momument and information centre (NT) on the left.

The Ashridge Estate covers a huge area of 6 square miles along the main ridge of the Chilterns from Ivinghoe Beacon to Berkhamsted. Most of this is now owned by the National Trust, though the house, is now a management training college. The momument itself was errected 150 years ago by the 3rd Duke of Bridgewater, the one renowned for the building of canals. Superb views from the top. With shop and information centre open daily in the afternoon April to end of October, 14.00 to 17.00. There is a tea kiosk open summer weekends.

20.9 LEFT into Beacon Road, at Ringshall, signposted Ivinghoe. After long climb descend past Ivinghoe Beacon to T-Junction.

At over 700 feet there are fine views to be had across the Vale of Aylesbury. from Ivinghoe Beacon which marks the start of the Ridgeway Path.

23.5 LEFT at T-Junction , signposted B489 Pitstone/Tring. At next LEFT onto B488, signposted Tring. (Right to Ivinghoe and Youth Hostel).

On the right is Pitstone Windmill (NT) one of the oldest post mills in the country, open Sundays and Bank Holiday Mondays May to end of September, 14.00 - 17.00.

24.7   CONTINUE straight on at bend over Pitstone Hill to Aldbury, an unspoiled village with tea-rooms.

26.9   RIGHT at crossroads in Aldbury, signposted Tring. Pass Tring Station.

29.5   RIGHT at T-Junction and immediately STRAIGHT ACROSS roundabout by the Robin Hood, signposted Town Centre into Tring. By car park to right is the Nell Gwyne Cafe (closed Sundays). Follow road through traffic calmed centre.

Tring was little more than a hamlet until the coming of the canals and arrival of the Rothschild family in the 20th Century. Walter Rothschild collected an enormous number of stuffed mammals, birds, reptiles and insects. Bequeathed to the nation and now part of the Natural History Museum. Open daily.

30.0   STRAIGHT ON at this roundabout and next, signposted A41.

31.5   LEFT, signposted A4011 Wendover. Continue through to town.

Standing at the foot of the Chiltern escarpment, Wendover is an attractive town with many old houses. The 1537 Bradshawe Brass in the church manages to show all the Bradshawes including their twenty three grand childen!

34.6   LEFT at roundabout , signposted A413 Amersham then STRAIGHT ON past the Landon Tea Rooms, at the next into Ellesborough Road. Continue past station and over railway.

35.1   FORK LEFT at bend onto Ridgeway Path. Immediately FORK LEFT again on track for horses and mountain bikes. Continue along deeply sunken track up hill through beautiful beech woods. Any mud can be avoided by walking along the high banks.

36.1   RIGHT and lift bicycle over kissing gate and continue along footpath to the momument on Coombe Hill (NT).

If you do not wish to go up to Coombe Hill continue straight on rather than turn right. At 852 feet this is the highest point in the Chilterns and the momument is actually a a war memorial for the Boer War. Dramatic views can be had towards the Cotswolds.

36.3   LEFT from momument and continue LEFT along the main path. Follow through gap in the woods into clearing to gate and road.

36.7   RIGHT and continue down steep hill then LEFT at T-Junction, signposted Great Missenden. Continue down gradually descending road and cross railway before entering Great Missenden.

Pass the entrance to Chequers, the Prime Ministers country residence . It was built around 1560 and can be seen from the road, though it is wise not to linger too long! This ride meets Route 2 here coming from the opposite direction. Turn Right here if you wish to return to Seer Green via Princes Risborough and West Wycombe. Beware this is not for the faint hearted!

42.1   RIGHT at T-junction into Aylesbury Road, signposted Amersham/ London. Continue straight on at mini-roundabout through centre, past Abbey and Chiltern Hospital

43.4   RIGHT at T-Junction onto busy A413, signposted London/ Amersham. Continue under railway and past Deep Mill Diner.

44.2   RIGHT, signposted Little Missenden. Follow into the village.

The church of St John the Baptist is built around an Anglo Saxon core.The Medieval wall paintings are one of the chief attractions.

44.7   RIGHT after church. Climb long hill along narrow road.

46.2   LEFT at T-Junction and immediately LEFT at the next onto the A404, signposted Amersham. RIGHT into Penn Street and continue past The Squirrel and the sign for Winchmore Hill.

48.2   STRAIGHT ON at corner, signposted Winchmore Hill/Coleshill. Follow road round to LEFT past the Coleshill sign and continue up hill. **OS LR 175.**

49.5   STRAIGHT ON at junction signposted Beaconsfield into Magpie Lane. Continue downhill to The Magpie.

50.2   LEFT at T-Junction, signposted A355 Amersham. Immediately RIGHT into lay-by, and immediately RIGHT again, signposted picnic area. Start climbing hill.

50.5   RIGHT into marked bridleway under the barrier. Follow yellow arrows and horseshoe signs through woods. Going could be muddy in places but drier ways can be found to the side. Continue to metalled lane.

51.7   RIGHT and continue down narrow bumpy lane before RIGHT at T-Junction and LEFT at next. RIGHT to station

53.7   END

2 CHILTERN BOTTOMS RIDE

B ottoms is the local word describing the deep trench-like valleys that dissect the Chilterns. Clothed in beech woods they can be very beautiful, particularly in Autumn. After Beaconsfield, the route climbs to Penn and descends to Penn Bottom. After Great Kingshill there is Bryants Bottom before dropping off the Chilterns to Princes Risborough.

Led from afar by the golden ball on the church tower, there is much to see at West Wycombe, situated in the valley of the little River Wye. The route climbs out of the valley to Lane End before skirting High Wycombe and heading back with a long descent to Wooburn Green. A steep ascent into the beech woods, passing Beaconsfield to the south, completes the full circle to return to Seer Green.

This is a hilly but rewarding route. Some hills are long and testing, like the climb to Bledlow Ridge, but the steepest gradients are all downhill with fine descents to be enjoyed.

Maps	OS LR 175 & 165.
Distance	46.8 miles, none off-road.
Start/Finish	Seer Green Station where there is ample parking.

8.9 STRAIGHT ACROSS into New Pond Road. After Old Oak PH LEFT at T-Junction into Beech Tree Road and CONTINUE over double roundabout, signposted Prestwood, into Spurlands End Road.

10.3 LEFT signposted Great Kingshill/Prestwood then LEFT again into The Commons. Continue to A4128.

11.0 LEFT at T-junction by Red Lion PH and immediately RIGHT down Hatches Lane by village stores. Descend long hill.

11.9 CONTINUE over crossroads, signposted Bryants Bottom/Princes Risborough. Continue gradually uphill past The Gate and Bryants Bottom village.

13.9 RIGHT and continue climbing through the beautiful beech woods. RIGHT again at T-Junction in Hampden Row, signposted Prestwood/Great Missenden. Pass Hampden Arms PH and entrance to Great Hampden.

Near Great Hampden church Grimms Ditch can be viewed. Cropping up in many places in the Chilterns, this mysterious earthwork is lost in the mists of antiquity. Some say it was built before, others after Christ.

The church contains a memorial brass to John Hampden, the Great Patriot whose refusal to pay the notorious Ship Tax eventually sparked off the English Civil War. The house is a private residence.

15.2 LEFT at crossroads, signposted Butlers Cross. There is a fast descent before LEFT again at T-Junction, signposted Princes Risborough. Follow gradually climbing road.

Route 1 is joined here. Turn right for a shorter ride back to Seer Green via Great and Little Missenden.

16.4 LEFT signposted Askett/Princes Risborough. Continue climb then descend through Cadsen past The Plough PH on the left.

18.3 LEFT onto Upper Icknield Way, signposted Whiteleaf.

The Icknield Way originated from the time of Neolithic Man and, dating back over 3,000 years, is the oldest road in the country. Following the base of the Chilterns meant that the earliest travellers would be close to the spring-line.

19.0 RIGHT at T-junction into Peters lane. Descend to Monks Risborough then LEFT at next onto A4010 and continue to Princes Risborough.

It's worth visiting the church at Monks Risborough. Inside there is a modern sculpture of St Dunstan inflicting grievous bodily harm upon The Devil.

Outside are beautiful thatched cottages and, close by, a medieval dovecote.

19.9   STRAIGHT ACROSS roundabout, signposted Town Centre. RIGHT
       at the Market Hall and past church and manor (NT).

Sir John Betjeman called Princes Risborough 'a first impression of untidy
Metroland below the Chilterns', but it is an attractive enough place, the more
so for the traffic calming measures in the High Street. The manor house,
owned by the National Trust, is open only by prior arrangement with the
tenant (08444 343168). It dates from the 17th Century, is built of red brick and
has a fine staircase.In Bell Street on A4010 are tea rooms combined with an
antique shop.
    Route 3 starts from the station.

20.2   CONTINUE straight on at car-park onto metalled private road with
       footpath. LEFT at T-Junction then RIGHT into Picts Lane,
       signposted Bledlow.

21.0   RIGHT at T-junction and continue over railway bridge, signposted
       Bledlow. Then RIGHT into Upper Icknield Way, signposted
       Bledlow/Chinnor.

22.6   LEFT at T-junction, signposted Bledlow Ridge/Radnage. Climb long
       steep hill onto Bledlow Ridge.

24.1   RIGHT at T-Junction followed by LEFT signposted Radnage.
       Descend hill and follow road round past church.

The church of St Mary is one of the most unspoiled churches you will find
anywhere, with its Saxon font, medieval tiles and fine 16th Century brasses.

25.4   LEFT into Bottom Road, signposted High Wycombe /West
       Wycombe. Continue along this very attractive valley lane gradually
       descending.

27.9   RIGHT at T-Junction and aim towards West Wycombe, the golden
       ball on top of the church serving as a landmark. Before reaching A40
       there is a garden centre where teas are served.

It is difficult to believe that West Wycombe was faced with demolition in
1929. Now the whole village, with its 17th and 18th Century buildings along
with the hill is owned by The National Trust. The Bread Oven Tea Room in
located in the village store.
    The church, open Sundays only, and planned on the lines of a drawing room,
was the 18th Century creation of the notorious Sir Francis Dashwood, founder
of the Hell-fire Club He is said to have used the golden ball on top for card
parties. The open air mausoleum, close by on the same hill, was also his
creation.

Unspeakable orgies were supposed to have been held in West Wycombe Caves, which are entered on the hillside opposite the garden centre and perpetuated by the commentary and special effects. In fact they are old mines enlarged to produce material for a new road. Open most weekends, especially in Summer. Cafe here as well.

West Wycombe Park NT again bears the handiwork of the notorious Sir Francis. He had strong classical architectural interests and rebuilt the original house in various styles. Inside are frescoes and painted ceilings; outside a landscaped garden. Open Sundays to Thursdays, June to August, 14.00 to 18.00. Grounds only Sunday, Wednesday and Bank Holidays, April - May.

28.7   RIGHT at T-Junction onto A40 after garden centre. (Left to West Wycombe and an easy though very congested route back to Seer Green through High Wycombe.) **OS LR 175.**

29.2   LEFT into Bullocks Farm Road and climb steep hill to Wheeler End. Continue past Chequers and over A40 to Lane End.

31.1   LEFT at T-Junction in to Park Lane. Recross M40 and descend to RIGHT turn into Horns Lane. Climb hill.

34.6   LEFT at T-Junction by M40 into Cressex Road. STRAIGHT ON at mini-roundabout and CONTINUE over next roundabout with A4010, signposted Cressex Industrial Estate.

35.9   LEFT at T-Junction with mini-roundabout. STRAIGHT ON at next then LEFT at roundabout to A404 down 10% hill.

36.4   RIGHT turn with care into Daws Hill Lane, signposted Flackwell Heath. Continue mainly downhill to this large modern village. STRAIGHT ACROSS mini-roundabout, signposted Wooburn Green. Take great care on the final 20% descent to T-Junction.

40.6   RIGHT at T-Junction at Wooburn Green. Immediately LEFT and LEFT again by Queen and Albert PH. Then immediately RIGHT and RIGHT again into Windsor Lane, signposted Glass Craft. Climb steep hill through beautiful beech woods.

41.1   RIGHT at T-Junction at top of hill, then LEFT, both signposted to Wooburn Common and Rare Breeds Centre. Then LEFT by Royal Standard PH into a beautiful narrow lane with grass growing down the centre.

Continue straight on if you want to visit Odds Farm which specialises in the conservation of rare and endangered breeds of British farm livestock. Tea rooms in the stables. Open April to October, 10.00-17.00.

43.0 LEFT at T-junction then LEFT onto A355. Continue over M40 along dual carriageway to roundabout.

44.4 RIGHT onto A40 signposted Gerrards Cross. LEFT, signposted Jordans. Descend 12% hill.

46.3 LEFT signposted Seer Green/Beaconsfield. LEFT up Farm Lane to Seer Green Station.

46.8 END

3 VALE, HILL & WATER

Princes Risborough lies at the foot of the Chilterns and throughout this ride they are always there on the sky line. This is an open and gently undulating route through the Vale of Aylesbury to Cuddington, then progressively more hilly through Long Crendon to Brill at 603 feet. From Brill it's downhill and then in a more gentle mode through Boarstall to Waterperry and Dorchester.

Here we meet the Thames and follow it for a short distance before the Chilterns, like an ever present magnet, lead the way up up their wooded slopes to Cookley Green and through Christmas Common to the highest point of the route at 835 feet. Thence it is a rapid descent to Kingston Blount and back to Princes Risborough at the foot of the hills.

This route can be best described as easy going with hilly interludes, the climbs to Brill and Cookley Green being long but not particularly steep.

Maps	OS LR 165, 164, 175, with a lot of overlapping.
Distance	65.2 miles of which 1 mile at Waterperry is off-road but rideable.
Start/Finish	Princes Risborough railway station - plenty of parking.

Railway Access

Princes Risborough is served by trains mainly from London Marylebone and occasionally Paddington. In the opposite direction, trains from Birmingham via Banbury and also from Aylesbury.

Places to see

Cuddington village.

Courthouse (NT) & village - Long Crendon.

Village & windmill - Brill.

Duck Decoy & Tower (both NT) - Boarstall.

Gardens & church - Waterperry.

Abbey - Dorchester.

Cycle Museum. - Benson.

Watlington Hill (NT).

Chiltern Sculpture Trail.

Refreshments

Tea rooms - Bell Street, Princes Risborough.

Annie Bailey's Eating House - Cuddington.

Waterperry Gardens.

Little Chef, Waterside Cafe, Abbey Tea Rooms - Dorchester,

Riverside Cafe - Benson.

Good range of pubs, particularly at Long Crendon, Brill, Dorchester and Benson.

VALE, HILL & WATER

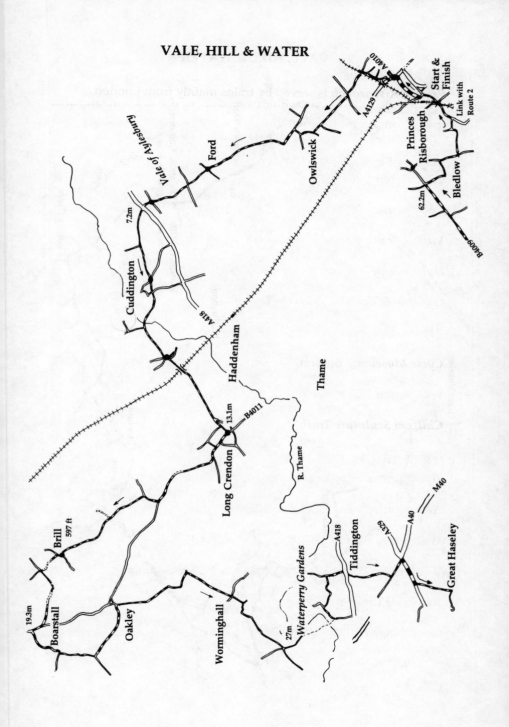

VALE, HILL & WATER

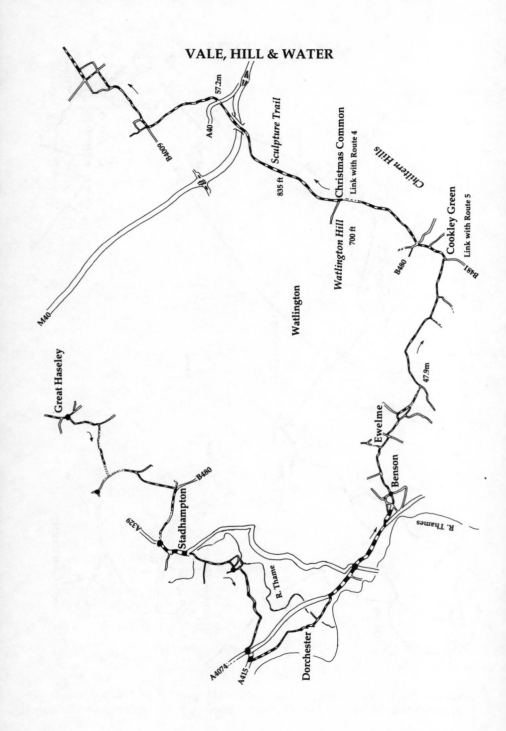

3 VALE, HILL & WATER

Starting from Princes Risborough Station this route joins nicely with Route 2, the Chiltern Bottoms Ride. An overnight stay would give a fine weekends cycling.

0.0   LEFT from Princes Risborough Station. **OS LR 165**. RIGHT at T-Junction and immediately left into Manor Park Avenue. Continue along private road with footpath, past entrance to car park, church, and Manor House (NT).

0.7   LEFT at Market Hall then LEFT again at roundabout, signposted A4129 Thame.

1.0   RIGHT into Wellington Avenue by low bridge sign. Immediately LEFT into Westmead then LEFT at T-Junction and immediately LEFT at staggered crossroads. Continue under railway.

2.1   LEFT at T-Junction onto B4009. Immediately RIGHT, signposted Owlswick. Continue through village with its tiny green and Shoulder of Mutton PH.

3.6   LEFT at T-Junction, through Ford.

6.2   CONTINUE over staggered crossroads, signposted Dinton and pass through village.

7.2   STRAIGHT ACROSS staggered crossroads over A418, signposted Cuddington/Long Crendon. Continue to Long Crendon.

Cuddington is an attractive village of picturesque cottages, particularly near the church where you will find Anne Baileys Eating House if you like your food in style.

Difficult to believe that the picture postcard village of Long Crendon was once an important market town and wool trade centre. The Court House, one of the first buildings to be acquired by the National Trust as far back as 1900, was used for the Manorial Courts from the reign of Henry V until recent times. The top floor can be viewed Wednesday afternoons and weekends, April to end of September, 11.00 to 18.00. At one time the village was a centre for lace making and the manufacture of needles.

13.1   RIGHT at T-junction onto B4011 signposted Bicester.

15.1   RIGHT and climb long hill to Brill.

A restful place where attractive red-brick cottages coil round the hill. Brill was once connected to London by the Metropolitan line. Attempts were also made to make the village into a popular spa. A chalybeate spring was exploited in the 1830s and though a pump room was built, the place was ignored by those who mattered and eventually decayed.

17.6   LEFT into Windmill Street by Sun Inn signposted Boarstall.
        Continue past windmill and descend hill.

The Pheasant Inn faces the windmill in a dramatic situation overlooking the lower lands to the south west and an extensive pockmarked landscape caused by old clay workings. Though not in working order, this post mill, dating from 1688 is open to the public 14.30 to 17.30 on afternoons, April to September.

18.1   LEFT at crossroads. Descend hill.

19.3   RIGHT at T-Junction onto B4011 signposted Bicester. Then LEFT signposted Boarstall. Follow road through village.

The Duck Decoy NT at Boarstall dates from the 18th Century and is in working order and set in thirteen acres of natural woodland along with a nature trail. Open April to end of August, weekends, 10.00 to 1700 and Wednesdays 16.00 to 19.00. Boarstall Tower NT is the stone gatehouse of a fortified manor house long since demolished. Its three stories were converted to become a substantial dwelling in its own right. Open May to end of September, Wednesdays, 14.00 to 18.00, by written appointment with the tenant.

20.4   LEFT then LEFT again at T-Junction before M40 signposted Oakley.
        Continue to village.

22.3   RIGHT by Royal Oak PH signposted Worminghall. Follow road through to the village and continue STRAIGHT ON at crossroads signposted Waterperry.

26.7   LEFT at corner signposted Waterperry Horticultural Centre only.

Open all the year round and once the practical working ground for the former Waterperry Horticultural School there are an enormous variety of plants for sale and display. Also a very useful tea shop. Close by is the small church of St Mary, dating from Saxon times, with box pews, a 17th Century triple deck pulpit, and a palimpest or recycled brass used once then turned round and used the other side.

27.0   RIGHT onto footpath by side of red-brick house. Walk through two gates and keep straight on over track to dilapidated picnic site.
        LEFT here and continue through gates to drive from manor.

27.4   RIGHT onto drive which eventually becomes bridleway. Pass South Lodge, cross bridge, go past Waterstock Mill to metalled road.

28.0   LEFT at T-Junction and continue through Waterstock, then RIGHT at T-Junction, signposted Tiddington.

29.1   RIGHT onto A418 and immediately LEFT signposted Sandy Lane Farm then RIGHT at T-Junction signposted Postcombe to A329 at crossroads by Three Pigeons PH.

30.8   RIGHT at crossroads onto A329, signposted Wallingford. Cross M40.

31.4   LEFT signposted Great Haseley. Follow road through both Great and Little Haseleys until LEFT at T-Junction, signposted Chalgrove.

35.6   RIGHT at T-Junction onto B480 signposted Oxford. Continue into Stadhampton. **OS LR 164.**

36.8   LEFT by double mini-roundabout onto A329. Continue past Crown PH then LEFT at T-Junction signposted A329 Wallingford.

37.3   RIGHT signposted Drayton. Continue over bridge into village. After church with wooden steeple LEFT signposted Dorchester.

40.6   STRAIGHT ACROSS roundabout past Little Chef, signposted A415 Abingdon then LEFT signposted Dorchester and Waterside Cafe. Then RIGHT at T-Junction into Dorchester and past abbey.

Dorchester dates back to Roman times and a church was built when St Birinus in 635 AD converted the West Saxon King and his court to Christianity. It became the cathedral for Wessex until the Norman Conquest. In 1170 it was given to the Augustans who started the great abbey that dominates this attractive village. Of the very impressive windows inside one dates from the 16th Century and creates in stone and glass a family tree showing the descent of Christ from Jesse. Close by in the monastery guest house is a small museum, open Tuesday to Saturday, May to September along with the Abbey Tea Rooms, open from Easter to September, 15.00 onwards.

43.0   RIGHT a T-Junction onto A4074 signposted Reading. Follow this road straight across the roundabout to the next when it is LEFT signposted B4009 Watlington/Benson. Continue through Benson and past airfield.

The Riverside Cafe is just up the road towards Reading if in need of refreshment. In Benson there is a privately owned museum of veteran cycles ranging from 1818 to 1920. Check with the local tourist information centre at Wallingford (0491 26550) if interested in viewing.

47.0   RIGHT by Shepherds Hut into Ewelme after watercress beds and village hall then turn LEFT. Keep STRAIGHT ON at bend, signposted Swyncombe/Cookley Green. Continue past church.

Ewelme is a show place village largely built in brick and flint, but the chief attraction must be the remarkable grouping of church, almshouses and school, virtually unchanged since their construction between 1435 and 1450. The church is built completely in the Perpendicular style of architecture. Alice, Duchess of Suffolk, and grand-daughter of Geoffrey Chaucer the poet was renowned for her good works. She founded the almshouses that are gathered round a cloister reached by steps from the church. They are still supported by the funds left in 1475. Next door is the school founded in 1437 and claiming to be the oldest church school still in existence.

47.9   LEFT at T-Junction and LEFT at next both signposted Swyncombe/ Cookley Green and continue up long hill onto the Chiltern ridge. **OS LR 175.**

51.2   LEFT at T-Junction after top of hill at Cookley Green signposted B481 Watlington. Meet Route 5 here.

52.9   RIGHT and immediately LEFT signposted Christmas Common. Follow road through this hamlet and past The Fox and Hounds PH. Through Cowleaze Wood and past the Chiltern Sculpture Trail before crossing the M40 in a deep cutting. **OS LR 165.**

This flat road runs along the very top of the Chiltern ridge but trees obscure the view. If you wish to see what has been previously hidden then turn left at Christmas Common to Watlington Hill (NT), 700 feet up on the escarpment.
   The Chiltern Sculpture Trail can be followed on two walks with the idea of inviting the visitor to experience contemporary art in a forest setting. So don't be surprised if you see a giant picnic table - it serves as a shelter!

   Meet Route 4 along this road.

57.2   STRAIGHT ACROSS A40 on staggered crossroads onto single track road signposted Kingston Blount. Descend steep hill.

58.6   RIGHT at T-Junction onto B4009 and follow through Chinnor signposted Princes Risborough.

62.2   RIGHT at crossroads, signposted Bledlow. Continue into village past pub before RIGHT turn at T-Junction, signposted Bledlow Ridge.

63.3   LEFT into Oddley Lane, LEFT at T-Junction and after crossing over railway, LEFT again into Picts Lane, all signposted to Princes Risborough. Meet Route 2 along this road.

64.9   LEFT onto B4444. Continue to station.

65.2   END

4 THE THAMES & CHILTERNS EIGHT

U sing an unequal figure of eight, this ride takes in the Thames valley to the south of the river and the Chilterns to the north.

Starting from Taplow Station, the Thames is first crossed at Maidenhead and, after Pinkney's Green, recrossed at Marlow. From Marlow it is into the hills for Fingest and up to the final ridge at Stokenchurch. Near Christmas Common the highest point of 835 feet is reached. Thence a descent to Turville, and back to Marlow through Bockmer End. Once over the Thames a bridleway leads to the top of Winters Hill before a nice descent to Cookham. After the last climb of the day it is mainly downhill past Cliveden back to Taplow Station.

For the most part this is a hilly route, 10% being the norm on some of the long drags, but the climbing is compensated by fine views from the top before the descent.

Maps	OS LR 175, 165.
Distance	45.3 miles, of which 2.2 miles is off-road but rideable.
Start/Finish	Taplow Station. Marlow is a good alternative. Both sections are designed to be ridden separately.

Railway access

Taplow is served by an hourly service from London Paddington on the local stopping service to Reading. On Sundays use Maidenhead or Burnham.

Marlow may be reached by an hourly service on the branch line from Maidenhead - not on Sunday during winter.

For a few extra miles *Eton* and *Windsor Riverside* provides an alternative for those who wish to travel from London Waterloo via Clapham Junction and Richmond.

Places to see

Bisham.

St Peter's Street - old buildings and much more in Marlow.

Church & village - Fingest.

Chiltern Sculpture Trail.

Watlington Hill (NT).

Village - Turville.

Winters Hill.

Village & Stanley Spencer Gallery - Cookham.

Cliveden Gardens (NT).

Refreshments

Riverside Gardens Cafe - Maidenhead.

Court Garden Leisure Complex - Marlow.

Tea rooms - Cookham.

Tea room - Clivedon Gardens, visitors only.

Kings Arms PH - Skirmett, also serves afternoon teas.

Useful pubs at Fingest & Christmas Common.

THAMES & CHILTERN EIGHT

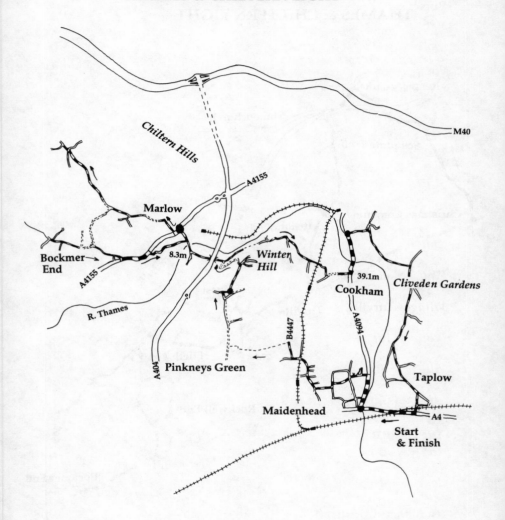

THAMES & CHILTERN EIGHT

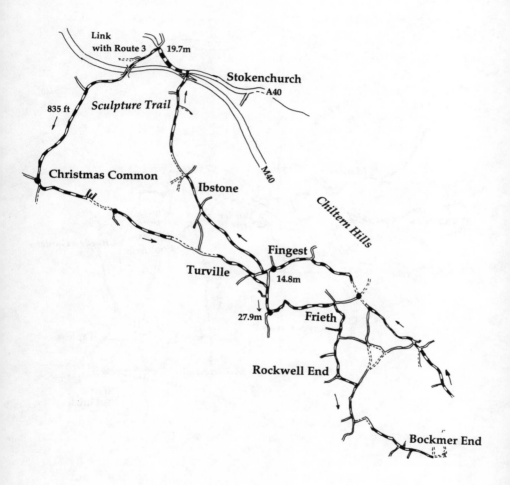

4 THAMES & CHILTERNS EIGHT

0.0 RIGHT from Taplow Station. **OS LR 175.** Pass under railway then RIGHT at staggered crossroads onto A4. Follow under railway, over Thames to outskirts of Maidenhead.

1.2 RIGHT at roundabout, signposted A4094 Cookham. Pass Riverside Gardens, where the cafe is open seven days a week, and continue to Boulters Lock and Boulters Inn.

2.0 LEFT into Ray Mill Road East. CONTINUE on same road over crossroads then LEFT at T-Junction and immediately RIGHT into Ray Mill Road West.

3.1 RIGHT at T-Junction into Cookham Road B4447. Follow over two mini roundabouts and over railway before RIGHT at mini-roundabout signposted Cookham.

4.2 LEFT onto Road Used as Public Path. Continue over metalled road into Hindhay Lane along firm though bumpy track. Keep RIGHT through yard at Hindhay Farm then LEFT past new housing development to Pinkneys Green (NT), one of several areas given by local residents to the National rust in 1934.

5.4 RIGHT at T-Junction then STRAIGHT ON at corner signposted Cookham Dean/Winter Hill.

7.1 LEFT at T-Junction into Quarry Wood Road. After initial climb descend 10% hill through woods taking care around two very sharp bends. Pass under A404.

If you just want a short ride, at the bottom of the hill keep straight on at bend into Quarry Wood, signposted No Through Road and follow route described later.

8.3 RIGHT at T-Junction and continue over bridge to Marlow. After bridge CONTINUE straight on through High Street over mini-roundabout (Right here and right again to St Peter Street.)

Left instead of right before the bridge will bring you to Bisham church which contains many memorials to the Hoby family both inside and out. In a medieval version of Home Alone Lady Hoby punished her young son for not doing his schoolwork properly by locking him in a cupboard, then forgot about him completely when called away to another part of the country on urgent business. On return she found he had starved to death.

Marlow Bridge, suspended above the Thames, was built by Tierney Clarke who also built the bridge that joined up Buda with Pest. Marlow is an old town with strong monastic connections. St Peter Street contains many old buildings including The Old Parsonage, one of the finest medieval buildings in Buckinghamshire. There are strong literary connections as well - Percy Bysshe Shelley lived there at the same time as his wife completed Frankenstein. T.S. Elliott and Jerome K Jerome were other residents. Marlow Place was once occupied by George II. The population of Marlow has trebled since the Second World War through an increase of commuters wishing to capture something of its rural atmosphere.

8.8   LEFT at next roundabout, signposted A4155 Henley. Then RIGHT into Oxford Road by pub, signposted Bovington Green/Frieth. It's a long ascent up into the Chilterns but fine views are to be had to the hills beyond.

12.9   STRAIGHT OVER crossroads and a downhill stretch where it's LEFT at the T-Junction, following the signs to Fingest.

Set in a deep, dry, chalk valley Fingest is often used as an illustration for a typical Chiltern village. Yet the massive twin-gabled church tower is unusual in itself. Built in early Norman times with walls over a yard thick it makes the rest of the church appear tiny in comparison. Across the road is The Chequers pub with its pleasant gardens.

14.8   RIGHT then RIGHT again following signs to Ibstone up a steep 10% hill past the privately owned windmill that overlooks the village of Turville. Continue through the long straggling village of Ibstone, past The Fox PH before crossing the M40 on the outskirts of Stokenchurch. **OS LR 165.**

19.0   LEFT at T-Junction onto A40 signposted Oxford. Continue towards 300 foot concrete tower crowned with radio dishes and probably the most prominent feature of the Chilterns.

19.7   LEFT signposted Christmas Common, just before Oxfordshire sign. Continue over M40 along wooded ridge on road to Christmas Common and The Fox and Hounds pub. **OS LR 175.**

Meet Route 3 here. The Chiltern Sculpture Trail and Watlington Hill are described in the commentary for Route 3.

23.1   LEFT at Christmas Common signposted Northend/Turville. STRAIGHT ON at Northend and down superb though steep 10% drop along the single track road.

Turville is another very attractive village with its quaint cottages - a mixture of brick, flint and tile, or half timbering and thatch. The church, close to The

Bull and Butcher PH, is full of memorials and the whole village is overlooked by the impressive windmill that was passed earlier on the ride and is now a private residence.

27.1   RIGHT onto single track road marked unsuitable for motors. It is metalled but beware of potholes. Then RIGHT at the next T-Junction into Skirmett, where afternoon teas are served at The Kings Arms PH.

27.9   LEFT after The Old Crown PH signposted Freith. Continue along single track road and up steep hill. Then RIGHT at crossroads in Freith, signposted Pheasants Hill before LEFT at bend by Rockwell End, signposted Farm Shop.

30.9   RIGHT at T-Junction followed by LEFT turn after Springfield Farm. Continue past Bockmer End down steep hill and up another, though fortunately not as long. This runs through a beautiful avenue of beech trees.

33.4   RIGHT at T-Junction, signposted Marlow at top of hill then LEFT at next onto A4155 to Marlow. Continue down hill.

34.5   RIGHT after Hare and Hounds PH into Pound Lane. Follow road into Marlow past the Court Garden Leisure complex. The Tourist Information Centre is in the car-park, and facing the river is a cafe and bar.

35.4   RIGHT at mini-roundabout into the High Street and cross the bridge over the Thames, then STRAIGHT ON at bend, signposted Cookham Dean - light vehicles. Pass under A404

36.2   LEFT into Quarry Wood marked No Through Road at bottom of hill where road swings round to right. Follow uphill onto bridleway which becomes a narrow path as it passes to the right of   Quarry Clyffe House. This in turn leads to a driveway that continues uphill and becomes metalled later.

You are now on Winter Hill. The view to the north across The Thames to Marlow and the Chiltern Hills is impressive but it is very noticeable how obtrusive the A404 is, ploughing its way to High Wycombe.

37.2   LEFT at T-Junction then follow road mainly downhill over railway. Again it is LEFT at the next to enter Cookham.

Cookham has strong artistic connections for it was the birthplace and home of Sir Stanley Spencer RA. There is a gallery where you can see some of his paintings and drawings. You can also see his version of the Last Supper in the parish church and more of his work at the Sandham Memorial Chapel near Newbury, visited on Routes 6 and 7. Cookham itself is an attractive village to linger in with tea rooms and pubs.

39.1   LEFT at T-Junction onto A4094 by Stanley Spencer Gallery. Cross the River Thames. Continue to Bourne End.

39.9   RIGHT, signposted Hedsor/Taplow. Climb hill past The Garibaldi Inn before RIGHT at T-Junction into Hawks Hill, again signposted Taplow. Continue up steep 10% hill.

41.4   RIGHT at T-Junction, signposted Taplow. Continue past Cliveden House (NT).

Cliveden House, built in 1851 and once the home of Lady Astor is now a country house hotel but the gardens, high above the Thames, have spectacular views. There are tea rooms for visitors. Open daily March to December, 11.00 to 18.00 or 16.00 when the days are shorter.

43.9   LEFT near white cottage into Hill Farm Road. Pass through Taplow village. Descend hill before turning RIGHT into Station Road, signposted Maidenhead. Then, before passing under railway, RIGHT to station.

46.3   END

5 TO THE MAHARAJAH

Tis ride starts in the Thames valley at Reading and after Caversham it is an enjoyable ride along bridleways through the film-set village of Mapledurham. Elephants in the Chilterns?... That is what you see supporting the dome of the Maharajah's Well at Stoke Row, having conquered a steep but gradual climb through woods and fields via Goring Heath and Checkendon.

Now firmly on the Chiltern Ridge there is no option but to go down once the highest point of 700 feet is reached near Cookley Green. Past Russell's Water, through open commonland and then a plunge into Stonor and a long, slight descent to Henley-on-Thames. Then back to the hills. Greys Court is a fascinating place, before Kidmore End and the descent to Caversham. Once again over the river to Reading.

Flat stretches with hilly interludes would be the best description. The steepest and longest is to Goring Heath but fine descents compensate, and the woods are beautiful.

Map	OS LR 175.
Distance	37.2 miles. Of this 3.3 miles is off-road and easy to ride.
Start/Finish	Reading Station. Car parking there and in town.

Railway access

Reading is served by inter-city and local trains from London Paddington and a more cycle friendly service from London Waterloo. Also trains from Guildford, Basingstoke, Newbury, Oxford.

Henley-on-Thames is served by a branch line from Twyford, but not on Sundays in winter.

Places to See

Blake's Lock Museum - Reading.

House & Watermill - Mapledurham.

St Peter and St Paul church - Checkendon.

Maharajah's Well - Stoke Row.

Stonor House.

Henley-on-Thames.

Greys Court (NT).

Refreshments

Gorge Cafe - by Caversham Bridge, Reading.

Goring Heath.

Schoolhouse Tea Rooms - Stoke Row, (not Sundays).

Tea rooms - Stonor House, for visitors only.

Tea rooms - Greys Court, for visitors only.

The Herb Farm - Soning Common.

A good choice of pubs, especially in Henley-on-Thames.

TO THE MAHARAJAH

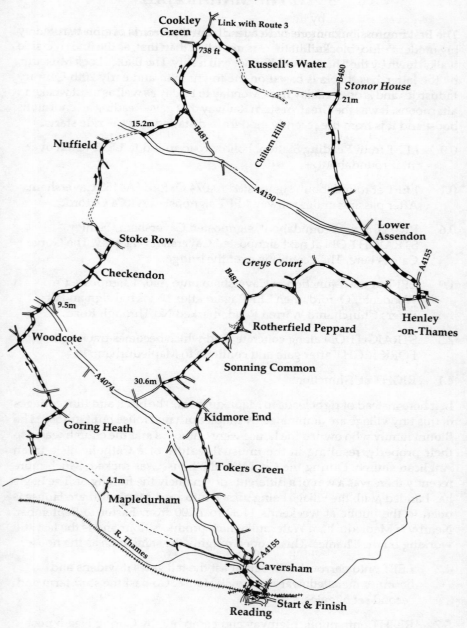

5 TO THE MAHARAJAH

The first impression one gets of Reading from the train is of a place ruled by big modern office blocks. But there is more to it than that, as the fine riverside walks down by the Thames and Kennet will testify. The Blakes Lock Museum, by the latter, has displays based on the towns 19th and early 20th Century industries and is open all day from Monday to Friday as well as most weekend afternoons. It was the Great Western Railway that gave Reading an enormous boost and it is from the recently modernised station that the ride starts.

0.0   LEFT from Reading Station. Follow road round to LEFT again over mini-roundabout.

0.1   LEFT at roundabout, signposted A4074 Oxford/A4155 Caversham. After passing under railway LEFT signposted A4074 Oxford.

0.6   RIGHT at next roundabout, signposted Caversham/Henley. STRAIGHT ON at next signposted Caversham/Henley. The Gorge Cafe is here. Then continue over the bridge.

1.0   LEFT at the T-junction in Caversham onto A4074 signposted Woodcote/Oxford, then LEFT again after 12.5% hill sign and St Peters Church into Warren Road, marked No Through Road.

2.3   STRAIGHT ON along concrete road which becomes track and FORK RIGHT after gate and continue to Mapledurham.

4.1   RIGHT at T-Junction.

Left here instead of right leads to Mapledurham. The brick and flint cottages of this tiny village are dominated by Mapledurham House built in 1588. The Blount family who owned the house were Catholics and the church was also their property, resulting in the unusual feature of a Catholic aisle in an Anglican church. During the Civil War the house was sacked. Much more recently there was a war of a different sort - namely the filming of The Eagle has Landed with the village being turned into a set. Mapledurham House is open to the public at weekends 14.30 to 17.00 from Easter to September. Nearby is Mapledurham Watermill which produces flour and is the last still working on the Thames. This is open roughly the same time as the house.

4.2   LEFT onto narrow bridlepath. Past the tall gates it widens and becomes metalled near Hardwick House. Go past the stud farm and second set of gates.

5.7   RIGHT onto public highway and climb hill. By Goring Heath post office, where there are tea rooms, LEFT at crossroads.

7.5 STRAIGHT ON at next crossroads onto single track road. RIGHT after the Woodcote sign. Pass pub and then RIGHT again at the T-Junction marked as part of Oxfordshire Cycle Way.

9.5 RIGHT at T-Junction on A4074 and immediately LEFT, signposted Checkendon/Oxfordshire Cycle Way. Follow through village.

Checkendon is another fine example of a Chiltern brick and flint village. The church of St Peter and St Paul is Norman. At the end of the chancel are 12th Century wall paintings of Christ and the Apostles. As well as the pub are the recently opened Schoolhouse Tea Rooms, not open Sundays.

11.3 LEFT at T-Junction signposted Nuffield. Continue through the village.

Right instead of left leads into Stoke Row. The village might be considered nondescript but for the Maharajah's Well. This was a gift to the village in 1863 from the Maharajah of Benares to his friend Edward Reade of Ipsden House who had been his advisor. Water had always been difficult to obtain here and this well was sunk by hand 346 feet through the chalk. The gold dome and the elephants supporting the windlass are certainly striking.

15.2 RIGHT at T-Junction signposted A4130 Henley. Immediately LEFT onto single track road signposted Park Corner then LEFT at T-Junction onto B481. Continue through Cookley Green. Having climbed to the top of the Chiltern Ridge this ride now joins Route 3 for a short distance.

17.9 RIGHT, signposted Russell's Water/Maidensgrove. Continue through Russell's Water past the Five Horseshoes PH and over a flat stretch of common before the steep descent through the woods.

21.0 RIGHT at T-Junction onto B480. Continue on a gradual downhill run through Stonor and Middle Assendon to Lower Assendon.

A left turn instead of the right leads to Stonor House. The Lord and Lady Camoys have been there since the 13th Century and the house dates from around 1190, built near a prehistoric stone circle recreated in the grounds and surrounded by a deer park. The red bricks give the house a pleasing face so that it fits into the surrounding countryside. The family were Catholics and suffered much for it in the 16th and 17th Centuries and an exhibition is dedicated to the Jesuit Martyr, Edmund Campion, who was sheltered here in 1581. Teas are available for visitors. Open afternoons April to September excluding non bank holiday Mondays and Fridays.

23.0 LEFT at T-Junction and follow A4130 into Henley along Golden Mile.

Henley-on-Thames is in a beautiful situation surrounded by wooded hills. The first ever boat race between Oxford and Cambridge took place here in 1829 followed by the first regatta ten years later. There are many old houses in the town such as the 15th Century Chantry House. A good place for refreshments with a wide choice of eating and drinking places, not surprising with Brakespear's Brewery in the town.

25.2 STRAIGHT ON at roundabout signposted Reading, then into one-way system that leads past brewery, to follow the river as far as the bridge and church. Then RIGHT at traffic lights and carry straight on at the next, signposted Peppard passing the Town Hall where the Tourist Information Centre is situated. It's a long hill out of the town before dropping past the entrance to Greys Court.

Greys Court (NT) is worth visiting. It is really two houses - one was rebuilt in the 16th Century and added to later while the original dank castle was left to fall into a state of ruin. A wander around the grounds will reveal a Tudor donkey wheel for raising well water and the Archbishop's Maze. Also tea-rooms in the Cromwellian Stables. The house itself is open, April to September, Monday, Wednesday, Friday, the grounds daily except Thursdays and Sundays. Opening hours for both 14.00 - 18.00.

29.5 LEFT at T-Junction signposted B481 Reading. Descend steep 14% twisting hill. On the other side RIGHT and carry on up hill.

By carrying straight on into Sonning Common, The Herb Farm is reached where teas are available in addition to a wide range of herbal products - there is also a maze. Open daily except Mondays and over Christmas.

30.6 RIGHT then STRAIGHT OVER crossroads and LEFT at next after The Reformation PH at Gallowstree Common, following signposts to Kidmore End.

32.9 RIGHT by church and well at Kidmore End signposted Tokers Green. Continue through hamlet and down hill into Caversham.

Wells were always of great importance in the Chilterns. There is one instance of beer actually being cheaper than water so it is not surprising that the one at Kidmore End was kept locked, with keys obtainable for a deposit of 6d.

36.1 LEFT down Priests Hill then RIGHT at T-Junction in bus/cycle lane.

36.3 RIGHT and follow signs to town centre crossing once again over Caversham Bridge and continuing over two roundabouts, under railway before LEFT signposted Railway Station.

37.2 END

6 BEYOND THE ROMANS

This ride starts from the isolated station of Winchfield and takes in much of the gently rolling countryside on the Hampshire/ Berkshire border. It heads north to the old Roman town of Silchester along quiet roads through unpretentious scenery before entering the Kennet valley at Aldermaston. From here it is up into extensive heathland and a wooded undulating area at Burghclere.

Closer and closer the North Downs come, but they are not climbed and after Kingsclere they slip away. Continue on through Sherborne St John, past The Vyne, through to Newnham and the Basingstoke Canal. From Up Nately to Greywell it is a short downland excursion before Odiham and the final miles past Winchfield church to the station.

A pleasant cycle through gently rolling countryside of woods and fields giving a strange feeling of remoteness at times. There are no major hills.

Maps	OS LR 186, 175, 174.
Distance	61.1 mile. No off-road. Can be shortened very easily.
Start/Finish	Winchfield Station on line between London and Basingstoke. Car parking.

Railway access

Winchfield is served by the stopping service between London Waterloo and Basingstoke - half-hourly during the week and hourly on Sundays.

Bramley or *Basingstoke* could be used as escape points.

Places to see

West Green Garden (NT) - Hartley Wintney.

Wellington Country Park - Risley.

Stratfield Saye House.

Roman town & museum - Silchester

Sandham Memorial Chapel (NT) - Burgclere.

The Vyne (NT) - Sherborne St John.

Basingstoke Canal & Greywell Tunnel.

Georgian houses, church & castle - Odiham.

Refreshments

Wellington Country Park - Risley, for visitors.

Tea rooms - West End Green, near Stratfield Saye Village.

Little Chef - on Newbury end of by-pass (A339) at Kingsclere.

Tea rooms - for visitors to The Vyne, Sherborne St John.

Tea rooms - by Basingstoke Canal, Winchfield Hurst.

A good scattering of pubs in this area which should fill any gaps in the refreshment chain.

BEYOND THE ROMANS

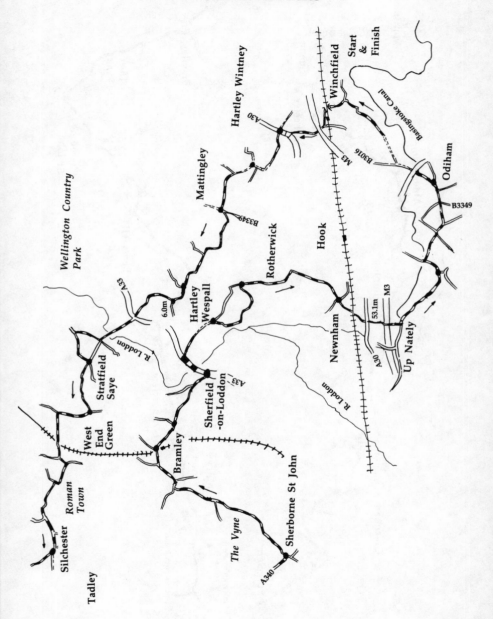

BEYOND THE ROMANS

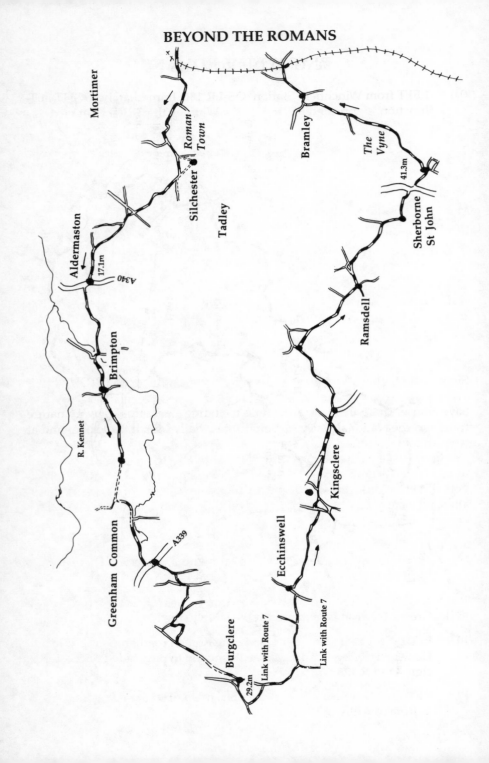

6 BEYOND THE ROMANS

0.0 LEFT from Winchfield Station. **OS LR 186.** Immediately RIGHT at T-Junction, signposted B3016 Hartley Wintney then RIGHT at next onto A30.

1.1 LEFT into Thackers Lane signposted West Green. Continue past West Green House (NT).

West Green House dates from the 18th Century. Though small it has great charm and a very attractive garden.

2.3 LEFT at T-Junction signposted Dipley/Mattingley. Then LEFT at the next onto B3349, signposted Alton. Immediately RIGHT signposted Chandlers Green/Stratfield Turgis.

The lanes around here twist and turn through flatish, uneventful yet very restful countryside and with a suprising feeling of remoteness considering how close it is to large settlements such as Fleet or Basingstoke.

6.0 RIGHT signposted Stratfield Turgis and STRAIGHT ACROSS the busy A33 by The Wellington Arms PH.

Signs point to the Wellington Country Park, three miles to the RIGHT but if you are interested in visiting it is best to take the small roads past Stratfield Saye House. There are many attractions including a miniature railway, nature trails and the National Dairy Museum. Open daily March to October and at weekends other times.
  Stratfield Saye House is off to the right through the lodge gates. It was built in 1630 and has been home to the Dukes of Wellington ever since the nation voted the first duke the money to buy an estate 'worthy of a national hero' after his victory at Waterloo. Open May to September, 11.30 to 16.00 daily except Fridays.

8.4 LEFT at T-Junction then RIGHT at crossroads in Stratfield Saye village by New Inn and former infant school, signposted Silchester/Mortimer.

10.2 RIGHT at T-Junction by The Four Horseshoes PH in West End Green. Teas can be obtained at the shop to the left.

10.9 LEFT signposted Silchester along the Roman road known as The Devils Highway. LEFT again at T-Junction to pass faded Silchester sign. **OS LR 175.**

12.4 RIGHT at T-Junction to pass remains of amphitheatre and long line of Roman walls.

Unlike other important Roman settlements Silchester decayed over the centuries. By the Middle Ages its role was taken over by Reading. Most of the outer walls still stand and there is medieval church built inside.

13.4   LEFT signposted Silchester. Follow round to T-Junction, passing the left turn to the modern settlement of Silchester.

The left turn to the modern Silchester also passes the small, unpretentious building next to the parish hall, which is the museum and is worth visiting to know more about the Roman town, though the more important finds are housed in the County Museum in Reading.

14.0   RIGHT at T-Junction and immediately RIGHT into Stoke Road, signposted Aldermaston.

15.2   LEFT at large roundabout and immediately RIGHT signposted Aldermaston. Follow through the wooded heathland. **OS LR 174.**

17.1   RIGHT at T-Junction onto A340 and Aldermaston village.

Situated in the Kennet valley, Aldermaston still has many pleasant brick and tiled cottages. Apart from the Aldermaston Peace Marches of the 1960s the village is well known in horticultural circles as the place where the William Pear was first grown.

17.3   LEFT at the roundabout by The Hinds Head PH and following the signs to Brimpton, RIGHT at T-Junction followed by LEFT.

19.4   RIGHT on top of the hill by The Three Horseshoes PH and follow road through Brimpton onto a high open stretch of common.

21.7   STRAIGHT ON at junction onto road that runs beside Greenham Common airfield where the slogans of the peace protesters are now fading from the surface. At T-Junction RIGHT.

23.9   LEFT onto A339, signposted Basingstoke. Shortly RIGHT and then LEFT at T-Junction following Ecchinswell signs.

24.9   RIGHT signposted Adbury/Newtown. Follow lane through beautiful wooded stretch of countryside. After it drops to bridge and ford LEFT at T-Junction then RIGHT to avoid the farm.

26.4   LEFT at T-Junction at top of hill. Continue past entrance to Adbury House to Burgclere. At T-Junction by church LEFT signposted Sandham Memorial Chapel.

29.2   LEFT again, signposted Ecchinswell. Go straight on to view the Sandham Memorial Chapel. Meet Route 7 here.

On the Berkshire/Hampshire border and close to the foot of the downs, Burgclere was often a base for William Cobbett in his Rural Rides. Perhaps the village is remembered now more for the Memorial Chapel (NT). It was built in the 1920s as a memorial to the First World War and is notable for the paintings by Stanley Spencer of war scenes in Salonica which cover the walls. Open April to end of October 11.30 to 18.00 Wednesday to Sunday plus Bank Holiday Mondays. Weekends only in November and March.

29.8　RIGHT at T-Junction, then LEFT and LEFT again at T-Junction, following signs into Ecchinswell.

32.1　RIGHT in the village. For the first few yards this road runs close to a very clear stream, a hallmark of the county where streams flow from the chalk hills. Continue into Kingsclere, then RIGHT into Popes Hill, marked No Through Road and RIGHT after barrier into the town centre.

Kingsclere at the foot of the chalk hills was an important local road junction. Now time has passed it by with the construction of a new by-pass for the traffic between Basingstoke and Newbury so it is possible to admire the fine old buildings. The church weather vane is in the shape of a bed-bug or louse. Legend has it that King John gave it as a present to the local monks after spending a night at their unhygienic quarters!

34.2　RIGHT by The George and Horn PH, marked No Through Road, into Basingstoke Road. Continue to No Entry sign at end before LEFT onto footpath and RIGHT at by-pass.

35.6　LEFT signposted Wolverton and, after passing through village RIGHT, signposted Ramsdell.

38.8　LEFT at crossroads by church and continue through Charter Alley and Monk Sherborne, **OS LR 175**, to A340.

41.3　RIGHT at T-Junction and immediately LEFT into Sherborne St John. At staggered crossroads it is LEFT again, signposted The Vyne and continue through village, round to the right. Follow road past The Vyne (NT).

The Vyne is a Tudor mansion house with the earliest classical portico to a country house in England which was added in 1654 and looks rather out of place. However, it is well worth visiting if only to view the wainscotting and Tudor chapel with its Renaissance glass. Tea room for visitors. Open daily, except non Bank Holiday Mondays and Fridays, April to October, 13.30 to 17.30.

44.3　RIGHT at T-Junction, signposted Bramley Station. Continue through the expanding village of Bramley to Sherfield-on-Loddon.

47.0   LEFT at T-Junction by The White Hart PH, marked No Through
        Road, and LEFT again on main road A33.

47.6   RIGHT signposted Hartley Wespall. In the village RIGHT at
        staggered crossroads along narrow lane.

50.0   RIGHT at T-Junction by The Fox PH. Continue through Rotherwick
        to Newnham, **OS LR 186**. STRAIGHT ACROSS crossroads,
        signposted Nately Scures. Descend hill, under railway to the A30.

53.1   CONTINUE straight across A30 to cross M3 and Basingstoke Canal.

This section of the canal has recently been restored. It never proved very
profitable from the time it was opened in 1794 and further west it has mostly
disappeared.

53.7   LEFT at T-Junction at Up Nately. Continue past church with its
        Norman arch and over the hill while the canal goes the easy way
        through a tunnel. By The Fox and Goose PH at Greywell turn
        RIGHT and continue up hill.

A footpath on the left immediately after this last turning leads to the entrance
of the Greywell Tunnel. This proved a major expense to the builders of the
canal and a headache to those trying to restore it. Apart from the roof having
collapsed it is also the home to a colony of about 2,000 bats of five different
species, some rare.

56.0   LEFT at T-Junction and immediately RIGHT signposted Odiham.
        STRAIGHT ON at junction up West Street to junction with B3349
        and STRAIGHT ACROSS into Odiham High Street.

Odiham has many Georgian houses and other old buildings including the
fine Perpendicular church .With a population of only 250 Odiham was once
the largest town in Hampshire after Winchester.

57.8   LEFT into No Through Road, signposted Basingstoke Canal, after
        High Street. Cross the canal by the former Cricketers PH and
        continue to end of road.

58.2   STRAIGHT ON through subway and immediately LEFT to join
        B3016. There turn RIGHT and, after cattle grid, RIGHT signposted
        Winchfield Church.

60.5   LEFT at T-Junction after church and continue to station.

61.1   END.

7 WATERSHIP DOWN

T he quiet station of Micheldever up in the Hampshire Downs between Basingstoke and Winchester is the start. We go northwards across those rolling open hills to the Test Valley and Overton. Then more climbing through the wide open fields, past coppices and belts of trees. At the top, the ridge is followed to Watership Down at 779 feet.

The hard gained height is shed by the plunge towards Burgclere and a further descent to Kintbury by the Kennet and Avon Canal. The Downs beckon again to Inkpen and then a climb to over 900 feet near Walbury Hill. Over the hill and down, down to Combe, Hurstbourne Tarrant and St Mary Bourne along a winding valley. Up and over to Whitchurch to revisit the River Test once more. Only a few miles across the Downs remain before the circle is completed at Micheldever.

This ride has some long but rewarding hills but nothing too steep apart from the climb from Inkpen. Ample compensation in the long descents and fine views.

Maps	OS LR 185, 174.
Distance	46.7 miles. Of this 1.7 miles off-road but rideable.
Start/Finish	Micheldever Station.

Railway access

Micheldever station is served by the stopping service between London Waterloo and Southampton, at hourly intervals. Sunday service is limited.

Basingstoke is an alternative.

Kintbury is served by trains from Reading to Bedwyn.

Overton and *Whitchurch* are on the Salisbury line where new turbo trains have **very** limited cycle accommodation.

Places to see

Watership Down (779 feet).

Sandham Memorial Chapel (NT) - Burgclere.

Highclere Castle.

Hollington Herb Centre.

Kennet and Avon Canal - Kintbury.

Walbury Hill (974 feet) & *Combe Gibbet.*

Silk Mill - Whitchurch.

Refreshments

Tea rooms - Hollington Herb Centre.

Tea rooms - Kintbury.

Tea rooms - Whitchurch Silk Mill.

WATERSHIP DOWN

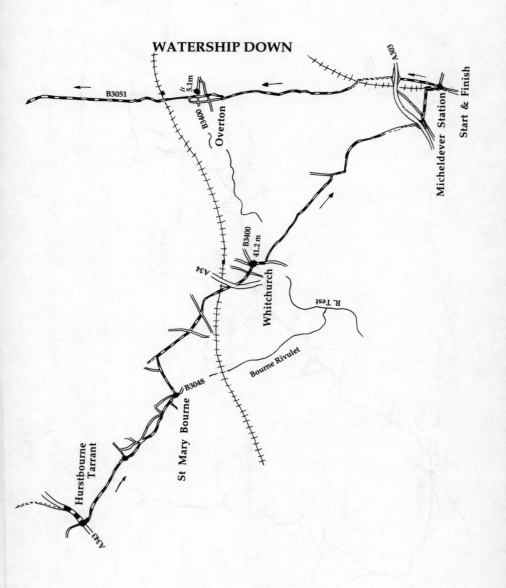

WATERSHIP DOWN

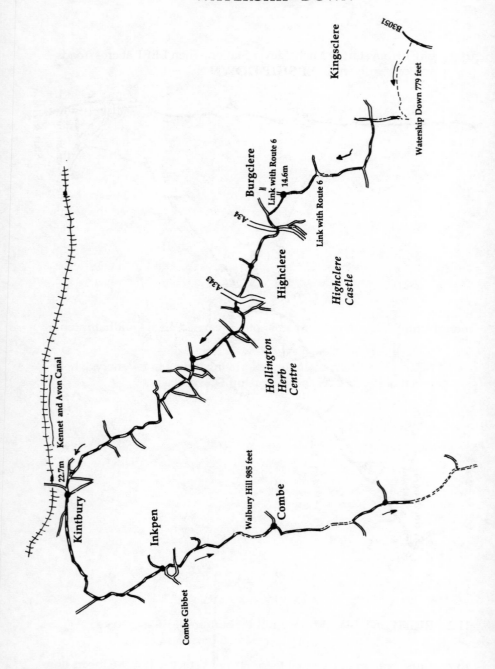

Kingsclere

B3051

Watership Down 779 feet

Burgclere

Link with Route 6

14.6m

A34

Link with Route 6

Highclere

Highclere
Castle

A343

Hollington
Herb
Centre

Kennet and Avon Canal

22.7m

Kintbury

Inkpen

Walbury Hill 985 feet

Combe

Combe Gibbet

7 WATERSHIP DOWN

0.0   LEFT from start at Micheldever Station. Then LEFT at crossroads
       and over railway.

Micheldever Station is in an isolated position three miles from Micheldever
village and formerly with nothing but a pub and a few houses, although
some new development has taken place. The building itself dates from 1840.
If saving 0.6 mile is of great concern then there is a short cut by turning left
instead of right in the subway and joining the road to Overton via the oil
terminal. But check there are no shunting trains.

0.3   LEFT signposted Overton. Follow this road over the Downs before
       dropping into the Test valley and Overton. Follow road through to
       village centre and traffic lights at crossroads with B3400.

Though it does not look it, Overton started life as a planned town; set up by
the Bishop of Winchester in 1200. It became important as a centre for the
cattle and wool trade. Imagine 18,000 sheep gathered there in the market
place. With the Test rising nearby and providing a source of power, the
manufacture of silk was established in the 19th Century and today the
manufacture of the paper for bank notes is carried on at Quidhampton.

5.1   STRAIGHT ACROSS onto B3051 at traffic lights and continue over
       railway climbing again into the rolling downland scenery, where
       much of Richard Adams Watership Down is set.

8.7   RIGHT at T-Junction, signposted B3051 Kingsclere and up the hill.
       OS LR 174.

9.5   SHARP LEFT by the car park sign at the top and follow track over
       Cannon Heath Down to Watership Down 779 feet. Where track
       becomes a wide grassy field follow the fence on the right.

Good views at the beginning and near the trig point. The horse gallops
bordering the track are strictly private.

10.9   RIGHT near the trig point and descend steep narrow bridleway to
       metalled road.

Alternative is to swing left of the trig point and then right onto the same
road, which might be a wiser option in wet weather.

11.2   RIGHT and descend steep hill. At bottom LEFT signposted
       Sydmonton, then RIGHT signposted Burgclere.

13.7   LEFT onto road Unsuitable for Heavy Vehicles. Route 6 meets here.

14.6   LEFT into Spring Lane and LEFT again, signposted Highclere. Pass the Sandham Memorial Chapel (NT), described in Route 6.

15.5   RIGHT over A34, signposted Highclere. Descend hill.

Highclere Castle can be reached by carrying straight along the A34. It is the ancestral home of the Earl of Caernarvon. The house bears a striking resemblance to the Houses of Parliament for both were designed by Sir Charles Barry and built in the same period of the 19th Century. The place might seem familiar for it has been used on many TV programmes. The interior and gardens along with various exhibitions can be visited from July to September, Wednesdays to Sundays plus Bank Holidays, 14.00 to 18.00

17.2   STRAIGHT ACROSS A343, signposted Kintbury and Herb Garden.

The Hollington Herb Centre has a fine collection of herbs and scented plants within its walled garden. There is a shop and free admission to the tea room. Open middle of March to end of September.

18.9   LEFT at T-Junction, LEFT at next, following signs to Kintbury

Situated on the Kennet & Avon Canal, Kintbury was known for the production of whiting - an important ingredient in paint. In the church is a brass to a certain John Gunter, who, on his death in 1624, had managed to live in the reigns of five different monarchs. It is peaceful down by the canal apart form high speed trains roaring past. There is a pub down by the lock and a railway station nearby. Also a tea shop in the main part of the village.

22.7   LEFT at T-junction in village, signposted Hungerford/Inkpen. After continuing through village LEFT signposted Templeton/Inkpen. Continue through former gates into the grounds of Inglewood House which is now a health hydro.

25.0   LEFT at T-Junction, signposted Inkpen/Combe. Continue past The Swan Inn before turning RIGHT at T-Junction and immediately LEFT signposted Upper Inkpen/Combe Gibbet. Here the climbing begins in earnest under the shadow of the Downs ending on a 1 in 6 gradient for the final stretch up to almost 900 feet.

At the top of this massive chalk escarpment dramatic views are to be had. To the left is Walbury Hill, the highest point in Berkshire. From the top a huge sweep of country can be seen, from the Chilterns in the North East to Wiltshire in the West.

To the right up a stony track and visible for a long way stands Combe Gibbet. It was originally erected in 1674 to hang a man and woman for the murder of their children and served as a warning to any potential wrong doers. The whole area now is a favourite spot for hang-gliding.

27.9 CONTINUE straight on at the top of the hill, signposted Combe/ Linkholt. The first part of the descent is quite steep before the tiny remote hamlet of Combe is reached. By the little Norman church of St Swithin and the manor house is a very sharp left-hand bend. The descent becomes very gentle and it's an idyllic road to be cycling down on a fine summer day as it twists beneath the downland hills. **OS LR 185.**

33.7 RIGHT at T-Junction, signposted A343 Andover into Hurstbourne Tarrant.

The church, which dates from 1190 has a remarkable wall-painting of 'The Three Living and the Three Dead', representing three kings meeting three skeletons. William Cobbet thought the village, called Uphusband in his writings, was worth going many miles to see, though he saw the plight of the labouring classes as one of the worst he had seen anywhere.

34.3 LEFT by The George and Dragon PH, signposted B3048 St Mary Bourne. Follow road to village.

St Mary Bourne is another beautiful village. With its long main street, flanked by attractive old houses and with its clear chalk stream completing the picture, it is definitely a place to linger in.

37.7 LEFT by The George PH and up the hill. After road levels out LEFT at T-Junction and immediately RIGHT onto road with low bridge sign. Descend into Whitchurch passing under three bridges.

41.2 FIRST RIGHT at roundabout, signposted Silk Mill. Continue and cross the River Test.

Whitchurch grew up as an important river crossing and had its heyday in the coaching era, hence the Georgian houses. Now it is by-passed by the main road and one of the railway lines is closed. The silk mill was built on the banks of the Test in 1800 and today manufactures silk for items like the Queen's Council Gowns, or items like coloured taffetas for academic gowns and theatrical costumes. The old power loom utilises the energy produced by the water wheel. Shop and tea rooms. Open all year, Tuesday to Sunday plus Bank Holidays from 10.30 to 17.00.

41.5 LEFT up Micheldever Road into more rolling downland scenery. RIGHT at T-Junction and pass under A303. Then LEFT and immediately RIGHT following signs to Micheldever Station.

46.7 END

8 RIVER & GARDENS RIDE

This route is designed to avoid the busy roads that are sometimes associated with Surrey, the closer to London it comes. There is nothing to hinder the enjoyment of cycling by the Thames from Hampton Court to Walton. You encounter a slightly built up area around Weybridge then progress to the Wey Navigation for another long stretch of car-free riding by the quietly flowing water.

The riverside path is forsaken for Ripley and a trip into the Surrey heathland to Chatley Heath. Then to Cobham, and Esher before the circle is completed at Hampton Court.

This is a flat ride, with only slight hills involved. A great deal is off-road which needs to be ridden with due consideration for others as the paths are also popular with walkers.

Maps	OS LR 176, 187, 186.
Distance	24.1 miles. Of this 12.7 miles is off-road, most of which is along river and canal towpaths which should offer easy riding except after very wet weather. The section to Chatley Heath can be sandy and should be walked while the stretch from Cobham is easily rideable.
Start/Finish	Hampton Court Station.

Railway access

Hampton Court on the end of the line from London Waterloo.

Weybridge, Addlestone, Byfleet, Cobham & Esher could be used as escape points.

Places to see

Royal Horticultural Society Gardens - Wisley

Semaphore Tower - Chatley Heath.

Painshill Gardens - Cobham.

Claremont Park (NT) - Esher.

Hampton Court Palace.

Refreshments

Coffee Shop - at Marina & open-air *snack bar* at bridge, Walton-on-Thames.

Watson's Bakery & tea rooms - Ripley.

Tea stall - at entrance to Wisley Gardens.

Tea bar - in car-park, Boulder Mere.

Tea rooms - weekdays only, Cobham and for visitors to Painshill.

Good choice of pubs - *The Seven Stars* near Ripley is popular with cyclists.

RIVER & GARDENS RIDE

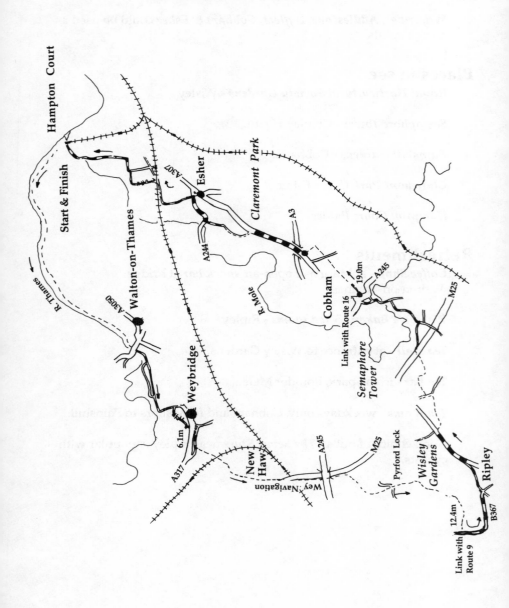

8 RIVER & GARDENS RIDE

0.0 START from Hampton Court Station. **OS LR 176.** Cross road and take A3050, signposted Walton. Follow towards Thames.

0.2 RIGHT at war memorial onto the towpath. It is loose in places but rideable enough. Watch out for pedestrians and fishermen, particularly at weekends.

4.7 CROSS OVER footbridge where towpath divides to pass Walton Marina, where there is a coffee shop, then CONTINUE under Walton Bridge, past open air snack bar.

4.9 CONTINUE onto metalled road along Desborough Channel, a navigational short-cut to avoid a twisty section of river, and follow into Weybridge.

5.5 RIGHT after St Maurs School into Portmore Park Road, through gates into former estate but now a residential area.

6.1 RIGHT at mini-roundabout onto main road A317. Cross bridge and take FIRST LEFT down a short stretch of bumpy road to T-Junction by the Wey Navigation.

The River Wey and Godalming Navigation NT is one of the earliest waterways to be built. Cutting off the awkward stretches of the river Wey it was built as far as Guildford in 1653 and later extended to Godalming in 1763. Its entire length of 19.5 miles is managed by the National Trust. The tow-path is used a lot by walkers and there is nothing to say that cyclists cannot go on it as well. Obviously, consideration needs to be shown to all fellow users. Since some parts can be muddy, or narrow, it is wise to let your speed match that of the flowing water and let the miles drift slowly by.

6.3 RIGHT at T-Junction onto what used to be the old main road. Note how the water level of the river on the left is higher.

6.5 LEFT over footbridge onto towpath Go under railway and past the tall impressive former mill at Coxes Wharf, now luxury flats, and continue to main road A318 at New Haw.

7.8 CROSS main road at New Haw. A left turn will take you to New Haw Station. Continue towards Byfleet and bridge that carries the old main road.

9.0 TURN LEFT onto old main road, then swing round to RIGHT to regain towpath other side of buildings. Then pass under new road and continue to Pyrford Lock. **OS LR 187.**

This stretch includes the junction with the Basingstoke Canal that is mentioned in Route 6. A signpost points out that it is 31 miles to Greywell, far less as the crow flies, an indication of its very twisting course. After the collapse of the Greywell Tunnel in 1932 the canal was abandoned and left to rack and ruin. Surrey and Hampshire County Councils bought their respective sections in 1973 and 1976 and began a massive restoration programme, now more or less complete.

10.5   CONTINUE straight on along towpath by Pyrford Lock. Positioning makes The Anchor a popular pub for food and drink. CROSS weir at Walsham Gate. Then after a more open stretch, the remains of Newark Priory can be seen before turning RIGHT over footbridge to opposite bank and reaching B367. **OS LR 186** for short stretch.

12.4   LEFT at bridge and continue past Royal Seven Stars PH into Ripley. **OS LR 187**. Route 9 carries straight on along the towpath.

13.5   LEFT at T-Junction in Ripley. Almost opposite is Watson's Bakery. Continue to very brief meeting with A3.

Ripley, on the Portsmouth road, was prosperous in the coaching days, until the advent of the railways. It underwent a revival in the 1870s through the increasing popularity of cycling along this road, considered to be one of he best in the countryside. The Anchor PH became enormously popular both for refreshments and as an overnight stop and it was not uncommon to see two to three hundred bicycles stacked outside.

14.9   LEFT signposted Wisley Gardens then LEFT again towards entrance.

There is a tea stall by the entrance, open at weekends. The gardens themselves, with 250 acres devoted to ornamental plants, vegetables, and fruit are world famous. Open Mondays to Saturdays all year except Christmas. Sunday is restricted to RHS members only.

15.1   LEFT onto footpath, signposted Elm Lane to cross A3 by footbridge. On other side RIGHT then LEFT and CONTINUE onto track in woods. This can be muddy in places but the worst is avoidable.

15.9   LEFT at road then RIGHT into car park, marked Semaphore Tower and follow Red Path onto Chatley Heath and the tower.

Carry straight on if refreshments are required from the tea bar in the Boulder Mere car park. The Semaphore Tower was part of a system designed to carry messages rapidly between London and Portsmouth and other places. On a clear day it only took 45 seconds to signal the hours of one-o-clock from Greenwich to Portsmouth and back again, but fog was another matter, and the whole idea proved something of a nine day wonder in the end. Surrey

County Council restored the tower in 1989 and it is now open to the public on weekends from April to September.

16.7 CONTINUE from tower onto metalled road and descend past gate to bridge crossing M25. On the other side RIGHT and continue to next T-Junction. Then LEFT and follow road past The Plough PH.

18.3 LEFT at T-Junction and RIGHT at the next in Cobham after bridge and church.

A left turn here leads past the entrance to Painshill Park. This 18th Century landscape garden has recently been restored and is well worth visiting, though opening hours are limited to Sundays only April to September.

19.0 LEFT into Hogshill Lane by cleaners, then FORK RIGHT past No Through Road sign. FORK LEFT onto bridleway before Ferndown Gardens.

19.6 STRAIGHT OVER metalled Icklingham Road to join Burstead Close then FORK RIGHT into further unmetalled section. STRAIGHT over Fairmile Lane into Green Lane and follow to end.

20.3 FIRST LEFT in front of fire hydrant sign onto bridleway, signposted Portsmouth Road.

20.5 RIGHT onto main road A307. Cross A3 before LEFT into West End Lane. Follow downhill to West End village and roundabout.

Close by is the entrance to Claremont Park NT. This is another fine example of an 18th Century landscape garden, with lake and turf amphitheatre. Very attractive in autumn. Open daily all year round except for Mondays November to March. Tea rooms for visitors.

21.6 RIGHT onto main road A244 and follow uphill to Esher. LEFT on green by war memorial into More Lane, marked with low bridge warnings. Descend hill and immediately after passing under railway. **OS LR 176.**

22.2 LEFT into Woodend and STRAIGHT ACROSS crossroads into Grove Way which is followed to T-Junction.

23.2 LEFT and follow Ember Lane past Ember Court, which is a training centre for mounted police, into East Molesey. There FORK RIGHT at mini roundabout in front of police station, signposted Hampton Court, then STRAIGHT ON at next to reach main road opposite railway station.

24.4 END

9 WEYSIDE TO NEWLANDS

From Effingham Junction it is through gently rolling woods and fields to Send and the quiet waters of the Wey Navigation until Trigg's Lock is reached. Beyond Sutton and Jacobswell, Guildford is reached. Past the cathedral on Stag Hill, looking down on the city, then through the centre and up the other side to Pewley Down. From here there are fine views looking back over Guildford.

Continue along the North Downs to Newlands Corner and to Combe Bottom, the highest point at 600 feet. That height is soon lost in the descent through Sheepleas, and despite a couple of hiccups it is downhill most of the way through East Horsely to Effingham Junction.

For the most part a reasonably flat ride with no major climbs except from Guildford up to Pewley Down.

Map	OS LR 187, 186.
Distance	25.6 miles. Of this 6.5 miles is off-road in two sections - along the Wey Navigation, which can be rough in places, and on the North Downs.
Start/Finish	Effingham Junction Station.

Railway Access

Effingham Junction is served mainly by services from Waterloo to Guildford that run half hourly during the week and hourly on Sundays. Also from Epsom and, except on Sundays, Thameslink from Luton via Kings Cross to Guildford.

Guildford on London Waterloo to Portsmouth line, served by Thameslink and also from the east via Redhill and Dorking.

Places to see

Cathedral, Castle, High Street, museums - Guildford.

Countryside Information Centre - Newlands Corner.

Refreshments

Wheelers Rest - near Send.

Cathedral Refectory - plus plenty of other eating places as well - Guildford.

Tea bar - Newlands Corner, by Countryside Information Centre or indoors at *The Barn* across the A25.

A good choice of pubs including the *Seven Stars* near Ripley and *The Fox and Hounds* in Sutton.

WEYSIDE TO NEWLANDS

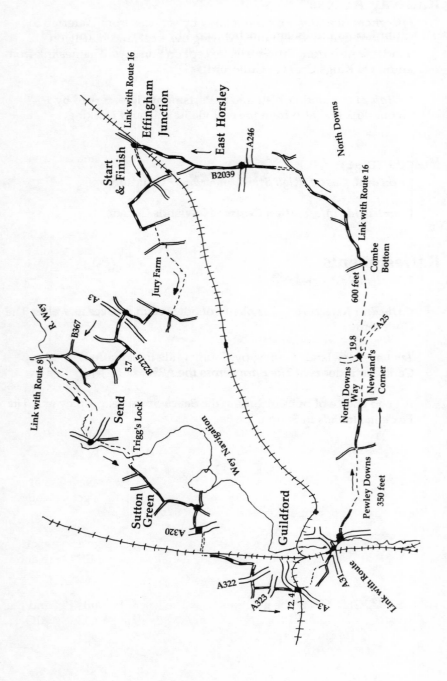

9 WEYSIDE TO NEWLANDS

0.0 LEFT from Effingham Junction and LEFT in front of The Lord Howard PH, signposted East Horsley. **OS LR 187.**

0.4 RIGHT before crossing railway, signposted Drift Golf Course. RIGHT again at staggered crossroads, signposted Ockham. Then SECOND LEFT into Green Lane.

2.2 LEFT at T-junction into Long Reach. Then RIGHT onto bridleway, which can be muddy after wet weather. LEFT onto metalled road.

2.8 FIRST RIGHT onto concrete road through Jury Farm. Continue along this public bridleway past next farm to Hungry Hill Lane.

4.2 RIGHT at crossroads then LEFT into Gambles Lane. Wheelers Rest, a hugely popular refreshment stop for cyclists, is on the left up the drive. Follow to right past mobile home park before LEFT for bridge over A3.

5.7 LEFT at T-Junction by Ripley Nursery. **OS LR 186.** RIGHT after The Jovial Sailor PH into Send Common Road. STRAIGHT ON at corner by green, signposted Pyrford.

6.7 LEFT at bend past large gravel pit, then RIGHT at T-Junction by Papercourt Farm. LEFT at next by The Seven Stars PH. Follow to bridge with traffic lights over Wey. Join Route 8 here.

7.7 LEFT onto left hand towpath by river. Later cross footbridge to other side. Path is sandy in places.

9.6 LEFT and then RIGHT at Send to cross A247 by The New Inn at Cartbridge. After the lock at Worsfold Gates the path goes through a rough and potentially muddy section to Triggs Lock.

10.6 RIGHT before the keeper's cottage to cross footbridge and lock to a footpath which leads to a barrier by metalled road. LEFT here and continue to Sutton Green.

11.2 STRAIGHT ON at the junction, past The Fox & Hounds PH and the entrance to Sutton Place, once owned by the late Paul Getty. RIGHT at the T-Junction in Jacobs Well.

12.4   LEFT onto A320 before RIGHT at roundabout, signposted A322. LEFT onto bridleway immediately after passing under railway.

13.0   STRAIGHT ON at Grange Road in the outskirts of Guildford. RIGHT at traffic lights in front of grocers. Continue past the former Stoughton Barracks and STRAIGHT ACROSS into Shepherds Lane at the next traffic lights.

14.2   LEFT into Northway before descending to Aldershot Road. Here RIGHT and immediately LEFT into Southway.

14.9   LEFT onto metalled footpath near shops to pass under A3, over railway to entrance for Surrey University campus. STRAIGHT ON here and immediately LEFT up hill to cathedral.

The modern Cathedral of the Holy Spirit occupies a prominent position on top of Stag Hill overlooking Guildford. It was begun in 1936 and not finished until 1966. Refreshments at the refectory.

15.5   RIGHT before cathedral and down steps to follow path round side before RIGHT down more short flights of steps to Cathedral Close.

15.7   LEFT and continue down hill. Then LEFT at T-Junction into Madrid Road.

16.2   LEFT again into Farnham Road over railway. At traffic lights STRAIGHT ACROSS into one-way system (Station to left). KEEP RIGHT past entrance to North Street.

16.6   LEFT into High Street. Follow non-cobbled section RIGHT into Chapel Street past the ancient church of St Mary.

The High Street is cobbled at the top and contains many historic buildings. Controversial road schemes existed as far back as 1938 when it was proposed to demolish one side to improve traffic flow.

16.8   LEFT into Castle Street by The Kings Head PH. Continue up hill past entrance to Norman Castle before RIGHT into South Hill and immediately LEFT up the steep climb of Pewley Hill.

Only the keep remains of this impressive castle set in a beautiful garden. Grounds open all year round, castle April to September.
At the top of Pewley Hill is Semaphore House, which, like ChatleyHeath

(Route 8) formed part of the semaphore chain between London and Portsmouth. It was in use from 1822 to 1847 and is now a private residence.

17.4   CONTINUE along bridleway at top of Pewley Downs (350 feet). Fine views from here on a clear day. Keeping towards hedge on left side enter narrow stretch and continue to junction.

18.4   STRAIGHT ON along metalled road. At Albury Downs CONTINUE either on bridleway, which can be very muddy, through trees to left or on open footpath where cycling prohibited. There are fine views from here. Follow through to Newlands Corner.

Newlands Corner is a popular local beauty spot. The Countryside Information Centre is well worth visiting for finding out more about the area. There is a snack bar next to it. Across the A25 there is the more luxurious accommodation offered by The Barn

19.8   LEFT on the A25 and LEFT again onto North Downs Way and continue on well surfaced bridleway amongst the trees. **OS LR 187.** Then CROSS road for further short stretch. Here, at Combe Bottom and 600feet, is the highest point of the ride.

20.6   LEFT at next road and after flat stretch descend long hill through to Sheepleas. Join Route 16 from Portsmouth here and for rest of ride.

22.4   LEFT up Chalk Lane with width restriction and down to A246 at East Horsley. At The Duke of Wellington Tavern STRAIGHT ON to B2039 through East Horsley. RIGHT, signposted Effingham and continue to Effingham Junction. At Lord Howard PH turn RIGHT for station.

25.6   END

10 THE WAVERLEY RIDE

The steep but rewarding climb from Guildford covers the section of the North Downs known as the Hogs Back and attains a height of over 450 feet. It is then down to the lighter sandy soils to the south through which the river Wey flows - to be crossed several times during this ride.

The route continues through wooded heathland to Millbridge and into Alice Holt Forest, a fine example of commercial forestry at its best. Up to Binsted the route climbs into the Hampshire Downs before descending to the sandy soils and heavily wooded area around Frensham Ponds. A last sandy ridge is conquered before the final drop to Guildford.

This is quite an undulating ride. The longest and steepest climb is that out of Guildford. A good route for picnicing on a warm summer day.

Map	OS LR 186.
Distance	42.1 miles. Of this 1.4 miles is off-road along the North Downs Way which is generally rideable but has sandy patches which sometimes makes riding difficult.
Start/Finish	Guildford Station.

Railway access

Guildford has a frequent train service from Waterloo on the Portsmouth and Effingham Junction Lines. Also Thameslink from Luton & Kings Cross (not Sundays) and services from Redhill, Reading.

Godalming & Farncombe, as well as *Farnham & Bentley* on the Waterloo to Alton line are close to this route and provide escape points.

Places to see

Castle, Cathedral, museums - and much more besides, Guildford.

Church, Watts Gallery & Memorial Chapel - Compton.

Waverley Abbey (EH).

Rural Life Centre - between Tilford and Millbridge.

Alice Holt Forest.

Church - Binsted.

Frensham Ponds.

Loseley House & Estate - near Farncombe.

Refreshments

Watts Gallery - Compton.

Manor Farm Craft Centre - Seale.

Rural Life Centre - between Tilford & Millbridge.

Garden Centre & Country Park - Frensham.

Good choice of pubs such as *The Good Intent* at Puttenham or *The Rising Sun* at Tilford.

THE WAVERLEY RIDE

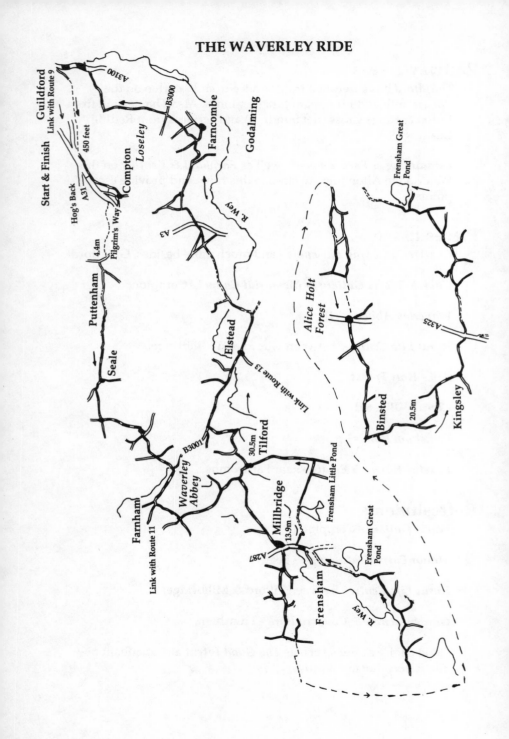

10 THE WAVERLEY RIDE

0.0   RIGHT from Guildford Station. **OS LR 186.** To avoid the rigours of the one-way system push along the pavement, over the traffic lights until the High Street on the left.

0.2   RIGHT up The Mount. A very steep climb past Guildford Cemetery where signs point to the grave of Lewis Carroll. Continue through barrier, before road flattens out onto the Hogs Back, on newly surfaced bridleway with no traffic apart from occasional New Age Travellers.

2.0   LEFT on A31. Immediately LEFT again, signposted Portsmouth/ Petersfield/ Compton. Descend hill then LEFT again just before joining the A3. Go past Watts Gallery, where teas can be obtained.

3.0   RIGHT onto North Downs Way, signposted Monkshatch Garden Cottages.

Straight on is Compton village itself. Interesting church with unique two storey Romanesque sanctuary added to the chancel in the 12th Century. The Watts Gallery contains a museum of the paintings by G.F.Watts (1817-1904) who lived in the village. In the cemetery is the burial chapel with a very striking Art Nouveau interior designed in 1896 by his wife .

3.2   KEEP TO LEFT after passing under both old and new versions of A3. The bridge that carries the former bears a cross, indicating that this section of track is regarded as a section of the Pilgrims Way.

4.4   RIGHT at T-Junction at end of sometimes sandy track by Harvesters. Then immediately LEFT into Puttenham, an attractive mixed brick and stone village. Pass The Good Intent PH and follow road to Seale in the lee of the Hogs Back.

7.1   SECOND LEFT in Seale village into Seale Lane near the Manor Farm Craft Centre, where teas are served. At crossroads LEFT into Binton Lane, signposted Elstead/Tilford and climb into sandy woodland.

8.7   CONTINUE over crossroads after chapel, signposted Waverley/ Tilford onto Botany Hill. Climb to top then STRAIGHT OVER staggered crossroads. Descend hill to junction with B3001.

9.6   CONTINUE straight on, past the turning to Waverley Abbey (EH).

LEFT after flat stretch by River Wey and climb through woods.

Waverley Abbey, in its sheltered position by the river Wey beneath pine clad hills was founded in 1128 and was the first home of the Cistercian order in England. It lasted until 1536. By the time Sir Walter Scott was staying the other side of the river in Waverley House, the hills must have looked so romantic that he named his Waverley Novels after them. They were also one of the childhood haunts of William Cobbett who recalled seeing a cat '...as big as a middle-sized spaniel dog...' disappearing into a hollow elm tree, and getting a beating when he related his story. Cats that size will not be seen today in these ruins, now run by English Heritage and reached by a riverside path. They are open, free of charge, all the year round.

10.8   LEFT at crossroads, signposted Tilford. Descend long hill to pass the entry sign to Tilford.

12.2   RIGHT, signposted Frensham. Continue past Rural Life Centre where there is a tea-room and Frensham Garden Centre where there is a coffee shop. Enter Millbridge, bearing left around the one-way system.

The Rural Life Centre, as well as being a handy refreshment stop, is also worth visiting in its own right, not only for displays of farming implements but for a wheelwrights shop, an arboretum and narrow gauge railway. Open April 1st - September 30th 11.00-18.00, Wednesday to Sunday including Bank Holidays.

13.9   RIGHT at T-Junction by the Mariners pub then LEFT, signposted Shortfield/Dockenfield.

The Village Workshop further up the road has an interesting collection of artefacts including old bicycles.

14.1   LEFT at T-Junction then RIGHT after the Holly Bush, signposted Broomfield/West End. Then LEFT past West End House.

15.7   LEFT at T-Junction then RIGHT where road comes in from left onto well defined track leading into Alice Holt Forest.

16.0   RIGHT at T-junction onto forestry road. KEEP RIGHT at next junction, before LEFT onto Horse Ride. This can be muddy but it is not long before gravelled track is reached and another LEFT turn leads to the visitors centre.

Alice Holt is a fully working forest with a long pedigree which included providing timber for the Royal Navy. There are forestry trails and a great variety of wild life. Drinks machines at the visitors centre.

16.5 FOLLOW metalled road from visitors centre then RIGHT at T-Junction. At Halfway House PH CONTINUE over the A325 and descend to The Jolly Farmer PH.

17.5 STRAIGHT ACROSS, signposted Binsted/Alton. This road climbs into the Hampshire downland. It is fairly gradual but there are several steeper pitches. Continue into Binsted. At top of hill and after The Cedars and by the converted oast houses, LEFT past church for a mostly downhill run.

The large aisle Norman/Early English church contains a Crusaders tomb. A more modern counterpart, Viscount Montgomery, is buried in the church yard.

20.5 LEFT and continue past The Straits - a large poultry farm. Then RIGHT signposted Kingsley. Continue on long descent. LEFT at T-Junction onto B3004, signposted Bordon.

22.9 CONTINUE over staggered crossroads on A325 by the New Inn, signposted Headley. After the country club LEFT signposted Frensham and follow the river Wey for a short distance.

24.4 LEFT at T-Junction, signposted Churt/Frensham. Continue past Frensham Great Pond to Frensham village.

Frensham Great Pond covers 108 acres, big enough for the testing of the first sea-plane in 1913 and for sailing and wind surfing today. Together with the Little Ponds this sandy heathland has been designated as the Frensham Ponds Country Park with rangers to manage the fragile environment. Hotel and restaurant by the side of the Great Pond, refreshments elsewhere in the high season.

27.1 LEFT at the T-Junction onto A287 then downhill before turning RIGHT signposted Frensham Little Pond. Continue past pond over more sandy heathland.

Frensham Little Pond is the more attractive of the ponds and is beautiful in summer with its waterlillies. Both were created by the Bishop of Winchester in the 13th Century to provide fresh fish..

29.2   LEFT at T-Junction, signposted Farnham and continue to Tilford.
RIGHT after church, signposted Elstead to cross the green in front of
the Rising Sun PH.

Tilford is situated at the junction of two arms of the river Wey, hence it has
two medieval stone bridges which are probably the work of the monks of
Waverley Abbey.

30.5   RIGHT to cross bridge before RIGHT again into Whitmead Lane.
Continue around steep hairpin bend and up hill before RIGHT onto
B3001 for fast descent past The Donkey PH to cross the Wey yet
again by another medieval bridge. Pass through Elstead.

34.3   LEFT and LEFT again and cross the Wey for the final time over
narrow restricted bridge. Continue up hill past Pepper Harrow
before passing under A3 and up hill.

37.2   RIGHT at T-Junction, signposted Godalming. LEFT into Twycross
Road, signposted Farnham.

38.4   STRAIGHT ACROSS into Elizabeth Road (Farncombe Station to
right) and then SECOND LEFT into Perrior Road before RIGHT at
T-Junction into Warren Road.

38.7   CONTINUE over crossroads into Furze Lane. On reaching B3000
RIGHT and immediately LEFT into Stakescorner Road. Follow past
entrance to Loseley House, through Littleton and up hill with sharp
right turn through sandy cutting. Thence it is down all the way into
Guildford.

Loseley was built in 1562 on the sandy ridge that occupies the Pilgrims Way.
The estate is noted today for its high quality ice-creams and other dairy
products. Open to public from beginning of June to October, Wednesday to
Saturday plus Bank Holidays. Shop and restaurant as well.

41.2   LEFT at bottom of hill onto A3100 at Olde Ship Inn. Continue into
Guildford to station after second set of traffic lights.

42.1   END

11 WATERCRESS RIDE

This ride starts in the Wey valley at the historic town of Farnham before climbing into the rolling Hampshire Downs. Through the woods towards Golden Pot and the highest point of the ride is reached at over 700 feet. From here it is mainly downhill to The Candovers and a long gradual descent through one of those dry valleys so characteristic of the chalk landscape.

Up and over the valley to the River Alre and to New Alresford before a long climb from Bighton to Medstead and a memorable drop to Farringdon from a high of 650 feet. Then once again into the Wey valley near Bentley and a final sortie with the Downs before Farnham once again.

This can be termed a hilly route and although some of the climbs are long they are very gradual and therefore not strenuous. Pedalling easily upwards in a low gear is a perfect way to see ones surroundings. After all who wants to hurry in country like this?

Maps	OS LR 186, 185.
Distance	57.1 miles. No off-road.
Start/Finish	Farnham Station on line from Waterloo to Alton.

Railway Access

Farnham is served by trains from Waterloo to Alton, half hourly during week and hourly on Sundays.

Alresford is on the Mid Hants Steam Railway - The Watercress Line - to Alton. Cycles can be taken on the Watercress Line making a novel different return journey.

Bentley is close to the route and on the Waterloo to Alton line.

Places to see

Castle & town - Farnham.

The Candovers.

The Grange - near Northington.

The town & the Watercress Line - New Alresford.

Massey's Folly - Farringdon.

Jenkyn Place Gardens - Bentley.

Refreshments

The Forum & The Maltings - and many other places in Farnham.

Tea rooms - at the railway station and in New Arlesford.

Little Chef - Four Marks.

Wide choice of pubs - *The Golden Pot* is in a good position.

WATERCRESS RIDE

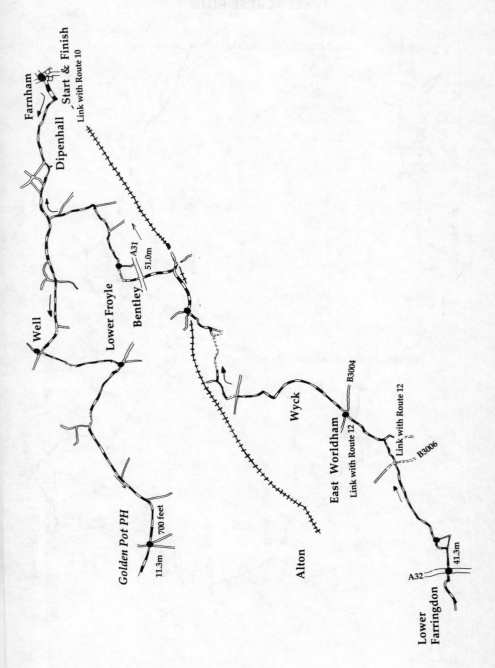

Farnham

Dipenhall   Start & Finish
Link with Route 10

Well

Lower Froyle
Bentley
A31
51.0m

Wyck

East Worldham
Link with Route 12

B3004

Link with Route 12
B3006

Golden Pot PH
700 feet
11.3m

Alton

Lower
Farringdon
A32
41.3m

WATERCRESS RIDE

Golden Pot PH
700 feet
Southrope
A339
Lasham
Alton
Medstead
Four Marks
Lower Farringdon
A32
41.3m
600 feet
Watercress Line
Preston Candover
19.9m
Chilton Candover
Brown Candover
B3046
Northington
The Grange
Bighton
Old Alresford
New Alresford
28.4m
B3047

11 WATERCRESS RIDE

0.0   STRAIGHT ON from Farnham Station into the town after traffic lights. **OS LR 186.** Plunge into one-way system keeping to the left lane past The Maltings and turning LEFT into West Street.

Farnham is set in the broad valley of the Wey and is one of the most attractive of Surrey towns. It is dominated by its castle which has been continuously occupied from 12th to 20th Centuries by the Bishops of Winchester. The huge shell keep is run by English Heritage and is open April to September. Castle Street and West Street have many Georgian houses, dating from the time that Farnham boasted the largest corn market in the country outside London. William Cobbett, whose Rural Rides painted such a graphic description of rural poverty in the early 19th Century was born in Farnham in 1762 and was buried in the churchyard after his stormy and controversial life ended in 1835. Coffee shop in The Maltings. Other cafes in town.

0.9   RIGHT into Crondall Lane, signposted Dipenhall. Follow road up long gradual hill which drops then climbs again to the Hampshire Downs. At Dippenhall turn LEFT, then RIGHT and STRAIGHT ON to follow signs to Well.

5.9   LEFT at crossroads at Well (literally!), signposted Froyle along narrow road and down steep hill. By the Prince of Wales PH RIGHT, signposted Golden Pot and ascend long easy hill past the lovely brick built cottages of Lower Froyle into the woods where there are wide views through gaps in the trees. Highest point of ride is reached at over 700 feet.

11.3   CONTINUE over crossroads with B3349 by the Golden Pot PH, signposted Shalden/Lasham. Follow past airfield where there is much glider activity as well as a collection of ex-RAF planes close to the road.

13.3   RIGHT and continue to Southrope. LEFT at T-Junction past the Fur & Feathers PH and a small office block - an example of rural diversity.

14.6   RIGHT at T-Junction onto A339, then LEFT at crossroads and LEFT again, following signposts down to Preston Candover. **OS LR 185.**

19.9   LEFT at T-Junction onto B3046. Continue through the Candovers to Northington, up and over Abbotstone Down where there is a picnic site, before descending to Old and then into New Alresford.

Preston Candover is the largest of the Candover trio - a place of well tended thatched cottages, rural high-tech industry and a pub - The Purefoy Arms. At Chilton Candover there is no visible church but an underground Norman crypt chapel was discovered in 1927. Brown Candover is the last of the villages.

After Northington signs point to The Grange which is approached down a long bumpy driveway. This house, built 1665 to 1673 was inspired by Greek architectural ideals and is based on The Partheon at Athens. By 1970 it had become a ruined empty shell but the Government, realising its importance, decided to spend half a million pounds on the restoration of its exterior. Run by English Heritage it is open all the year round.

New Alresford was in fact built in 1200 by Bishop Godfey de Lucy of Winchester, a man of big schemes. He established this town with the idea of making the River Itchen navigable all the way to the sea at Southampton. To regulate the water he constructed a huge dam across the tributary Alre to create a 200 acre lake with gates and sluices. The road between Old and New Alresford still runs on top of this though now only about 60 acres of reed fringed and coot inhabited water remain.

Apart from the tree-lined Broad Street New Alresford s other main attraction is the Watercress Line, a steam powered railway which runs all the way to Alton. It operates weekends and Bank Holidays between Easter and the end of October and daily last week of July to end of August. Bicycles are carried free and with NetWork SouthEast connections at Alton it is possible to travel all the way back to Farnham this way. For information ring 0962 734866. Refreshments can be obtained at the station and elsewhere in the town.

28.4   LEFT at T-Junction in New Arlesford and continue along the old main road (B3047) to Bishops Sutton. By The Ship PH turn LEFT, signposted Bighton. Continue past watercress beds and over railway and switch backs to Bighton.

31.6   RIGHT at T-Junction, signposted Medstead. Continue along valley and up very long though fairly easy hill then RIGHT at T-Junction, signposted Four Marks, into Medstead. RIGHT after church and village shops into South Town Road. Follow round to pass under railway.

36.7   LEFT at T-Junction with A31 (Little Chef about half a mile to the right). Then immediately RIGHT through the scattered modern hill top settlement of Four Marks. After passing school on right, LEFT into Willis Lane. Climb hill. At crossroads STRAIGHT ACROSS at high point of 650 feet and down long descent to Lower Farringdon. **OS LR 186.** Meet Route 12 here.

41.3 CONTINUE over crossroads with A32, signposted to church, and LEFT into Church Road, signposted East and West Worldham.

Gilbert White of Selborne was curate at the church here for 24 years. The Reverend Massey was rector for no less than 62 years and one of his abiding passions was building. Between 1870 and 1900 he engaged himself, with the minimum of labour, in the construction of that huge red brick building opposite with no idea what it was to be used for. With its terracotta panels and seventeen bedrooms Massey's Folly is unique. It was put to use as a school and serves as a village hall today.

43.7 CONTINUE over crossroads with B3006 at the turnpike cottage. Route 12 joins here and leaves at the next junction, so forming a convenient route to Alton.

45.0 RIGHT at T-Junction with B3004 by The Three Horseshoes PH then LEFT, signposted Wyck. Pass through village to crossroads and STRAIGHT ACROSS, signposted Mill Court.

48.0 RIGHT by classical style lodge house and up hill. Then LEFT and LEFT again at T-Junction.

50.3 LEFT, signposted Bentley. Pass the turning to Bentley Station on right and continue to crossroads with A31 at Bentley.

Bentley is the scene for the popular real-life story of country folk on Radio 4 - 'The Village'. For the horticulturally inclined the garden at Jenkyn Place displays roses and a large collection of rare plants. Open April to September, Thursday to September plus Bank Holidays.

51.0 STRAIGHT ACROSS busy main road (CARE) by memorial hall. Climb hill and before footbridge turn RIGHT and then STRAIGHT ON at next corner, signposted Pennyland. It's a very quiet peaceful lane up onto the downs so do not be surprised to find large numbers of pheasants wandering on it!

52.9 LEFT at T-Junction, signposted Wimble Hill House before RIGHT at T-Junction to retrace the first part of the route through Dippenhall and down Crondall Lane to Farnham.

56.2 LEFT at T-Junction into Farnham. After Castle Street on left RIGHT into South Street and continue over traffic lights to station.

57.1 END

12 THE HANGER RIDE

The River Wey rises near Alton and into the hills this route must go. From Farringdon the first long climb is to around 650 feet, before eventually descending from the Downs to the River Itchen at Cheriton. Onwards and upwards to the Meon Valley, sometimes called Little Switzerland, towards Petersfield with the high wooded scarp face of the chalk hills looming ahead. The hills are finally scaled on the long twisting climb from Steep and the highest point of the ride is reached at Warren Corner. After the descent to Selborne the Downs are left behind on the way back to Alton.

This is a hilly ride with several long climbs, the most prolonged being that from Steep. The gradients tend to be gradual and compensation is ample with long descents and fine scenery in one of the most attractive areas of Hampshire.

Maps   OS LR 186, 185, 197.

Distance   42.7 miles.

Start/Finish Alton Station.

Railway access

Alton is at the end of the line from Waterloo via Aldershot. Service generally hourly. Also served by Watercress Line from New Alresford.

Petersfield, on the Waterloo to Portsmouth line could be an escape point.

Places to see

Curtis Museum, Allen Gallery - Alton.

Jane Austen's House - Chawton.

Battle of Cheriton memorial & village - Cheriton.

Hinton Ampner House & Gardens (NT).

Church & village - East Meon.

The Wakes Museum, Romany Museum, church - Selborne.

Refreshments

Station Cafe - closed on Sundays, and plenty of other places in Alton.

Coffee shop - Chawton.

Tea rooms - for visitors to Hinton Ampner House.

Bush House tea rooms, Queens Hotel - Selborne.

Wide choice of pubs throughout the route.

THE HANGER RIDE

Start & Finish
Alton
East Worldham

Chawton

Link with Route 11

Lower Farringdon

Watercress Line

Link with Route 11   5.0m

Selborne

Ropley

Warren Corner
806 feet

14.9m

Cheriton

A272

Hinton Ampner

28.5m

West Meon

R. Meon

Petersfield

East Meon   Ramsdean

A31

B3004

B3006

A32

12 THE HANGER RIDE

0.0   LEFT from Alton Station where there is a cafe close by though it is
        closed on Sundays. **OS LR 186.** RIGHT into Paper Mill Lane then
        LEFT into main street.

William Cobbett remarked how the hills of Hampshire began at Alton and in
that particular year how bad the hops were in the area. Brewing is still a
major industry of Alton - Harp lager is a product of the town. In the 19th
Century Dr William Curtis established an extensive local history collection
which can be seen in The Curtis Museum in the High Street. Also in the
same area is The Allen Gallery where a large collection of ceramics are
displayed. Both open Tuesdays to Saturdays.
 In the last century, eight year old Fanny Adams was murdered by a solicitor's
clerk. It so struck public imagination that the phrase Sweet Fanny Adams
became part of the English language, coined originally by naval ratings
disgruntled by the inferior quality of the tinned meat they were issued with.
Her grave can be seen in the churchyard.

0.7   STRAIGHT ON at junction past church with spire then LEFT at
        roundabout after railway bridge, marked No Through Road. Follow
        via subway under A31 to Chawton village where there is a coffee
        shop as well as Jane Austin's House.

Jane Austin lived in this red bricked house, built around 1690, from 1809 to
1817. There is a museum with a collection of her personal belongings.
Open daily from April to October; Wednesday to Sunday, November,
December, March; weekends only in January and February. Hours 11.00 to
16.30.

1.6   STRAIGHT ON in Chawton. At end of road up steps to join A32 and
        LEFT to Farringdon.

3.5   RIGHT at crossroads and continue up long hill, to over 650 feet. **OS
        LR 185.** Meet Route 11 here.

5.0   LEFT at crossroads on top of hill then RIGHT into Hawthorn Lane.
        Descend hill before RIGHT at T-Junction and immediately LEFT,
        signposted Kitwood/Lyeway.

6.9   LEFT at T-Junction, signposted Ropley. CONTINUE along Swelling
        Hill and after primitive Methodist chapel LEFT, signposted Ropley
        Church.

8.7   RIGHT at T-Junction in Ropley village. Continue past church and
        LEFT after parish hall then RIGHT at T-Junction before LEFT into

Park Lane along delightful twisting road amongst folds of downs.

11.5 STRAIGHT ON at Manor House Farm past memorial to the Battle of Cheriton. Descend to Cheriton itself.

The Battle of Cheriton, fought in 1644, was one of the turning points of the Civil War when the Roundheads routed a Royalist force and '20,000 soldiers hazarded their lives'. Cheriton itself is an attractive village by the side of the infant river Itchen. Truffle hunting has not always been the domain of the French - it was carried out in this country as well and Cheriton is reputed to have been the last place in England where specially trained dogs sniffed out this rare delicacy from the ground.

14.9 LEFT at T-Junction and continue through village, before LEFT onto A272.

16.6 RIGHT after passing entrance to Hinton Ampner Gardens (NT), signposted Hinton Ampner. Climb hill through village and past tradesmen's entrance.

Hinton Ampner House has been rebuilt several times, the last after it was gutted by fire in 1960. In 1793 one of the main reasons for a new house was because the previous was haunted! Today there is a fine collection of regency furniture and formal gardens to wander around in. Tea rooms for visitors. Open April to September, Tuesday and Wednesday plus weekends during August, with the gardens only open all the weekends plus bank holidays 13.30 to 17.30.

17.2 FORK LEFT and continue through avenue of trees, then LEFT by cottage and LEFT again at junction in woods. After long easy climb RIGHT at crossroads signposted West Meon and descend to village.

21.2 LEFT by the Red Lion PH and immediately RIGHT signposted East Meon. Continue past the Thomas Lord pub, named after the founder of Lords cricket ground who is buried in the village churchyard, and past the chapel ruins on the hill, to East Meon. The Meon Valley is often described as Little Switzerland.

William Cobbett was taken very much by the beauty of this village, situated in the deep valley quite close to the source of the Meon, as well as the very fine Norman church with its impressive spire. Opposite is the old court house dating from 1450.

24.5 RIGHT by the church, signposted HMS Mercury, and continue through village. Who can argue with William Cobbett for it is still a very attractive place with the chalk stream flowing through. After the Izack Walton PH and Riverside Stores LEFT, signposted

Frogmore, along narrow lane. KEEP RIGHT, **OS LR 196.**

25.8 LEFT, LEFT and LEFT yet again before immediately RIGHT at Ramsdean, signposted Petersfield. Then it's downhill to Stroud.

28.5 RIGHT at T-Junction onto A272 by The Seven Stars PH before LEFT signposted Steep.

30.1 LEFT at crossroads by The Cricketers PH signposted Alton and up the long twisting 1 in 14 hill through the woods that seem to hang on the steep scarp slope leading to the downs. Hence the local name of Hanger.

32.2 RIGHT after The Trooper PH, signposted Warren Corner. This is the highest point of the ride at 806 feet. Descend past the church at Priors Dean. Opposite the manor farm LEFT, signposted Colemore/ Newton Valance. **OS LR 186.**

33.9 RIGHT down sunken lane with thickly hedged banks. A sharp climb and then it opens out to give wide views to the north-east. LEFT at T-Junction, then RIGHT at staggered crossroads, down steep hill (1 in 7) past Selborne Hanger to Selborne itself.

William Cobbett visited Selborne as a result of reading Gilbert White's book 'The Natural History and Antiquities of Selborne'. White's home The Wakes is now a museum which was purchased by R.W. Oates, uncle of the famous Captain Oates who died on Scott's ill-fated Antarctic expedition in 1912. So now the bottom floor is devoted to Gilbert White and the first to the Oates Memorial Museum. Open end of March to beginning of November, Wednesday to Sunday plus Bank Holidays 11.00 to 17.30.

The church has a fascinating stained glass memorial window showing St Francis with the 82 birds depicted in White's book. The author himself is buried outside.

The Romany Folklore Museum is open all the year round and has an exhibition of gypsy history. Teas can be obtained at the Bush House Tea Rooms and the Queens Hotel is useful for morning coffee.

36.9 LEFT at T-Junction at bottom of hill onto B3006, signposted Alton. Follow through Selborne until, by old toll house, RIGHT at crossroads, signposted West Worldham. Join Route 11 here until next junction.

40.7 LEFT at T-Junction by the Three Horseshoes PH onto B3004. Pass under by-pass into Alton and immediately after railway bridge RIGHT to station.

42.8 END

13 THE WAGGONER'S RIDE

This ride starts with a climb almost from the start at Godalming, to leave the Wey valley before crossing the river at Eashing and following it at a discrete distance to Elstead. More climbing leads to wooded sandy heathland and some twisting and darting amongst the hummocks along Sailors and Green Lane. The assault on the Greensand Hills is via Whitmoor Vale to reach Greyshott, at 662 feet, - the highest point of the ride. Cycle on past the tree shrouded ponds of Waggoners Wells, up to Bramshot Chase then down, down to Haslemere in its deep valley. The hills are regained but at a lesser height and it is not long before Godalming and the Wey is reached once again.

A hilly route, particularly the first part up to Greyshott and Haslemere. But a small price to pay for the sheer delight of riding along the sunken twisting lanes, the woods, and the rolling countryside.

Map	OS LR 186.
Distance	33.1 miles. Of this 2.2 miles are off road. The section out of Waggoners Wells can be muddy.
Start/Finish	Godalming Station on London to Portsmouth line via Guildford.

Railway access

Godalming is served hourly by stopping trains between London and Portsmouth.

Haslemere, with a more frequent service, could also be used as an alternative start or escape point, as could *Witley* or *Milford*.

Places to see

Museum & the Cyclists Touring Club HQ close by - Godalming.

Eashing Bridge (NT).

Waggoners Wells.

Educational Museum - Haslemere.

Oakhurst Cottage (NT) - Hambledon.

Winkworth Arboretum (NT).

Refreshments

Cafe - weekdays only, by Godalming station.

Coffee Bar - High Street, Godalming.

Little Chef - Milford.

Little Chef - Bramshott Chase.

Darnleys Restaurant & tea room - Haslemere.

Tea room - Winkworth Arboretum.

Good range of pubs along the route.

THE WAGGONER'S RIDE

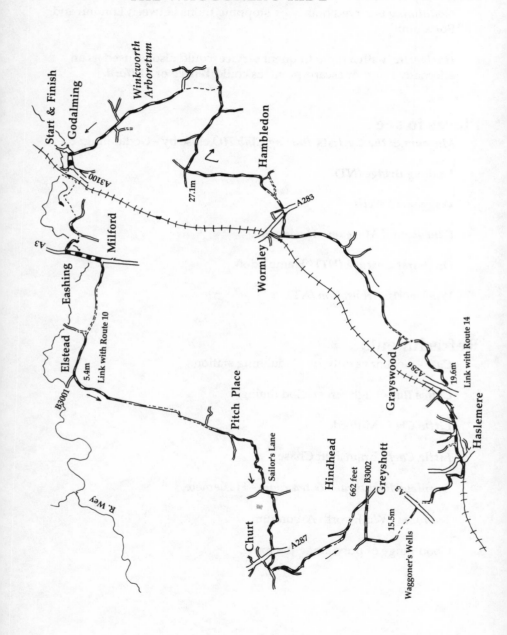

13 THE WAGGONER'S RIDE

0.0   LEFT from Godalming Station. **OS LR 186.** There is a useful cafe
        nearby if here on a weekday, or a coffee bar in the High Street as
        well as other alternatives. LEFT and LEFT again into Westbrook
        Road, passing under the railway.

0.2   LEFT after bridge onto bridleway, though signposted as a public
        footpath, to Eashing. Pass station again and follow track round to
        right, where it becomes deeply sunken as it climbs steep hill. After
        farm it becomes metalled.

1.4   RIGHT turn at T-Junction and continue through Upper Eashing.
        Then LEFT down hill, signposted Restricted Bridge, into Eashing
        and over bridge to old A3.

Eashing Bridge (NT) is a medieval double bridge over the Wey, perhaps the
best of the series between Guildford and Farnham built by the monks of
Waverley Abbey. Their work involved building rounded downstream cut-
waters to prevent eddying and wear from a river which could well have
been stronger than the one flowing today.

2.4   LEFT onto old A3 which runs beside the new road. SECOND
        RIGHT at roundabout, signposted B3001 Elstead. Cross over new A3
        and over the next roundabout to continue into Elstead, past The Star
        & The Woolpack PH to the village green. Going straight on at the
        first roundabout leads to Milford where there is a Little Chef. Meet
        Route 12 at Elstead.

5.4   LEFT at village green, signposted Thurley/Churt/Hindhead.
        Continue along this gradually climbing road through sandy wooded
        heathland to reach Pitch Place.

8.5   LEFT into Sailors Lane. Follow this beautiful roller-coaster
        wriggling lane, which becomes Hyde Lane, to a LEFT turn at T-
        Junction by the Hindhead sign. Continue up hill.

10.2   RIGHT into Green Lane for more steep but very short hills including
        one marked with a double arrow on the map. Watch out for gravel
        on the bends. When Green Cross Lane is reached LEFT and continue
        to A287.

11.4   RIGHT onto A287 and immediately LEFT before the Churt sign to
        descend steep hill to T-Junction by bridge. There LEFT to cross into
        Hampshire. Climb hill before LEFT into Hammer Lane, signposted
        Whitmoor Vale.

12.1 LEFT yet again into Whitmoor Vale Road and continue along beautiful twisting road through narrow steep sided valley. It's not as secluded as one would think with houses here and there in splendid isolation. Continue down hill to ford which is either very shallow or non-existent.

13.6 RIGHT at T-Junction to face steep climb up to Greyshott village.

In Greyshott The Fox and Pelican pub was opened in 1899 to encourage the sale of non-alcoholic drinks, but they sold alcoholic beverages as well, under the counter! To improve peoples minds it even had a library of books donated by George Bernard Shaw, who rented a house nearby. He used the local post office where the assistant was a young lady called Flora Thompson, who became famous herself for 'Lark Rise to Candleford'.

14.3 RIGHT at staggered crossroads in Greyshott onto B3002, signposted Bordon. Then LEFT, signposted Waggoners Wells. Descend hill.

Wagoners Wells (NT) are a series of small lakes or ponds once used as reservoirs for iron-smelting. Their waters eventually feed into the river Wey. Surrounded by woods, it is a beautiful place for a picnic.

15.5 STRAIGHT ON where metalled road swings right into car-park. Then FORK RIGHT onto Right of Way, and continue uphill along sunken track which could be muddy after wet weather. It becomes metalled once the houses are reached.

16.2 LEFT onto A3 at Bramshott Chase, with a Little Chef nearby to the right. Immediately RIGHT (CARE) by the Surrey border sign. At crossroads LEFT signposted Haslemere. Descend Woolmer Hill (1 in 7) where a faded sign warns cyclists of danger from stones that might have tumbled down the steep banks into the road. Continue into Haslemere.

17.4 RIGHT by The Royal Oak PH into Crichmere Road, then LEFT by railway bridge.

18.1 STRAIGHT ON at crossroads with traffic lights, signposted B2131 Haslemere. Immediately RIGHT at T-Junction . Continue past The Red Lion PH and cross under railway and pass station, where Route 14 starts.

19.0 LEFT into Tanners Lane, then LEFT again over railway bridge. Followed by RIGHT at T-Junction by Church Green, with the church on left. Follow to A287.

Haslemere Educational Museum is to the right in the High Street. It celebrated its centenary in 1988. The collections deals with geology, zoology, history and it is a good place to learn something about the area. Open Tuesday to Saturday all year round. Also in the High Street is Darnleys Restaurant/Tea Room.

19.6   STRAIGHT ACROSS A287 into Three Gates Lane, then RIGHT to continue along it until LEFT at T-Junction into Clammer Hill. Follow to the east of Grayswood.

23.2   LEFT at T-Junction, signposted Whitley Station. Once there RIGHT at crossroads.

24.9   STRAIGHT OVER crossroads with A283 into Hambledon. Continue through village with its deep sunken lanes, past The Merry Harriers PH.

To the right, soon after crossroads is Oakhurst Cottage (NT). This is a very small timber framed cottage, which has been restored and furnished as a cottagers dwelling. Open April to October, weekends plus Wednesdays, Thursdays, Bank Holidays, 14.00 to 17.00. By appointment only 0428 684733.

27.1   RIGHT at crossroads into Salt Road, signposted Hascombe. Long climb through woods followed by steep descent. By Marepond Cottages LEFT, into narrow lane with width restriction. This beautiful lane gradually ascends through a fold in the hills. Continue to brow of sudden drop.

28.9   LEFT onto bridleway. This is stony at first but becomes metalled with potholes after gate. Continue to B2130 where LEFT to pass Winkworth Arboretum (NT) and descend long hill into Godalming.

Winkworth Arboretum is hillside woodland with many rare trees and shrubs. It slopes down to two lakes. Well worth visiting in Spring for bluebells and azaleas and Autumn for colour. Open all year during daylight hours. Tea-room in car-park open daily April to November and weekends some other times of the year.

32.5   CONTINUE over crossroads with traffic lights at bottom of hill, signposted Town Centre Servicing. Swing LEFT into the pedestrianised High Street to the old town hall known as The Pepperpot.

At one time Godalming was the centre of the Surrey wool industry and in an important position on the Portsmouth turnpike road when that was opened in 1749. Thankfully traffic is now diverted away from the High Street so that it is possible to appreciate the old buildings. Godalming did score a first in history, namely being the first town in the world to have a public electricity supply - in 1881.

Notoriety came in the 18th Century when a certain Mary Tofts claimed that she had given birth to a litter of eighteen rabbits. Incredible as it may seem, she was believed by some of the most prominent physicians of the day as well as the King himself. Much of the towns history is told in the excellent little museum close to The Pepperpot.

All cyclists who are members of the Cyclists' Touring Club will know that the organisation has its headquarters out on the Guildford road. The shop is open weekdays and a few Saturdays and is an excellent place to buy books, maps and various cycling accessories including clothing.

32.8   RIGHT from The Pepperpot down Church Street, signposted Station. Push here as it is one way. Continue past church. THIRD RIGHT to station.

33.1   END

14 BLACKDOWN TO ROTHER

Taking in Surrey, West Sussex, and Hampshire this route immediately takes to the hills from the start in Haslemere. It reaches a height of 775 feet on its twists and turns through the woods around Blackdown. Long downhill stretches aid progress to Lurgashall and further south from where the walls of Petworth Park are followed before Tillington and Petworth itself are reached. From here to Midhurst and Woolbeding is the valley of the Rother before long climbs over Woolbeding Common and past Hollybourne to the final run in to Haslemere.

A hilly route with climbs which tend to be long rather than particularly steep - all the more to enjoy the woodlands and views over three counties.

Maps	OS LR 186, 197, 196.
Distance	33.4 miles. One very short stretch of track near Haslemere.
Start/Finish	Haslemere Station on Waterloo to Portsmouth line.

Railway access

Haslemere is served by both fast and slow trains from London Waterloo and Portsmouth.

Liphook is a possible escape point.

Places to see

Educational Museum, Dolmetsch Workshops - Haslemere.

Petworth House & Park (NT).

Watermill & nature trails - Burton.

Cowdray Park & ruins of house - Midhurst.

Hollycombe Steam Collection.

Blackdown - the road over is particularly attractive late May when the rhododendrons are in full flower.

Refreshments

Darnleys Restaurant & tea room - Haslemere.

Tea & Coffee - Lurgashall Winery.

Tea rooms - at house entrance and elsewhere in Petworth.

Ye Olde Tea Shop - and other places in Midhurst.

Tea rooms - for visitors to Hollycombe Steam Collection.

There is a wide choice of pubs such as *The Noahs Ark* at Lurgashall or *The Three Moles* at Selham.

BLACKDOWN TO ROTHER

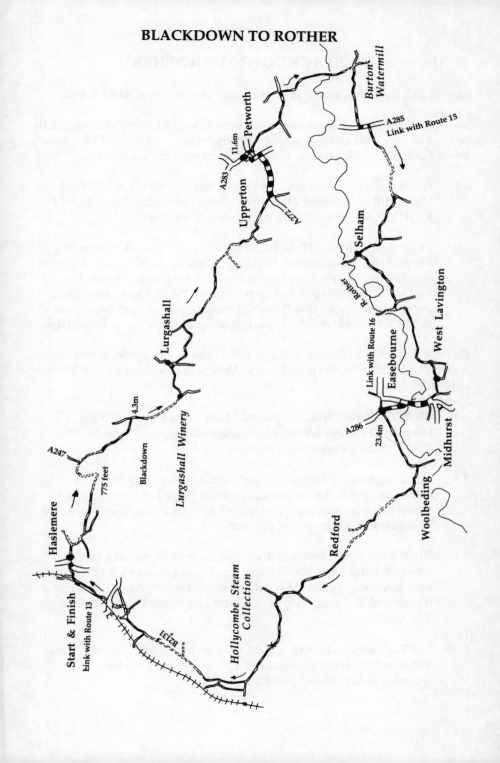

14 BLACKDOWN TO ROTHER

0.0   LEFT from Haslemere Station towards town centre. **OS LR 186.**

Since Route 13 from Godalming passes here as well, Haslemere could easily
be used as a base for an enjoyable weekends cycling. See Route 13 for details
about Educational Museum in the High Street on A286 for Milford.

0.8   Follow signs for Petworth, and leave town on B2131. RIGHT into
       Haste Hill, signposted Blackdown Rural Industries. Immediately
       RIGHT again up steep hill, signposted Blackdown.

1.0   LEFT then STRAIGHT ACROSS five-ways crossroad, signposted
       Blackdown/ Roundstreet. LEFT again into Tennyson Lane. Climb
       steadily up the slopes of Blackdown, to a height of 775 feet. The
       narrow road is surrounded by woodland, beech trees, laurels and
       the rhododendrons that flower so profusely in spring. Swing round
       to LEFT near Aldworth House before long descent past Roundstreet.

Blackdown is in West Sussex, and at 918 feet is the highest point in the county.
Alfred Lord Tennyson, the poet, lived at Aldworth House for the last 23 years
of his life.

4.3   RIGHT at T-Junction, signposted Midhurst/Lurgashall. Pass
       Lurgashall Winery where a coffee sign is displayed outside. Meet
       Route 16 from Portsmouth here.

5.4   LEFT, signposted Lurgashall and continue to village which is
       centred round its broad green, an idyllic place for a picnic on a
       warm summer day, especially with the village pub, The Noahs Ark
       being in such a convenient position.

6.1   RIGHT after pub, then LEFT at crossroads by Signpost Cottage.
       After Old Mill Farm RIGHT again at T-Junction. **OS LR 197.** Follow
       very long wall by the side of the Petworth estate. After a stiff climb
       it is downhill through Upperton, past The Horse Guards PH to
       Tillington.

10.5   LEFT at crossroads onto A272. Continue past pedestrian entrances
       to Petworth Park to roundabout. Follow one-way system past
       entrance to House and past church.

Petworth with its narrow streets is dominated by the magnificent late 17th Century House (NT) in the midst of the beautiful parkland designed by Capability Brown. Inside is a priceless collection of paintings, many by Turner and Van Dyck. The house is open April to October, daily except for non Bank Holiday Mondays and Fridays, 13.10 to 17.30. The park is open all year. Tea rooms by the entrance and can be used by non-visitors. Traffic twists and crawls through the narrow streets of the town. For years a by-pass has been planned and bitter battles have been fought to stop it being built in the park. The classic conundrum of improving one thing at the expense of another.

11.6   RIGHT after church, signposted A283 Pulborough. Then STRAIGHT OVER A272 and immediately LEFT into the very quiet High Street. Leave town.

12.6   LEFT at T-Junction, signposted Fittleworth, then RIGHT at crossroads, signposted Sutton, then after crossing the River Rother at Shopham Bridge, RIGHT at the next crossroads, signposted Duncton.

Pass Burton Watermill where an 18th Century water turbine produces stone ground wholemeal flour and breakfast cereal. There is a nature trail around the pond and through woodland.

15.9   LEFT at T-Junction onto A285, signposted Chichester, then RIGHT, signposted Selham/Grafton and continue along sandy heathland bordering the Rother valley.

18.4   RIGHT at T-Junction, signposted Midhurst and continue past The Three Moles PH to Selham before turning LEFT signposted Midhurst/South Ambersham.

20.2   RIGHT at T-Junction signposted Midhurst/Lodsworth then LEFT signposted West Lavington/Midhurst. Follow road until LEFT at crossroads to continue through West Lavington and up steep hill.

22.5   RIGHT at T-Junction and over the Rother into Midhurst then RIGHT into the main street where Ye Olde Tea Shop is open seven days a week.

Midhurst, like Petworth, is dominated by a big house - Cowdray Park. H.G.Wells once lived here and undoubtedly would have heard the curfew bell which still tolls at 20.00. There are medieval half timbered buildings in the town and stocks and pillory in the town hall. Cowdray Park is famous today for its polo playing. The house itself is in ruins. Built in 1530 it was destroyed by fire in 1793 partly because nobody could find the key to the shed where the fire appliance was kept! Open daily April to September, except Wednesdays and Thursdays, 13.00 to 18.00 along with the Cowdray Museum which is devoted to local history.

23.4 LEFT at roundabout, signposted A286 Fernhurst/Haslemere then LEFT at crossroads signposted Woolbeding. Once again meet Route 16 from Portsmouth.

25.1 RIGHT, signposted Liphook/Linch. Climb up and over Woolbeding Common before dropping to Redford and beyond.

28.5 RIGHT at T-Junction, signposted Liphook/Fernhurst. Continue up long hill and through arch by Hollycombe House. Pass right turn for Hollycombe Steam Collection. **OS LR 186.**

The Hollycombe Steam Collection is where everything seems to be driven by steam, including a fairground with roundabouts, organ, yacht, railway and tractors. There are woodland walks and refreshments to be had as well. Open all Easter weekend plus every Sunday and Bank Holiday Monday until October as well as daily during the last two weeks of August, 13.00 to 18.00.

30.7 RIGHT then RIGHT at T-Junction onto B2131. Follow to Hammer where RIGHT at roundabout, signposted Fernhurst.

33.6 LEFT into New Road after entering Camelsdale. Continue to short stretch of track over bridge. There RIGHT onto A286 and immediately LEFT up very short steep hill and LEFT at top into Kings Road, Haslemere. At end of road RIGHT at T-Junction to station.

This road passes close to the Dolmetsch Workshops where recorders and replicas of early musical instruments are made. Visits can be arranged (0428 3235) but not in Haslemere Music Festival Week at the end of July.

34.6 END

15 DOWN & WEALD

Petersfield lies close to the South Downs and it is from here that the ride heads eastwards on small twisting lanes. Through South Harting to Cocking and beyond they are always there, scarp face forward and clothed in woods. It might be a battle to get to the top of Duncton Down but from there it is a long descent through East Dean to Singleton. On to West Dean and it's up again, through the woods and over to East Marden. From here it is up to the highest point of the ride, 500 feet, at Uppark before reaching the crest and taking the plunge to South Harting. It is then back to Petersfield.

Chalk and cheese might be a fit way of describing the contrasting landscapes on this route. The cycling is easy enough on the twisting lanes at the foot of the Downs which eventually have to be climbed - hard work at times but tempered by joyous descents.

Map	OS LR 197.
Distance	44.3 miles. No real off-road though the section between Cocking and Heyshott is rough.
Start/Finish	Petersfield Station.

Railway access

Petersfield station is on the well served Waterloo to Portsmouth line - both fast and slow services call there at roughly two an hour.

Places to see

Petersfield.

South Harting.

St Andrew's Church - Didling.

Weald & Downland Open Air Museum - Singleton.

West Dean Gardens.

Uppark (NT).

Refreshments

Flora Twort Gallery & Restaurant - not Sundays, Petersfield.

Village Tea Rooms - Cocking.

Weald & Downland Open Air Museum - for visitors, Singleton.

Cream teas - Post Office & General Stores - West Dean.

A good choice of pubs - South Harting is well endowed as is the stretch between East and West Dean.

DOWN & WEALD

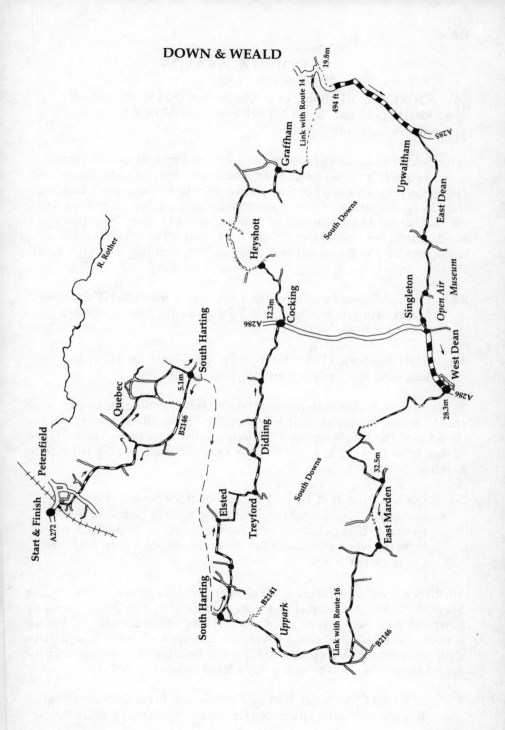

15 DOWN & WEALD

0.0   STRAIGHT OUT from Petersfield Station. **OS LR 197.** Immediately RIGHT past hospital. CONTINUE over old A3 onto B3146, signposted South Harting.

Petersfield is much quieter now traffic is diverted around to the west on the new by-pass. It is an old town, built around two squares - The Square and The Spain, linked together by Sheep Street with its timber framed buildings and Georgian cottages. Other attractions include a Physic Garden behind the High Street and a museum of Teddy Bears in Dragon Street (not open Sundays). Refreshments can be obtained at The Flora Twort Gallery & Restaurant or The Heath & Lake area park which is passed on the South Harting road.

2.4   LEFT at county boundary with West Sussex, then RIGHT signposted West Harting, before RIGHT at T-Junction, this time signposted South Harting.

4.0   LEFT signposted West Harting then RIGHT and RIGHT again, following signposts to South Harting.

Route 16 from Portsmouth meets at South Harting where the church spire stands above the many roof levels of the surrounding houses. In the churchyard the author Anthony Trollope is buried. He moved down to the village from London in order to escape the asthma that plagued him in London.

5.1   LEFT at T-Junction, keeping to the foot of the South Downs that tower above on the right and following signs to Elsted. RIGHT signposted Treyford/Cocking. Pass through Treyford village where there is a wooden figure of St Christopher to point the directions. Continue to Cocking.

Further on, a right turn leads to the tiny church of St Andrew. Known as The Shepherd's Church it is a picture of simplicity with its 13th Century roughly hewn oak pews. There is no electricity and candles are used for light at the services. With little in the way of valuable fittings it is hard to imagine that theft has become a major problem. However the bell was stolen one year, the font cover another, and most recently a large number of roof tiles.

12.3   STRAIGHT ACROSS A286 by The Blue Bell PH at Cocking or right if interested in the Village Tea Rooms just up the road. Immediately

RIGHT by the post office and stores, marked as No Through Road. Follow narrow, metalled potholed road to Heyshott.

13.9 RIGHT at church. Continue through village past The Unicorn PH. RIGHT at crossroads, signposted Graffham. Continue past The White Horse PH to the village.

17.2 RIGHT at T-Junction, No Through Road, and follow road past church. CONTINUE through gates onto metalled driveway that leads past the Stud Farm. This is not a bridleway but a footpath so be prepared to push if necessary.

18.6 CONTINUE over crossroads at East Lavington onto private driveway with footpath through the grounds of Seaford College. RIGHT after passing the main building then LEFT through gates into public road.

19.8 RIGHT onto A268 and start on long 11% climb round a horseshoe bend to Duncton Down and a height of 494 feet. A long descent follows past the little church of Upwaltham on the right.

This section of the South Downs is heavily wooded in comparison with other parts. After climbing up the hill there is a view point near the top that offers a fine prospect if the trees do not eventually obstruct it.

22.5 RIGHT and continue mainly downhill following signposts through East Dean to Singleton, passing The Hurdlemakers and The Fox PH on the way.

26.8 LEFT and continue past The Fox & Hounds PH to A286. Here LEFT and follow past entrance to the Weald & Downland Open Air Museum to West Dean, passing West Dean Gardens, before crossroads by The Selsey Arms PH.

William Cobbett experienced Singleton soaked to the skin and wondered if it was a good cure for whooping-cough. What he would have made of this museum is just a matter of conjecture. For over 35 historic buildings from coast and countryside have been rescued from destruction and rebuilt on this site. The 16th Century market hall is the centre piece for a growing small town. There are animals, craft exhibitions and refreshments for visitors. Open daily March to October, 11.00 to 18.00, Wednesdays and weekends at other times of the year.

West Dean Gardens is where there is not only an extensive downland garden to wander in, but an arboretum and a collection of mowers. Open daily March to October 11.00 to 18.00.

28.3 RIGHT at cross roads. (A left turn leads to the post office stores where cream teas may be had). Pass under old railway bridge and embark on long climb through woods. Descend and keep RIGHT past Stapleash Farm. Then down to The White Horse PH at Chilgrove where the pub sign of a cat does not match the name!

32.4 RIGHT at T-Junction, signposted B2141 Petersfield. Climb hill before LEFT signposted East Marden. At the thatched Well turn RIGHT, signposted North Marden/Harting.

34.3 LEFT signposted Compton/Up Marden. Continue up hill past Bevis' Thumb, a Neolithic Long Barrow. Descend to junction.

Bevis of Southampton was a legendary giant - a Desperate Dan of his time who ate a whole ox every week with bread and mustard and drank two hogsheads (105 gallons) of beer to wash it down. He could also wade across to the Isle of Wight!

36.3 RIGHT signposted Harting then RIGHT again at T-Junction onto B2146. It's a steady climb past the entrance to Uppark (NT) before the 13% drop off the downs to South Harting.

Uppark was built in the late 17th Century. Lady Hamilton was bought there as a servant girl by a naval officer. It was offered to the Duke of Wellington for services rendered but he thought the hill too hard on the horses and ended up with Stratfield Saye instead. Sarah Wells, mother of H.G.Wells, worked there and her son spent one winter with her at the house. In 1989 Uppark was partially destroyed by fire and, at the time of writing, restoration work is still going on. The grounds are open April to September, sunday afternoons, 13.30 to 17.30.

40.0 LEFT onto B2146 signposted Petersfield, by The Ship PH. STRAIGHT OVER crossroads at Petersfield and LEFT to station.

44.3 END

16 PORTSMOUTH BILLY LINK RIDE

Portsmouth Harbour is the start point for this ride and the coast is followed through Southsea before a short ferry crossing to Hayling Island. The old railway line is now a scenic cycling route close to the shoreline of Langstone Harbour to Havant. From here it is over the South Downs to South Harting, then it's Weald country. The River Rother is crossed and Bexley Hill is climbed. By Cranleigh there is yet more former railway in the form of the Downslink path. After this is an excursion into the sandy hills around Farley Green before Shere on the river Tillingbourne is reached. This is only a respite before the North Downs. At over 600 feet, Combe Bottom is the highest point of the ride. From there is much gentler terrain to Epsom.

Although the first part from Portsmouth to Havant is very flat, the rest, with four ranges of hills to cross, is not easy. On the other hand the ride can easily be split into sections and linked with other rides in this book.

Maps	OS LR 196, 197, 186, 187.
Distance	74.4 miles. Of this 6.4 miles is off-road, mostly on old railway lines with good surfaces.
Start	Portsmouth Harbour Station.
Finish	Epsom Station.

Railway access

Portsmoutth Harbour can be reached by train from either London Waterloo or Victoria by NetWork SouthEast, or by much less cycle-friendly Regional Railways services from Salisbury, Bristol and beyond. Also there is direct access to the Isle of Wight ferry.

Havant, Petersfield, Haslemere & Effingham Junction stations are either on or within a few miles of the ride and provide links to Portsmouth or London.

Places to see

The old part of the city, tall ships in the harbour - and much more, Portsmouth.

Castle & D-Day museum - Southsea.

Museum & art gallery - Havant.

Stansted Park.

Uppark (NT).

Shere.

Refreshments

Cafes - wide range at Portsmouth and along the seafront at Southsea.

Stage Door Cafe - not Sundays, at museum, Havant.

Coffee & Tea - Fitzhall, between Elsted and A272.

Lurgashall Winery.

Bricks Restaurant - Smithbrook Kilns, near Cranleigh on A281.

Astor Tea Shop & Kinghams Restaurant - Shere.

PORTSMOUTH BILLY LINK RIDE

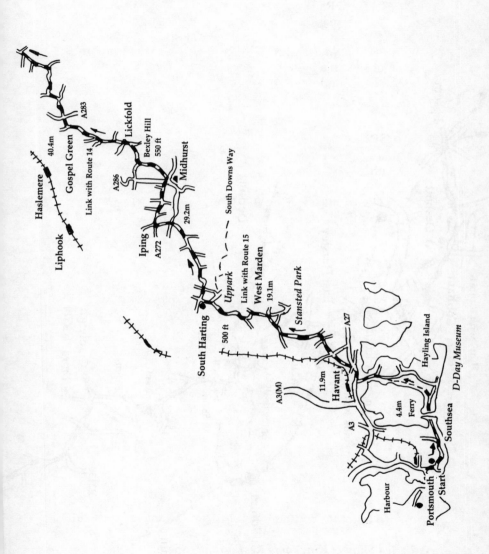

PORTSMOUTH BILLY LINK RIDE

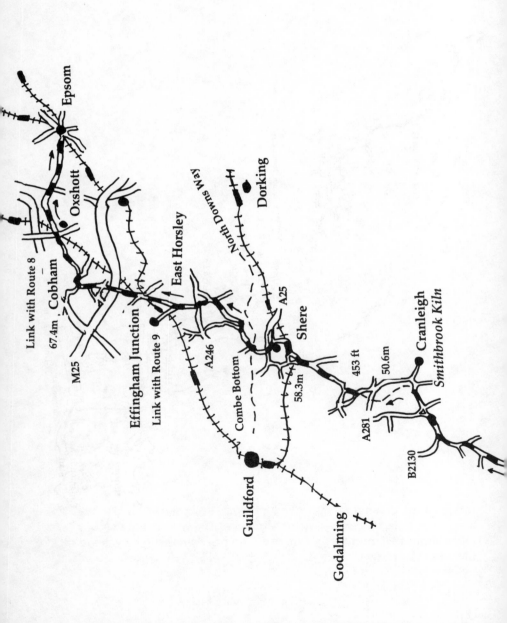

16 PORTSMOUTH BILLY LINK RIDE

0.0   RIGHT from Portsmouth Harbour Station. **OS LR 196.** RIGHT
        signposted Southsea/Seafront (HMS Warrior on left). After passing
        under the railway RIGHT at roundabout into Gun Wharf Road,
        marked No Through Road. Continue past the fish quay and by The
        American Inn go through the barrier into White Hart Road.

0.9   LEFT at T-Junction into Broad Street. Immediately STRAIGHT ON
        into the cobbled Battery Row. RIGHT at T-Junction to Penny Street
        and past ruined Royal Garrison Church (EH).

There is a vast amount to see in Portsmouth, far more than can be mentioned
in this book. As opposed to the large area rebuilt unimaginatively after the
last war, the old part this route goes through is still very attractive. Charles II
married Catherine of Braganza in 1662 at the Royal Garrison Church where
services are still held in the chancel. The Long Curtain and Kings Bastion on
the sea front are the only surviving remains of the ramparts and moat that
enclosed the town.

1.2   RIGHT at the crossroads by The Pembroke PH into Pembroke Road.
        RIGHT at roundabout into Pier Road and LEFT at next. Opposite
        the terminal for the hovercraft service to the Isle of Wight, turn LEFT
        and continue along Clarence Esplanade.

This is now Southsea which grew rapidly in the 19th Century as a seaside
resort from an initial beginning as a suburb for naval officers. On the right is
Southsea Castle, built in 1545 by King Henry VIII as part of his coastal
defences. It is open daily as is the D Day Museum close by which contains
the 272 foot Overlord Embroidery depicting the Allied Invasion of Normandy.

2.8   RIGHT onto South Parade by the pier and continue along the sea
        front to where the road bends away to left.

4.4   RIGHT signposted Hayling Ferry. RIGHT again at T-Junction and
        continue through marina to jetty.

It is accurate to say that this ferry runs every hour on the hour though there
are seasonal and local rush hour variations. The crossing to Hayling Island
takes about five minutes and there are no problems with bicycles, a rack of
the wheel twisting variety even being provided. This service is subsidised
by Hampshire County Council. Ring 0705 482868 for information.

AFTER crossing on the ferry CONTINUE past The Ferry Boat Inn and the Kench Nature Reserve.

6.6   LEFT down one way street and LEFT again at next T-Junction. STRAIGHT ON at junction by telephone box.

7.3   LEFT at crossroads, signposted car park and continue on cycle-way, bridleway, footpath known as the Hayling Billy Trail.

The Hayling Billy Trail follows the line of the old railway that connected the island to the mainland. The old tank engines that were used were known as Hayling Billys. The large building to the right at the very start of the trail was the old station. Services ceased in 1966 and the land reinstated for public use by the local council in 1986. The firm rough surface is perfectly rideable even with light weight tyres. The trail skirts the shore of Langstone Harbour, noted for the large number of wading birds, gulls, terns and other wild life. Undoubtedly fine views can be had across to Portsmouth and the hills beyond.

10.1   RIGHT before railway signal. The original bridge has been demolished so that it is now necessary to cross over on the main road. This trail, in common with most other cycle routes, is not particularly well signposted and care is needed to avoid straying off course. LEFT at car-park and follow piece of old road to join the A3023 by Texaco Garage then LEFT to cross Langstone Bridge and pass The Ship Inn at Langstone to opposite Mill Lane.

11.2   RIGHT to rejoin the Hayling Billy Trail. Pass under A27 to emerge by Havant Museum, housed in the old town hall.

This museum is well worth a visit. There is a replica of the Hayling Island waiting room that used to be at Havant station, machines for the making of gloves, and the important collection of firearms given by Hampshire inventor Cecil Vokes including rarities such as Buffalo Bills Winchester Rifle. Open Tuesday to Saturday, 10.00 to 17.00. There is the Stage Door cafe next door (not Sundays).

11.9   RIGHT opposite the Post Office then LEFT into Southleigh Road. Cross level crossing by Warburton station.

13.4   FORK LEFT into East Leigh Road and RIGHT at T-Junction. Immediately STRAIGHT ACROSS B2148 on staggered crossroads, signposted Chichester/Stansted House.

15.3 LEFT signposted Stansted House/Forestside/West Marden.

Stansted House is surrounded by beautiful parkland. 18th Century tapestries adorn this stately home. Open Easter Sunday and Monday then Sunday to Tuesday, May to end of September, 14.00 to 17.30.

17.8 RIGHT at T Junction, signposted Compton/West Marden on reaching Forestside after long climb through woods. Descend 14% hill before West Marden is reached, to just after The Victoria Inn.

19.1 LEFT at T-Junction onto B2146 signposted Petersfield. Continue through Compton and past Uppark House (NT) along classic downland road that gradually twists its way up hill among the folds of the South Downs. Route 15 joins near Uppark . Details of Uppark and South Harting are also included in the description for that route.

Over the crest of the South Downs it is a 13% drop to South Harting. Continue past the church and through village and follow signs to Elsted keeping along the foot of South Downs. Still following this road, pass the pub, built above a sunken section of lane and descend into the Rother valley past Elsted station, where the locomotive on the inn sign is about the only reminder of the former railway. Through the woods and then a sign points to a sharp right turn where coffee and tea is served in idyllic surroundings.

29.2 STRAIGHT ACROSS A272 on staggered crossroads, signposted Iping/Milland. Cross the Rother by the historic five arched bridge then turn RIGHT at crossroads, signposted Stedham/Woolbeding.

30.7 STRAIGHT ON at crossroads and RIGHT at T-Junction, following signs to Woolbeding. Meet Route 14 here.

31.6 LEFT, signposted Easebourne, marked as a single track road though most lanes are like that in this area. CONTINUE over A286, signposted Petworth/Cowdray Park to Easebourne where STRAIGHT ON to A272 before LEFT turn into Easebourne Street. It is a long climb past The White Horse PH and The Holly Inn up Bexley Hill to reach a height of over 550 feet. Then the road becomes sunken for a sudden, dangerous 1 in 6 descent (17%) to Lickfold.

36.6 LEFT at T-Junction signposted Lurgashall/Haslemere. Pass The Lickfold Inn and Lurgashall Winery (possible coffee stop) along wooded undulating road that eventually leads to Gospel Green.

OS LR 186. Meet Route 14 again along this road.

40.4   RIGHT at T-Junction at Gospel Green. CROSS A283 and following signs for Shillinglee Golf Course LEFT after the small lakes.

43.0   RIGHT at T-Junction signposted Plaistow then LEFT at next by telephone box. Next RIGHT following signs for Dunsfold. Continue past this village and The Sun and Rumpole pubs set on the spacious green.

48.1   RIGHT onto B2130 and OVER staggered crossroads with A281 following signs for Cranleigh. A left fork immediately before the main road leads to Smithbrook Kilns, a rural industry complex in an old brick works. Refreshments obtainable at Bricks Restaurant (not Sunday afternoons). There is also a cycle shop nearby.

50.6   FORK RIGHT before crossing old railway bridge and keep to LEFT on unmetalled road. In front of terraced cottages take path by the side of the telegraph pole, not the metalled one adorned with a No cycling sign. Drop to the Downslink path and LEFT under the bridge.

The Downslink path, so called because it links the North and South Downs, provides a quiet alternative to the metalled road. For practically all its length it utilises disused railway lines. The section between Guildford and Cranleigh was built in 1865 as part of the London, Brighton and South Coast Railway. One hundred years later it was closed, bought up by the local authority, and converted to its present use. This section, apart from the odd muddy patch is rideable.

52.7   RIGHT onto narrow path just before next bridge. Follow to metalled road where RIGHT. After crossing the Wey-Arun Canal and bridge over stream, LEFT, signposted Shamley Green/Wonersh.

53.6   RIGHT onto B2128 and immediately LEFT into Stroud Lane, signposted Farley Green. By pond RIGHT at T-Junction, and following signs to Shere, continue along narrow road up 1 in 7 climb into sandy heathland country. **OS LR 187.** Swing to left at Farley Green and descend hill. RIGHT into Brook Lane before level crossing to pass under the railway. After The King William IV PH RIGHT at T-Junction. Then LEFT at staggered crossroads by bridge over railway to descend past The Prince of Wales PH into Shere.

Some claim Shere to be England's prettiest village. The cottages are built of various materials and are mostly timber framed, many dating from the 17th Century. However, it is usually very busy at weekends. There is a choice of tea places, either Astors Tea Shop or Kinghams Restaurant.

58.3   LEFT into Lower Street just before crossing Tillingbourne river. Through ford, with footbridge provided, and up Rectory Lane. LEFT at T-Junction then OVER A25 on staggered crossroads, signposted East Clandon/East Horsley/Effingham. Climb North Downs through valley known as Combe Bottom. Towards the top a steep 1 in 7 section rears around a sharp left-hand bend to reach the highest point on the ride at over 600 feet. After flat stretch there is a long descent through Sheepleas woods. Route 9 joins at the top of the hill.

61.8   FORK LEFT into Chalk Lane with width restriction. Climb hill and descend through deeply sunken section to A246. There STRAIGHT ON and then RIGHT by The Duke of Wellington Tavern onto B2039, signposted East Horsley.

63.5   FORK RIGHT into Forest Road, signposted Effingham. Continue past Effingham Junction and over bridge into Cobham. Route 8 joins for a short distance.

67.4   RIGHT into Church Street after church, then RIGHT at T-Junction in front of record shop onto A246. Continue past water mill.

67.9   LEFT signposted Esher and immediately RIGHT onto private road, Mizzen Way. Continue over sleeping policemen. LEFT after gates and immediately RIGHT into Eaton Park Road. Keep to this further stretch of private road over more sleeping policemen to descend to Little Heath Lane.

69.4   STRAIGHT ON where road bends sharply round to right and follow line of railway on very rideable stretch of bridleway through woods. Descend to Oxshott station.

70.0   RIGHT onto A244 and after crossing railway immediately LEFT onto B280, Fairoak Lane, and follow over traffic lights, past church into Epsom. After railway bridge, LEFT to station.

74.4   END

17 THE VECTIS CIRCUIT

Vectis is the Roman name for the Isle of Wight. Measuring 23 miles by 13 it is a compilation of the best of South East scenery along with its own individual characteristics. This is an anti-clockwise coastal route from Ryde. It starts by following the more sheltered north coast at first through Cowes, through the former port of Newtown, to Yarmouth and out to Totland Bay, almost at the farthest point west. It returns via Freshwater Bay where the downs dominate. The Military Road is a spectacular corniche and the dramatic cliff scenery continues past Blackgang Chine and between Bonchurch and Shanklin. The circuit is completed with the final leg through Bembridge and Brading.

For a small island the Isle of Wight is deceptively hilly and it's a hard ride in one day. It is better to make a weekend of it and enjoy the route in stages.

Map	OS LR 196.
Distance	71.8 miles. Of this 2.7 miles is off-road on a reasonable rideable surface.
Start/Finish	Esplanade at Ryde Pier.

Railway access

Portsmouth Harbour from where the Passenger Ferry runs every half hour to hour and takes about twenty minutes. Ferries from Southampton to Cowes take about one hour and Lymington to Yarmouth 30 minutes. The car ferry from Portsmouth to Fishbourne can also be used. Cycles go free on the ferry but are prohibited on the Isle of Wight trains.

Places to see

Quarr Abbey - near Fishbourne.

St Mildred's church - Whippingham.

Clamerkin Farm Park - near Porchfield.

Old Town Hall (NT) - Newtown.

Yarmouth Castle.

Yafford Mill & Farm Park - near Brightstone.

St Catherines Oratory - near Chale.

Old Church - Bonchurch.

Windmill - Bembridge.

This list could go on and on - there is so much of interest on the island.

Refreshments

Plenty of choice of cafes and pubs throughout the island especially in resorts like Ryde, Cowes, Freshwater Bay, Bembridge or villages like Brighstone.

Smugglers Haven - outside Bonchurch is very useful being at the top of a long climb.

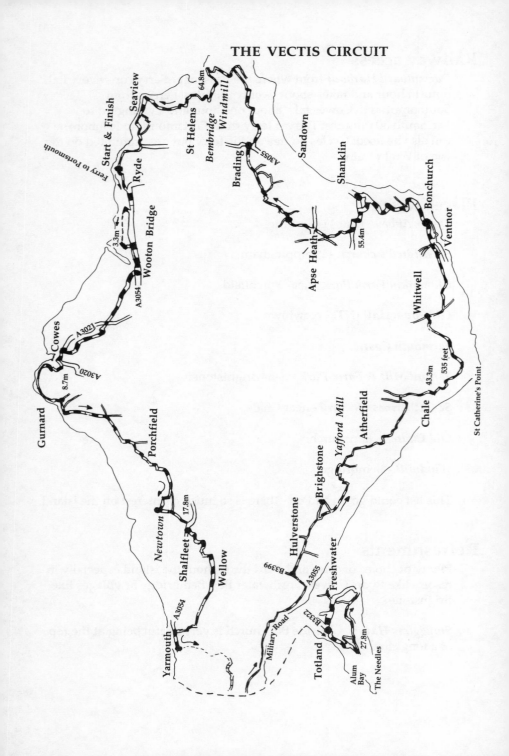

THE VECTIS CIRCUIT

Start & Finish

Ferry to Portsmouth

Seaview

St Helens

Bembridge Windmill

64.8m

Brading

A3055

Sandown

Shanklin

Ryde

Wooton Bridge

3.3m

A3054

Cowes

A3021

A3020

8.7m

Bonchurch

Ventnor

Whitwell

Apse Heath

55.4m

535 feet

43.3m

St Catherine's Point

Chale

Atherfield

Yafford Mill

Gurnard

Porchfield

Newtown

17.8m

Shalfleet

Wellow

A3054

Brighstone

Hulverstone

B3399

A3055

Military Road

Freshwater

B3322

Yarmouth

Totland

Alum Bay

The Needles

27.8m

17 THE VECTIS CIRCUIT

0.0   Ryde Pier Ferry Terminal. **OS LR 196.** Continue down the pier to Ryde. Built in Victorian times it used to carry a tramway as well as road and railway. The wooden planks can be slippery in wet weather and narow bicycle wheels can be caught between the planks.

0.5   CROSS pedestrian crossing and RIGHT up St Thomas Road, veering LEFT by Hotel Victoria.

Ryde is the largest of the island towns. As far back as 1800 it was becoming known as a pleasant place to visit and success was assured with the building of the pier and the ferry to Portsmouth.

0.7   RIGHT on hill into Spencer Road. Continue to the very end, exiting onto A3054 through narrow gateway. Follow through Binsted to crossroads at top of hill.

2.0   RIGHT into Church Road, then LEFT onto Quarr Road which is a bridleway. Metalled at first it becomes unsurfaced as it passes the ruins of the old Quarr Abbey with the new visible in the distance.

The church of the new Benedictine monastery was built between 1907 and 1914 and visitors are welcome. The ruins of the original monastery, founded in 1132, are scanty and incorporated in a farm.

3.3   LEFT at T-Junction by The Fishbourne Inn onto road from the car ferry. At traffic lights RIGHT to rejoin A3054 on Kite Hill. Follow to Wootton Bridge.

4.6   RIGHT on hill by garage into Rectory Drive. Follow twisting residential road. RIGHT at T-Junction and immediately LEFT into Footways.

5.1   LEFT and immediately RIGHT into Brocks Copse Road. Go down dale and up hill to A3021.

6.6   RIGHT at T-junction and immediately LEFT into Beatrice Avenue, signposted Royal Church of St Mildred which is situated by a sharp right hand bend.

This church was used by the Royal Family when they were at Osborne House. It was built between 1854 and 1862 in a unique Romanesque-Gothic style to a design said to be by Prince Albert himself.

7.9   LEFT at T-Junction into Victoria Avenue. Follow round to right before LEFT into Minerva Road. Continue into Clarence Road and pass Cowes Marina before entering one-way system which leads to Floating Bridge. Cross on ferry to West Cowes. Pedestrians and bicycles go free. The ferry from Southampton to Cowes provides an alternative way of getting to the island.

8.7 CONTINUE from ferry up Mill Hill Road. RIGHT into Victoria Road, signposted Town Centre, then RIGHT on hill into Granville Road.

9.5 OVER crossroads into Union Road and down hill to swing left into top part of High Street. Treat the sleeping policemen with due respect. Onto sea front and Castle Hill.

9.9 RIGHT on Castle Hill into Queens Road. Continue along seafront past seasonal open air snack bar to Gurnard Bay where there is a short but steep twisting hill.

11.1 RIGHT into Solent View Road. Descend steep hill into a shanty town of beach hut residences before heading inland and up hill.

13.1 RIGHT at roundabout, signposted Thorness/Yarmouth. Continue on Rolls Hill Road through Porchfield and past Clamerkin Farm Park .

Clamerkin Farm Park is a working farm with cows, sheep and rare breeds of pigs. Teas also available. Open daily Easter to end of September 10.30 to 18.00.

16.5 RIGHT, signposted Newtown and pass Old Town Hall (NT).

It is difficult to envisage that Newtown was once the capital of the island. With the harbour silted up and terminal decay setting in, Newtown was a classic example of a 'rotten borough' which still managed to send two members to Parliament until 1832. The Town Hall, standing alone, was built in 1699 and houses a museum of the borough's history. Open Monday, Wednesday, Sunday, April to September, `14.00 to 17.00.

17.8 RIGHT at T-Junction signposted Shalfleet/Yarmouth then RIGHT again at garage onto A3054. Continue through traffic lights into Shalfleet. By New Inn LEFT into Church Lane and RIGHT at T-Junction by the new Withyfields estate.

19.9 LEFT at T-Junction, then LEFT at next before RIGHT into Wellow Road, signposted Wellow/Thorley/Freshwater. After Wellow and Thorley RIGHT at T-Junction, signposted Yarmouth.

22.9 LEFT at T-Junction onto A3054 and follow into Yarmouth.

Yarmouth is another historic port and connected to the mainland by the ferry to Lymington. The narrow streets are laid out in a distinct rectangular pattern are are full of character. King Henry VIII built the castle after the town had been burnt by the French in 1527. Run by English Heritage it houses an exhibition and is open daily, from Good Friday to the end of September.

23.4 LEFT into Victoria Road. Continue to end by old railway station now used as a youth centre. RIGHT onto the former railway line, now a well surfaced bridleway.

There were once over fifty miles of railway on the Isle of Wight which, back in 1951, carried an estimated 3,000,000 passengers! Now only the line from Ryde to Shanklin remains along with the privately operated Isle of Wight Steam Railway. The line from Newport to Yarmouth and Freshwater was one of the first to close in the 1960s.

25.2 RIGHT onto metalled road. Follow into Freshwater after crossing River Yar, which has a namesake the other end of the island. By Post Office carry STRAIGHT ON and RIGHT at roundabout, signposted A3055 Totland. Climb hill.

26.7 LEFT at T-Junction into Totland. At the Tackle Box shop RIGHT into Granville Road. Follow coast line past road to beach and up steep hill.

27.8 RIGHT at T-Junction onto B3322, then SHARP LEFT onto Alum Bay Old Road, signposted Freshwater Bay (straight on for Alum Bay and The Needles). Gradually descend to Freshwater Bay past the thatched church of St Agnes. Join A3055 and follow the spectacular switchback Military Road.

Alfred Lord Tennyson, the poet, will always be associated with Freshwater Bay and his monument stands high on Tennyson Down, as much a beacon for sailors as anything else. The Military Road was a product of the French invasion scare in the 1860s and not actually surfaced until the 1930s. Now parts are in danger from erosion of the chalk cliffs and 'tiltmeters' have been installed at Compton Down to give warning of dangerous land movements. Freshwater Bay is a good place for tea shops, particularly in high season.

33.7 LEFT, signposted Brook/Brighstone then RIGHT onto B3399 signposted Newport. Continue through Hulverstone, Mottistone to the outskirts of Brighstone.

The garden at Mottistone Manor (NT) is beautiful, the mellow stone of the part 16th Century house contrasting vividly with the roses. Open March to September, Wednesdays & Bank Holiday Mondays only 14.00 to 17.30.

36.3   RIGHT into Galley lane, signposted Atherfield and STRAIGHT OVER crossroads into Mill Lane.

37.7   LEFT at Thorncross, signposted Yafford. Swing to RIGHT to continue past Yafford Mill and Farm Park.

Yafford Mill is a beautifully restored 18th Century water mill. There is also a collection of farm implements and rare breeds of livestock. Open daily Easter to end of September.

37.7   RIGHT, signposted Yafford and continue through this intricate network of small lanes. In village by pond LEFT signposted Atherfield then RIGHT signposted Atherfield/Chale. Follow through to Pyle and up Pyle Shute.

42.1   RIGHT signposted Chale Green then RIGHT at T-Junction by church onto B3399 into Chale village.

43.3   LEFT at T-Junction by church onto A3095, signposted Blackgang Chine, up Blythe Shute. Pass entrance to theme park and climb long 10% hill past view point where it is good to stop to see what has been climbed. From 535 feet it is down to Niton.

A chine is an island name for those deep valleys that cut into the cliffs. The one at Blackgang is over 400 feet deep. Now it is a fantasy theme park, a far cry from the original 1843 gardens. St Catherines Oratory (EH) is not far from the view point. Within the grounds of the demolished oratory is a 14th Century lighthouse.

45.4   CONTINUE over crossroads in Niton, signposted Whitwell. When there, RIGHT at T-Junction by church, signposted Ventnor. Enter the top end of what must be the hilliest seaside resort in the whole country.

49.0   LEFT at T-Junction into Gulls Cliff Road, signposted B3327 Wroxall. Then at next RIGHT into Ocean View Road and be prepared for long descent with steep 14% section at end.

50.5   RIGHT signposted Town Centre then immediately LEFT into St Boniface Road. Continue through Bonchurch village and up very steep and twisty Bonchurch Shute.

Bonchurch has two churches. St Boniface Old Church is very small and is a very complete example of a Norman church. The poet Swinburne is buried there. The new church is Victorian. There are tea rooms nearby.

51.0 RIGHT at the top of Bonchurch Shute onto A3055. Pass the entrance to the Landslip Pleasure Gardens where there is a useful cafe after such a long climb. Continue over spectacular switchback road with long descent to the outskirts of Shanklin. At Road Narrows sign and opposite Dale Cottage, turn LEFT into Rectory Road. Pass barriers and LEFT into Westhill Road. Follow to Victoria Avenue A3020.

55.4 LEFT and RIGHT after bends, and RIGHT at crossroads, following signs to Apse Heath.

56.4 STRAIGHT ON at mini roundabout by village stores, following signs for Brading. After Alverstone FORK LEFT past vineyard then RIGHT at T- Junction and RIGHT again at the next after descent of steep hill.

60.7 STRAIGHT ACROSS traffic lights, signposted B3395, Bembridge. Follow road past airfield. By inn LEFT, signposted St Helens/ Seaview/Ryde. Pass path to windmill (NT) into Bembridge itself.

Bembridge Windmill is the only one surviving on the island. Built in 1700 much of the wooden machinery can still be seen. Open April to October, daily except for Saturdays outside of July and August, 10.00 to 17.00. Bembridge itself is known as a yachting centre.

64.6 LEFT at T-Junction. Continue over embankment past harbour. There are plenty of tea places here in high season. After bridge with cycle path enter St Helens and SHARP RIGHT into Latimer Road.

66.3 RIGHT at T-Junction into Lower Green Road and RIGHT at next into Upper Green Road B3330.

67.9 RIGHT, signposted B3340 Seaview. RIGHT again into Old Seaview Road, follow down and along to seafront

A product of the Victorian age, Seaview still manages to maintain some of its period atmosphere with its 19th Century villas and shops.

68.8 VEER RIGHT into Bluet Avenue then RIGHT onto private toll road where bicycles go free. Continue along sea front until Battery Inn before left up Pickford Hill. There is a cafe on the right.

70.1 RIGHT at T-Junction signposted B3330, Ryde/Fishbourne, and RIGHT at next onto A3055. Follow round to esplanade. STRAIGHT OVER roundabout until opposite entrance to pier. RIGHT over pedestrian crossing, through pier entrance to reach ferry terminal.

71.8 END

18   FROM WINDMILL TO DRAGON

It's southward from Horsham through open and pleasing country that looks towards the South Downs on the horizon. The windmill at Shipley marks the turn to the east. Then the River Adur is followed at a distance through gently rolling country to Dial Post and by farm roads to Partridge Green. The estate at Shermanbury feels remote, a kind of 'Lost Domain'. Now it is north to enter the High Weald of Sussex up to Bolney and to Handcross at 500 feet. The nearby ruins in Nymans Gardens look truly romantic. Continue down to Slaugham and St Leonards Forest where once a dragon roamed, and where iron was bludgeoned and melted out of the rock. Then the return to Horsham.

This is mostly an easy ride except for the climbs from Bolney to Handcross and around the Hammer Ponds.

Maps	OS LR 187, 198.
Distance	34.8 miles of which 4.9 miles are off-road, a large proportion of which are on metalled farm roads.
Start/Finish	Horsham Station.

Railway access

Horsham is served by trains roughly half hourly from Victoria via Gatwick. Also hourly via Epsom but not on Sundays. From the opposite direction comes a one to two hourly service from Portsmouth and Bognor Regis.

Places to see

Causeway, museum - Horsham.

Windmill - Shipley.

Church - Shermanbury.

Nymans Gardens (NT) - Handcross.

Slaugham village.

St Leonard's Forest & the Hammer Ponds.

Refreshments

Cafe - off North Street in the park and elsewhere in Horsham.

Tea rooms - for visitors to the windmill, Shipley.

Coffee shop - at Old Barn Nursery, off A24, Dial Post.

Tea rooms - for visitors at Nymans Gardens, and at the Pine Loft in Handcross.

Good range of pubs throughout the route such as *The George & Dragon* at Dragons Green and *The Victory* at Staplefield.

FROM WINDMILL TO DRAGON

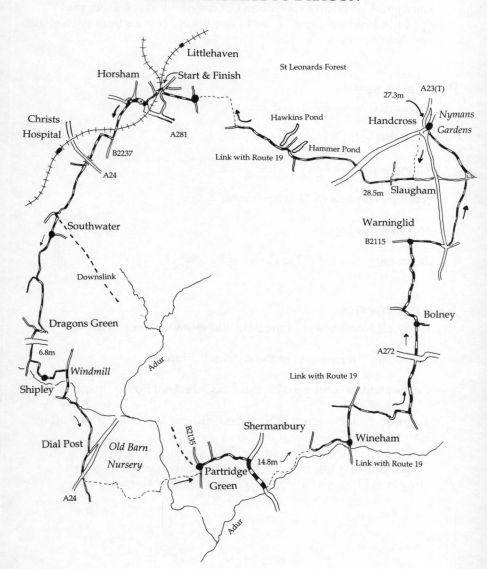

Littlehaven

Horsham   Start & Finish   St Leonards Forest

27.3m   A23(T)

Christs   Hawkins Pond   Handcross   Nymans
Hospital   Gardens

A281

B2237   Hammer Pond

A24   Link with Route 19   28.5m   Slaugham

Southwater   Warninglid

B2115

Downslink

Dragons Green   Bolney

6.8m   A272

Windmill   Adur   Link with Route 19

Shipley

Shermanbury   Wineham

Dial Post   Old Barn   B2135   14.8m   Link with Route 19
Nursery

Partridge
Green

A24

Adur

18 FROM WINDMILL TO DRAGON

0.0   LEFT from Horsham Station towards Town Centre, **OS LR 187,** down North Street. There is a cafe in the park to the right. Follow signs to Worthing B2237 RIGHT through archway and past the carpark on Albion Way before swinging round to the LEFT.

The old part of Horsham is disguised by the brashness of the new. The centrepiece is the causeway lined by houses three hundred years old. One is used as a museum for unusual items - where else can be seen a trap for catching four mice at once? Open all year Tuesday to Saturday, 13.00 to 17.00. The town also gave its name to the Horsham Slabs, used for roofing that would last for centuries and often longer than the buildings they were protecting.

1.6   RIGHT at The Boars Head PH, signposted Christs Hospital. Pass the road leading to the famous Bluecoat school with its distinctive uniform.

3.7   LEFT at T-Junction after Bax Castle PH and the old railway bridge which crosses over the Downslink path. KEEP LEFT for Dragons Green. **OS LR 196.**

6.3   RIGHT into Dragons Green, signposted Barns Green then turn LEFT by The George & Dragon PH, signposted Shipley.

The George & Dragon has a tombstone outside in memory of Walter Bount who lived at the pub in the last century. Because he was albino and epileptic he was shunned by other boys and he committed suicide after being accused of theft. The epitaph written on the tombstone offended the people of Shipley where he was originally buried, with the result that it was moved back home.

6.8   CROSS A272 and then LEFT, following signposts to Shipley and passing the windmill on the right, continue through the village.

Kings Mill is nearly 100 feet from ground to top of sail. Erected in 1879 it was purchased by Hilaire Belloc, the author and poet, in 1906 along with the adjoining house. A flamboyant figure he would doff his large black hat at the windmill and call it 'Mrs Shipley'! But it distracted him so much that he eventually shut it down. The mill is open from 14.00 to 17.00 first and third Sundays of month. There is a shop and teas for visitors.

8.3   RIGHT at T-Junction signposted Dial Post. Continue to village where RIGHT again past The Crown PH.

10.7   RIGHT onto A24 and immediately LEFT, signposted Ashurst by The Old Barn Garden Centre, where there is also a coffee shop. LEFT

again, straightaway, onto bridleway. Pass Manor Barn and
Sands Farm.

11.5   RIGHT at T-Junction onto metalled farm road. KEEP LEFT across
open stretch of land. Then RIGHT, LEFT and LEFT again around
Lock Farm, following the bridleway signs. RIGHT onto tarmac
section and follow through to Partridge Green.

13.6   LEFT at T-Junction on emerging from the West Grinstead Estate,
again crossing the Downslink path. RIGHT by The Partridge PH
onto B2116, signposted Hufford Trading Estate.

14.8   RIGHT at T-Junction onto A281, signposted Henfield.

15.5   LEFT opposite drive through gate into private road which is a
bridleway into Shermanbury Place Estate. This is metalled until the
rebuilt Elizabethan manor house and the very simple 12th Century
church that has outside steps leading to the organ loft. Afterwards
the drive degenerates into a grassy though still rideable track,
helping to empathise the general atmosphere of decay that
surrounds this estate despite the appearance of new signs. Continue
to the last gate.

16.9   RIGHT at T-Junction, then LEFT at next into Wineham. Join Route
19 from Brighton here.

18.5   RIGHT, after The Royal Oak PH into Bob Lane, signposted
Twineham/Burgess Hill. After this twisty lane, LEFT at T-Junction,
signposted Bolney.

21.0   CROSS A272 and continue up long hill past Bookers Vineyard. Still
climbing, RIGHT signposted Warninglid. RIGHT at T-Junction onto
B2115, signposted Haywards Heath.

24.4   LEFT, signposted Brighton after crossing A23 on bridge.
Immediately LEFT into Staplefield Lane and climb to Staplefield
where STRAIGHT OVER crossroads, signposted Handcross. On the
right, The Victory Inn provides excellent food. Then it is LEFT by
The Jolly Farmers PH and continue climb to Handcross, on B2114,
passing Nymans Garden (NT) on way.

Nymans is one of the best gardens to be found on the Sussex Weald, full of
rare plants, with fine views to the hills beyond. The house itself is in ruins,
destroyed by fire in 1947 and fits perfectly the idea of what a romantic ruin

should be like. Open daily except non-Bank Holiday Mondays and Fridays, April to October, 11.00 to 19.00. Weekends only in March, 11.00 to 19.00 or sunset if earlier. Teas available to visitors.

27.3   RIGHT at top of long hill, signposted A23 London, then LEFT to cross bridge (Coffee shop at Pine Loft in village). LEFT then immediately RIGHT onto bridleway on drive. Perfectly rideable surface though stony in places. It descends to the village of Slaugham past The Chequers PH onto the green overlooked by the church.

Slaugham looks almost too attractive and well kept. The lord of the manor did pay for the telephone wires to be hidden underground.

28.5   RIGHT and then STRAIGHT OVER crossroads by the pond, signposted Lower Beeding/Horsham. Route 19 from Brighton rejoins here.

29.9   STRAIGHT OVER A279 by The Wheatsheaf PH, signposted Bucks Head/Horsham into Hammer Pond Road. Continue into St Leonards Forest and past the three hammer ponds, approached by individual very steep descents of around 1 in 6.

William Cobbett might not have rated St Leonards Forest very highly but it is certainly a beautiful place with its wild flowers. At one time, according to legend, it was haunted by a dragon who was eventually slain by St Leonard. As late as 1614 a serpent, nine feet in length and spitting forth venom was seen. But really it is the ruins of the old iron workings that haunt the forest. The hammer ponds provided the power for the hammers that broke up the iron ore. Crossbow bolts, cannons, horseshoes were manufactured and there was even concern then about the stripping of the forests to feed the furnaces.

32.5   RIGHT onto bridleway after hill from third pond. **OS LR 187.** Continue along sandy but rideable track through gate. Then LEFT onto metalled road and STRAIGHT OVER crossroads into Hampers Lane and outskirts of Horsham.

33.8   STRAIGHT ACROSS staggered crossroads into Depot Road. RIGHT at T-Junction and LEFT at the next by Horsham Gates. Cross bridge to station.

34.8   END

19 SEASIDE RETURN

S tarting from Palace Pier this route was conceived as a return trip for those wishing to cycle back from the London-Brighton ride. The flat run along the seafront to Hove is a sweetener before the ascent to 673 feet on the South Downs near Devil's Dyke. It's downhill from here to Poynings and into the network of narrow, twisting and quiet lanes that head north and eventually climb to St Leonards Forest. It is gentler to Brockham under the shadow of the North Downs. The River Mole is followed through the Dorking Gap then the long drag of Little Switzerland. Once over the North Downs it is a well-earned descent to Epsom.

Not a particularly easy ride to complete in one go and again one which could be split. Horsham and Dorking stations could easily be used by those not wishing to travel further. The challenge of crossing both the North and South Downs and the pleasure of cycling through the woods and twisting lanes of the main roads make for very enjoyable riding.

Maps	OS LR 198, 187.
Distance	50.8 miles. Of this 0.9 miles is easy off-road.
Start	Brighton seafront at the Palace Pier.
Finish	Epsom station.

Railway access

Brighton is served by very frequent trains from London Victoria or by ThamesLink from Bedford via Kings Cross and London Bridge. Also services to Lewes, Eastbourne, Bognor Regis and Portsmouth.

Horsham and *Dorking* stations are conveniently situated on this ride to provide alternative start or early finish points.

Epsom has services through to Victoria, Waterloo, Dorking and, not on Sundays, Horsham and Guildford.

Places to see

Pavilion, Palace Pier - and much else besides, Brighton.

Views - across the weald from the top of the South Downs at Devil's Dyke.

St Leonards Forest.

Brockham.

Refreshments

Cafes & Pubs - Brighton and Hove.

Snack bar - at roundabout after Woodlands Drive on the way out of Hove.

Tea rooms & pub - Devil's Dyke.

Juggernaught transport cafe - weekdays only, Faygate.

Teas - at the church hall on Sunday afternoons in summer, Brockham.

Ryka's Family Restaurant - Burford Bridge.

Teas - at the church hall on Sunday afternoons in summer, Headley.

Wide choice of pubs. such as *The Dragon* at Colegate.

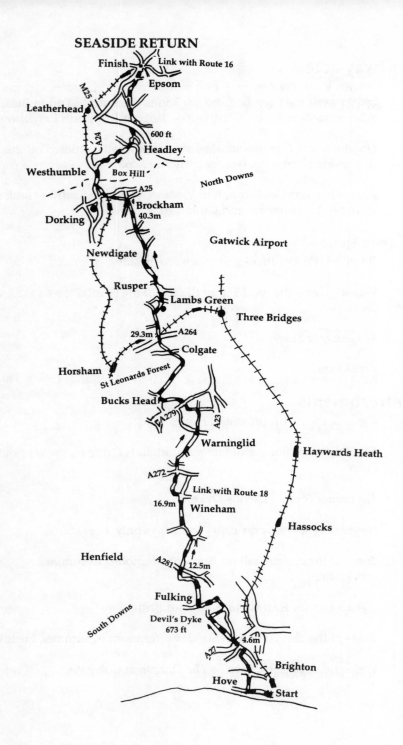

SEASIDE RETURN

Finish · Link with Route 16

Epsom

Leatherhead

M25

A24

600 ft

Headley

Westhumble · Box Hill

North Downs

A25

Brockham

40.3m

Dorking

Gatwick Airport

Newdigate

Rusper

Lambs Green

Three Bridges

29.3m · A264

Colgate

Horsham

St Leonards Forest

Bucks Head

A279

A23

Warninglid

Haywards Heath

A272

Link with Route 18

16.9m · Wineham

Hassocks

Henfield

A281 · 12.5m

Fulking

South Downs

Devil's Dyke
673 ft

4.6m

A27

Brighton

Hove · Start

19   SEASIDE RETURN

0.0   START from Palace Pier, Brighton. **OS LR 198.** RIGHT from Palace
       Pier and head westwards along the seafront cycle path into Hove.

Brighton has been an English seaside resort ever since Dr Richard Russell of
Lewes expounded on the health-giving potential of sea water and caught
the ear of Royalty. The Prince Regent left his mark with the Pavilion but the
town went more down market with the arrival of the railway, the day
excursion, candy floss, the piers - all part of London by the Sea. The Palace
Pier was built in 1899 and now restored to its former elegance along with a
whole range of traditional family amusements.
  Note the dramatic change in the surface of the cycle path, the style of the
buildings and the impressive streets of 19th Century buildings that join the
seafront, once the Hove boundary is crossed.

1.5   RIGHT into Grand Avenue, signposted Lewes/London. Continue
       up long gradual hill over three sets of traffic lights, the railway and
       then a fourth set.

3.4   RIGHT at T-Junction at bottom of dip into Woodlands Drive. This
       road becomes steep near the top where LEFT at T-Junction and
       STRAIGHT ACROSS the two roundabouts following the signs to
       Devil's Dyke. There is an open air snack bar by the first.

4.6   STRAIGHT ON at Junction, again signposted Devil's Dyke. This is a
       beautiful way across the South Downs. RIGHT, signposted Poynings
       if not going to Devil's Dyke. Having climbed to 673 feet from sea
       level it is time to descend a steep hill to the road at the bottom of the
       valley.

The Devil's Dyke looks down upon a deep cleft in the Downs caused,
according to legend, by a futile attempt of Satan to flood the low lands because
they had too many churches. Prehistoric man lived in the earthworks from
where there are extensive views. At one time there was a cable railway, a lift,
and the whole area threatened with brash development. Eventually it was
acquired by Brighton Corporation. Refreshments available.

7.3   LEFT at T-Junction, then by High Point LEFT again on very steep
       turn, signposted Poynings. Continue into village. After church LEFT
       at T-Junction, and follow sign to Fulking, past The Royal Oak PH on
       attractive road at very foot of the South Downs.

9.3   RIGHT into Clappers Lane on the outskirts of Fulking. Follow undulating, wooded lane past vineyard until LEFT into Holmbush Lane then RIGHT at T-Junction at Woodmancote.

12.5 RIGHT at T-junction onto A281. Immediately LEFT, signposted Blackstone. Continue through this pretty hamlet, protected by quite elaborate traffic calming measures.

14.4 LEFT at T-Junction onto B2116. Follow past turning for Music Farm and then Winterpick Mushrooms before RIGHT into Wineham Lane. Continue through Wineham and The Royal Oak PH. Join Route 18 from Horsham along this stretch of road.

16.9 LEFT, signposted Kent Street and CROSS A272 into Picts Lane and OVER staggered crossroads, signposted Warninglid/Slaugham.

19.9 FORK LEFT and LEFT at T-Junction, signposted Warninglid. Eventually climb steep hill past The Rifleman PH and Solomons Restaurant into the village. CONTINUE over crossroads by The Half Moon PH and down hill the other side towards Slaugham and Handcross.

22.4 LEFT at crossroads near pond and STRAIGHT ACROSS A279 by The Wheatsheaf PH into Hammer Pond Road, signposted Bucks Head, and continue to Hammer Pond down 1 in 6 hill before RIGHT at Bucks Head, signposted Colegate/Pease Pottage. **OS LR 187.** Rejoin Route 18 to Horsham at the first crossroads.

27.1 LEFT, signposted Colegate at top of long gradual climb through St Leonards Forest. Continue to village where LEFT at T-Junction, RIGHT by The Dragon PH into Tower Road, signposted Faygate. Long, fast descent but beware of roundabout at bottom.

29.3 STRAIGHT OVER roundabout with A264 into Faygate. On the right is the Juggernaught Transport Cafe. Open weekdays only. Pass The Holmbush Inn, the railway station, then up and over hill.

30.8 RIGHT signposted Lambs Green/Ifield. After The Lamb PH RIGHT at T-Junction, signposted Ifield and STRAIGHT ON at corner, signposted The Mount/Newdigate.

32.1 LEFT at top of hill, then RIGHT at T-Junction, signposted Charlwood. Follow long descending road until RIGHT into Broad

Lane, then LEFT into Shellwood Lane following signs to Brockham.

In many ways Brockham is the epitome of a picture postcard village - built around a large green with the church one end and a pub at the other, with Box Hill to the north to add a scenic backdrop. Teas are served at the church hall on Sunday afternoons, May to October, and are always popular with cyclists.

40.3   LEFT in Brockham after church into Old School Lane. After bridge, STRAIGHT ON to follow rideable bridleway past the golf course. Continue past golf club entrance to metalled section and A25 by Dorking sign. LEFT along A25 and, after Watermill, RIGHT into Pixham Lane before railway bridge and follow under bridge to roundabout on A24. Dorking railway stations are to the left. Otherwise STRAIGHT ACROSS signposted Vineyard and immediately RIGHT onto cycle track. Follow to left turn to West Humble, The Stepping Stones pub is just down there.

43.0   VEER LEFT to descend to and pass through subway. LEFT other side, across the approach to the roundabout on cycle lane, then RIGHT past The Burford Bridge Inn. Pass Ryka's Family Restaurant which is open all hours and is popular with the motorcycling fraternity. Ascend hill before dropping to Juniper Hall.

43.7   RIGHT into Headley Road. Prepare for long ascent up beautiful wooded valley known locally as Little Switzerland. RIGHT at T-Junction, signposted Headley. Climb hill then SHARP LEFT up Tumber Street. Continue along narrow hummocky road which later becomes Slough Lane.

46.5   LEFT at T-Junction at top of steep climb. Teas are available in Headley village hall to the right on Sunday afternoons in summer. Descend under A25 and across open downland.

48.1   RIGHT at crossroads, then LEFT into Headley Road, following signs to Epsom. Descend and follow past the hospital to town.

50.3   RIGHT at T-Junction onto A24 by garage. STRAIGHT ACROSS traffic lights and follow left lane, signposted B280 Chessington. LEFT at traffic lights and RIGHT before railway bridge to Epsom station.

50.8   END

20 UPS & DOWNS

The South Downs run either side of Lewes and the route is soon climbing off-road into these chalk hills to a height of 630 feet, where there are distant glimpses of the sea over the rolling contours. The South Downs Way is part used here. Telscombe, isolated in a fold, is reached before the long descent to the valley. Southease has a church with a round tower and the River Ouse is crossed by a bridge with wooden slats. Then to the South Downs Way again for another climb into the heights, reaching 623 feet by the radio masts. Down to Firle and Glynde, both villages dominated by their manors, past Glyndebourne and its Opera House, and back to Lewes.

The hills are long but the miles short on this route. The tracks are all very rideable, though they could be muddy after heavy rain. The countryside around West Firle and Glynde provides a pleasant contrast to the open landscape of the Downs.

Map	OS LR 198.
Distance	20.1 miles. Of this 9.0 miles are off road.
Start/Finish	Lewes Station.

Railway access

Lewes is on the line between Victoria, Eastbourne, and Hastings. Trains mostly hourly. Also linked by rail to Brighton and Seaford.

Southease has very few trains stopping while *Glynde* has an hourly service.

Places to see

Castle & the old town - with its jumble of streets and old buildings Lewes has a lot to offer including fine views from the Castle.

Model & Living History Centre - where the view can be seen in miniature in an audio visual exhibition, off Lewes High Street and open daily Easter to September.

Anne of Cleaves House - High Street, Southover.

Firle Place & church.

Glynde Place.

Refreshments

Old Needlemakers & Station Buffet - in West Street and at Lewes Station.

Tea rooms - for visitors, Firle Place.

Tea rooms - for visitors, Glynde Place.

There are not many pubs on this ride, most notable are *The Ram* at WestFirle and *The Trevor Arms* at Glynde. Also off the route at Rodmell and Ringmer as well as in Lewes itself.

Probably best to take your own refreshments. for this ride.

UPS & DOWNS

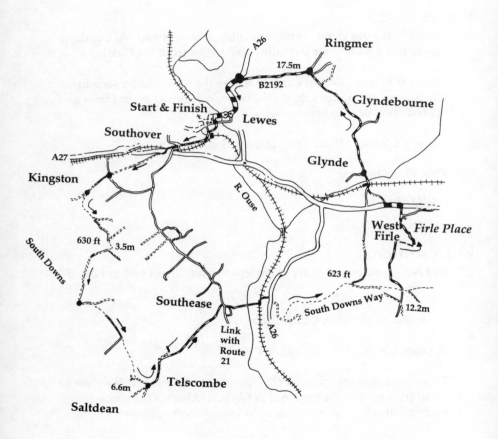

20 UPS & DOWNS

0.0   LEFT from Lewes station. **OS LR 198**. Immediately RIGHT to avoid crossing railway. Continue into Southover past church and Anne of Cleeves' House, now a museum.

Anne of Cleeves House is a 16th Centrury timber framed house that was part of Henry VII's divorce settlement to the said lady. She never actually lived there. Now it is a museum devoted mainly to English country furniture, kitchen and domestic utensils along with the Wealden Iron Gallery. Open daily Easter to end of October except for Sunday mornings. Along this road meet Route 21 from Newhaven to Purley.

0.6   VEER RIGHT at corner into Juggs Lane at corner after The Swan PH. This is a bridleway. Cross A27 on bridge over spectacular cutting through the chalk downland. Eventually the metalled section becomes a track across the fields leading through Kingston Hollow to Kingston village itself. This stretch is mostly rideable though it could be muddy in places.

1.8   STRAIGHT OVER crossroads into Kingston Ridge, marked No Through Road, and signposted bridleway to Woodingdean/ Rodmell. After metalled section with sleeping policemen pass through gate.

2.3   CONTINUE TO LEFT on obvious track up side of hill. At top LEFT to join the South Downs Way overlooking the grassy valley to the south and pass through the gate. STRAIGHT ON at next Junction on South Downs Way and STRAIGHT ON again where track comes up hill from left. Eventually reach 630 feet, the highest point of the ride.

3.5   RIGHT through gate where there is a seat carved out of a tree trunk, once again on the South Downs Way. Then STRAIGHT ON along concrete road by high pressure gas pipeline aerial marker. Here the South Downs Way is left. The surface becomes unmetalled again after farm building on right. Follow rideable track which gradually descends into valley to the second farm building on right.

4.6   LEFT past third farm building on right and fourth on left over open downland with views across to Saltdean.

5.6   STRAIGHT ON at next junction. Pass reservoir on right.

6.1 STRAIGHT ON along more indistinct track before cattle grid and CONTINUE through gate.

6.4 LEFT onto driveway from houses on right.

6.6 LEFT onto metalled road and downhill into the isolated downland village of Telscombe, past the Youth Hostel and church. There is a short uphill section before the final plunge into the valley of the Ouse. Meet Route 10 from Newhaven here.

8.6 RIGHT at T-Junction then immediately LEFT to follow signpost to Southease, No Through Road.

Southease church has a round tower, one of three in the Ouse valley. It is a very old building, some parts dating from before the Norman Conquest, and largely built of flint and rubble. A perfect setting on this small village green.

STRAIGHT ON past village green. Cross the Ouse on metal bridge with wooden slats and unmanaged level crossing by Southease Station where a train that stops is something of a rarity. Continue past Itford Farm.

9.5 RIGHT onto A26, and following South Downs Way signs, LEFT onto track by farmhouse. Continue through gate on the steep climb.

10.0 LEFT on hill, still on South Downs Way. Continue up long grassy climb with fine views to the north west. Pass through three gates, to reach a height of 623 feet by the radio masts, before a fourth gate.

12.2 PASS THROUGH final gate and immediately LEFT at car park onto metalled road that descends from the downs.

13.2 RIGHT onto rideable bridleway opposite track to farm. LEFT at T-Junction and pass farm buildings into West Firle.

In the church there are momuments to the Gage family who still reside in Firle Place at the other end of the village. Sir Thomas has the longest living memorial of them all. He is said to have bought back a plum from abroad and planted it in his garden to give us the greengage. The house itself contains many Old Masters and is open to the public from June to the end of September, Sundays, Wednesdays, Thusdays, and Bank Holidays, 14.00 to 17.00. Teas for visitors.

14.0   RIGHT at T-Junction after passing The Ram PH and the village stores. Continue past entrance to Firle Place to A27 where LEFT and RIGHT by Toll Gate Service Station.

15.1   RIGHT at T-Junction by The Trevor Arms PH then past Glynde railway station, through the village and up the hill, passing Glynde Place.

Glynde Place is an Elizabethan brick and flint house built around a courtyard. It has a large collection of bronzes, paintings, tapestries as well as a Rubens cartoon. Open June to end of September, Wednesdays, Thusdays and Bank Holidays as well as the first and second Sundays of the month. 14.15 to 17.30. Cafe for visitors. Continue past Glyndebourne Opera House up hill and down to B2192 near Ringmer.

17.5   LEFT at T-junction onto B2192 signposted Lewes. LEFT onto A26 and continue into town.

19.5   STRAIGHT ACROSS roundabout by entrance to tunnel. Cycling is prohibited here in the longest dry land road tunnel in the country.

STRAIGHT ON at roundabout by Tescos, cross bridge and follow one way sysem to LEFT and signs to station. STRAIGHT ON at traffic lights and up hill before LEFT to cross railway to station.

20.1   END.

21 TO THE PURLEY GATES

The South Downs rise behind Newhaven but through the gap in their defences, guarded by Lewes, flows the River Ouse and it is in this direction that this ride heads northward. Through Piltdown, home of the mythical man, then a long climb into the heathery bracken heathland of the Ashdown Forest which gives way to the woods and valleys of the Weald before Weir Wood Reservoir, the birthplace of the River Medway. After Lingfield the going is flatter and more open but with always the North Downs to come. Where the route joins the North Downs Way the high point of the ride is reached, at 616 feet. Then it's down and down through a long valley that is so unspoilt that its difficult to realise that London is only a few miles away. But soon suburbia comes for the final run in to Purley.

This ride can easily be split, with Lewes and Lingfield stations being particularly well placed as alternative access points. There are some hilly sections, particularly around the Ashdown Forest and the North Downs.

Maps	OS LR 198, 187.
Distance	53.6 miles. Of this 1.5 miles is rideable off-road.
Start	Newhaven Town Station.
Finish	Purley Station.

Railway access

Newhaven Town is served by a half-hourly service from Lewes, in turn reached by trains from London Victoria, Brighton to the west and Eastbourne from the east.

East Grinstead & Lingfield are early finish points an the line to London, via East Croydon.

Purley is on a frequent service to Victoria and to stations south.

Places to see

Fort - Newhaven.

Monk's House (NT) - Rodmell.

Standen (NT) - East Grinstead.

Church & village - Lingfield.

Yew tree in churchyard - Crowhurst.

Refreshments

Snack bar - ferry terminal, Newhaven and, for visitors, Fort Newhaven.

Tea rooms - at the old station, Barcombe Mills.

Tea rooms - Barkham Manor vineyard, Piltdown.

Little Chef - Nutley.

Tea rooms - for visitors, Standen.

Happy Eater - Felbridge.

Best Wishes Gift Shop - not Sundays, Lingfield.

Wide choice of pubs - *The Greyhound* at Lingfield serves good food.

TO THE PURLEY GATES

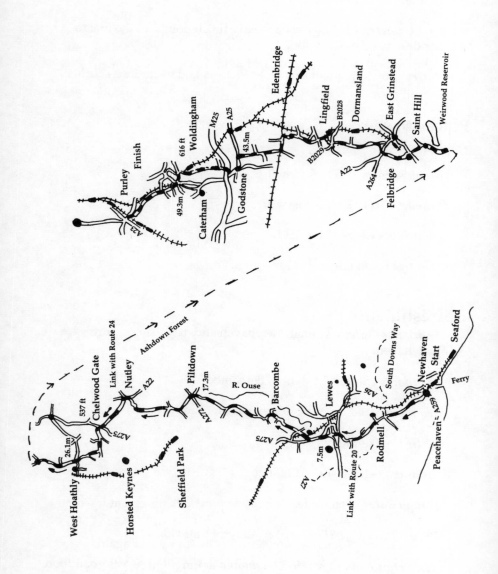

21 TO THE PURLEY GATES

0.0   LEFT from Newhaven Town station. **OS LR 198.** Cross Ouse and
       follow one-way system, signposted Town Centre.

Newhaven got its name in 1579 after a storm had altered the course of the
Ouse away from the old port of Seaford. In the 1860s the threat of invasion
by the French was considered to be so great that a fort was built out on a
headland with a commanding view of the whole bay. Fort Newhaven has
now been restored and is open Easter to early October, Wednesday to Sundays
and daily during school holiday periods. Refreshments for visitors to the
fort and also at the car ferry terminal though this cafeteria shuts when the
ferry has departed.

0.3   RIGHT into Meeching Road, signposted Town Centre South, to get
       away from the race track one way system. Immediately LEFT into
       the pedestrianised High Street and RIGHT onto main road again by
       the pedestrian crossing.

0.5   STRAIGHT ON where main road swings round to right. Follow
       signs to Piddinghoe, with its strong smuggling traditions, Rodmell
       and pass The Abergavenny Arms PH. Then cross over A27 on
       bridge and enter the part of Lewes known as Southover. Route 20
       crosses on its way to Southease from Telescombe

Monks House (NT) at Rodmell was where Virginia and Leonard Woolf lived
for many years having bought the house in 1919. The former, subject to
depression, drowned herself in the Ouse in 1941. Open April to end of October,
Wednesdays and Saturdays, 14.00 to 17.30.

7.0   LEFT at The Swan Inn, signposted East Grinstead/Brighton.
       Descend one steep hill and climb another. Cross Route 20 again at
       this turn.

7.5   STRAIGHT OVER crossroads near prison, signposted A275 East
       Grinstead. Follow this road to Offham through the gap in the South
       Downs.

8.9   RIGHT by the church, signposted Hamsey. Close to the Old Post
       Office, a convenient stopping place for coffee though at the time of
       writing it was up for sale.

9.9   RIGHT, signposted Barcombe. After church RIGHT again,
       signposted Barcombe Mills/Ringmer following road over former
       railway then LEFT at T-Junction, signposted Barcombe.

A right turn here leads to the Ouse and Barcombe Mills half a mile down the road. The mill itself has gone, ending its days as a button factory before being burnt to the ground. As well as The Anglers Rest PH there is a tea room and buffet at the old railway station.

12.7 RIGHT at roundabout in the main village of Barcombe. RIGHT again, signposted Piltdown passing the left turn for Barkham Manor Vineyard where ploughmans lunches and teas may be obtained.

17.1 LEFT at T-Junction near pond, then immediately FORK RIGHT, signposted Fletching.

There is a monument to the Piltdown Man at Barkham Manor. The skull found here in 1912 was for 41 years thought to be the oldest human remains to be found in the country. However tests revealed it to be nothing more than the skull of a young orang-utan! It was probably the biggest hoax ever to fall upon the world of archaeology.

17.3 CROSS A272 where there is a Little Chef to the left. Follow road to Fletching, a name meaning that it was a centre for the making of arrows, and where there is a good choice of pubs. Continue through village. At Fletching Garage STRAIGHT ON, signposted Nutley. Continue up long hill to the Ashdown Forest.

William Cobbett called Ashdown Forest '...the most villainously ugly spot I ever saw in England'. Perhaps it had been ravaged by the iron industry of past centuries. But now bracken and heather rule on this beautiful area of heathland.

21.9 LEFT onto A22 at Nutley. After cafe and Ganges Restaurant LEFT again, signposted Chelwood Gate. **OS LR 187.**

24.5 RIGHT at T-Junction onto A275, signposted East Grinstead and LEFT by The Red Lion PH. Then RIGHT signposted narrow road. Continue down this beautiful narrow lane as it twists its way though the woods to a ford and up the other side.

26.1 RIGHT at T-Junction and at top of long hill RIGHT at next, signposted West Hoathly. Continue to Tyes Cross.

27.6 RIGHT and immediately RIGHT at T-Junction. Then very quickly LEFT, signposted Saint Hill Green/East Grinstead/ Standen. Descend long hill to Weir Wood Reservoir before 12% climb after passing East Grinstead sign. Note how the tree roots entangle with the exposed rock, a common feature in this area.

30.2 LEFT, signposted Felbridge. Continue past Scientology College.

Keeping right and then right again leads downhill to Standen House (NT). This family house was built in the 1890s and is notable for the period interior with William Morris textiles and wallpapers. The hillside gardens give fine views across the valley of the infant Medway. Open April to end of October, Wednesday to Sunday and Bank Holiday Mondays 13.30 to 17.30 plus March weekends until 16.30. Tea room for visitors.

30.9 STRAIGHT OVER crossroads into Imberhorne Lane. Descend to Felbridge. VEER RIGHT at mini-roundabout.

32.7 RIGHT at traffic lights onto A22 (Happy Eater down road to left). Follow into East Grinstead if station required otherwise LEFT into unmetalled Yew Lane after garage (bridleway). This is rideable but with vicious sleeping policemen. RIGHT at T-Junction into unmetalled Lowdells Lane before STRAIGHT onto metalled road.

33.6 LEFT at T-Junction. Continue down hill through Felcourt, past Rentokil and up hill into Lingfield.

Lingfield is a large village, perhaps best known for its race course. The church contains some very fine tombs of the Cobham family and the area round about has a fine selection of buildings of the 16th to 18th Centuries. The village lock-up in the centre of the village always attracts attention. It was last used for this purpose in 1882 for a poacher.
 Teas can be obtained at either the furniture shop near the roundabout or at Best Wishes Tea Room & Gift Shop off to the right. Both not open Sundays. The Greyhound pub and others in the village also serve food. Lingfield also has a station for train services to Victoria and East Grinstead.

37.4 LEFT at roundabout, signposted Godstone/Crawley and immediately RIGHT by the lock-up, signposted library. LEFT at crossroads after the church then LEFT again at T-Junction into Crowhurst Road and, following signs, STRAIGHT ACROSS staggered crossroads through the scattered village of Crowhurst.

Outside St Georges Church at Crowhurst is an enormous yew tree, hollow inside and entered through a door.

41.9 RIGHT at T-Junction by The Bricklayers Arms PH. Continue under railway, then LEFT, signposted Tandridge/Godstone. Follow through to Tandridge village up 1 in 10 hill.

43.5 LEFT at top of hill into narrow lane then LEFT again onto A25. STRAIGHT ACROSS roundabout, signposted Godstone/Redhill. RIGHT into Flower Lane and up long hill onto North Downs, crossing over on flyovers the A22 and M25 respectively.

45.5 STRAIGHT onto bridleway where road swings round to right. This is part of the North Downs Way and is perfectly rideable. The highest point of the ride is reached at 616 feet. RIGHT at South Lodge onto metalled private road which also has bridleway status. Descend long gradual hill down valley through Woldingham School. It is amazing to think that such an unspoilt downland valley can exist so close to London. Pass under railway and at second bridge

48.8 STRAIGHT ON and follow road downhill to the busy Wapses Lodge Roundabout with A22.

Follow the A22 to RIGHT for a quick, though busy run past Whyteleafe South and Whyteleafe stations to Purley. Take RIGHT FORK at traffic lights before bridge to reach Purley station. The route which follows is longer, hillier, but quieter.

49.3 STRAIGHT ACROSS roundabout into Wood Lane. Visibility poor but subway can be used. Then RIGHT on hill immediately after crossing railway onto bumpy but rideable track,

49.9 LEFT at T-Junction by log cabin onto surfaced road. Continue up hill until RIGHT into Church Road.

50.5 OVER crossroads into Hornchurch Hill. Follow along Beverley Road and Valley Road into Kenley. After Kenley station.

52.0 LEFT into Hayes Lane. Follow into Park Road then RIGHT into Oaks Way.

53.0 RIGHT at T-Junction into Higher Drive and continue into Foxley Hill Road on crossing over railway. Descend to Purley. CROSS main road, using pedestrian crossing. Take zig-zag path before bridge which leads to car park at Purley Station. This avoids the busy one way system around Purley Cross.

53.6 END

22 THE LONG MAN RIDE

From Eastbourne this route soon climbs to Beachy Head at 536 feet, where the South Downs meet the sea in the most spectacular way. It is down along a twisting road to Birling Gap and a further sight of the sea where the Seven Sisters start their westward passage. Inland again to East Dean then up and over the Downs again before the long descent into the Cuckmere valley. This river is followed to the beautiful village of Alfriston, and through much gentler terrain before being crossed near Michelham Priory. The Long Man stands sentinel over the South Downs Way which is followed to a high point of 659 feet, overlooking Eastbourne. Soon the town is entered after a long and spectacular descent.

This is a very hilly route starting with a long 10% gradient and an even steeper one at East Dean. The final part along the South Downs Way can be hard particularly in bad weather, but the views are superb.

Map	OS LR 199.
Distance	32.5 miles. Of this 5.6 miles is off-road along the South Downs Way. Rideable but slippery in places when wet.
Start/Finish	Eastbourne Station.

Railway access

Eastbourne is served by trains from London Victoria, Brighton and Hastings. They run half hourly to hourly.

Berwick Station is a useful escape point for either Eastbourne, Lewes, Brighton and London.

Places to See

Cliffs & the sea - Beachy Head & Birling Gap.

Sheep Centre, Country Park & Living World Exhibition - Seven Sisters.

Church, Clergy House (NT) & Drusillas - Alfriston.

Michelham Priory.

The Long Man, Priory & church - Willmington.

The Wish Tower, Museum of Shops - Eastbourne.

Refreshments

Pub & Cafe - Beachy Head.

Cafe - at hotel, Birling Gap.

Tea rooms - for visitors, Seven Sisters Sheep Centre.

Copper Kettle & Badgers - and others, Alfriston.

Tea rooms - for visitors to Michelham Priory.

Plenty of choice in Eastbourne, including the railway station.

THE LONG MAN RIDE

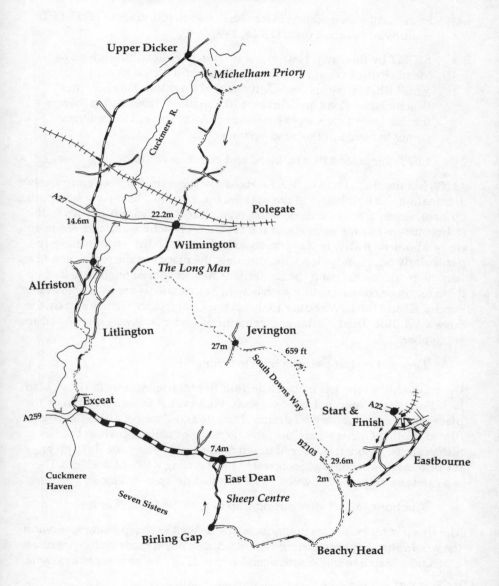

22 THE LONG MAN RIDE

0.0   From Eastbourne Station exit push across to roundabout and LEFT,
       signposted Beachy Head. **OS LR 199**.

0.3   RIGHT by the Town Hall opposite church. Follow through along
       Meads Road to next roundabout. There, still on the same road,
       VEER RIGHT, signposted University of Brighton. This becomes
       Beachy Head Road and climbs a 10% gradient from which there is a
       fine backward view over Eastbourne. After Upper Dukes Drive
       comes in from left this road becomes B2103.

2.0   LEFT signposted Beachy Head and continue climbing.

At 536 feet the chalk walls of Beachy Head rise sheer from the sea completely
dominating the lighthouse at the bottom, built in 1902. The view is superb
up here, suposedly as far as 60 miles on a clear day. Richard Jeffries in the
last century was rapturous about the breeze on Beachy head and wrote an
essay about it. But it is dangerous to go too near the crumbling edge,
particularly on a windy day. Unfortunately the place has the reputation of a
very high suicide rate and the Samaritans have a special telephone box up
there for those contemplating such action. Refreshments are available at the
Beachy Head Hotel. Next door to this is the Countryside Centre run by the
Sussex Wildlife Trust containing exhibitions and displays. Open April to
September.

        Descend on fast twisting road to Birling.

Up on the hill to the left is the Belle Tout lighthouse built in 1831 by 'Mad
Jack Fuller' and now not used as such. However it is recognisable as the
place where much of the BBC drama 'The Life and Times of a She-Devil' was
filmed. Birling Gap is where the famous range of cliffs known as the Seven
Sisters starts. Wooden steps lead down to the beach where the dirty green of
the tide-mark is in complete contrast to the dazzling white of the cliffs. There
is a cafeteria at the hotel, which has a decayed delapidated look.

        Continue inland after Birling Gap to pass the Sheep Centre.

The sheep centre is a working farm, where as well as sheep being shorn and
the wool spun, they are also milked, with cheese being made on the premises.
Open mid-March to mid-September, 14.00 to 17.00. Refreshments available.

7.0   LEFT, signposted East Dean village. Continue past church and green
       where there is The Tiger Inn along with the flint built cottages. The
       church has a Saxon tower.

7.4 LEFT at T-Junction onto A259. This is a busy road, not helped by the 1 in 6 ascent. However this can be made more pleasant by taking the metalled footpath just before the junction and push up the hill as far as Friston. There is a long descent after the church into Exceat and the Cuckmere Valley. Beware of 14% section at bottom.

On the right, in old barns, is the visitor centre for the Seven Sisters Country Park along with the Living World exhibition where living displays of wildlife, including butterflies and aquaria can be viewed. Open daily Easter to end October, 10.00 to 17.00. Teas can be had at Exceat Farmhouse.

10.2 RIGHT before bridge, signposted West Dean. Continue to Litlington. Just after The Plough and Harrow. LEFT onto metalled footpath. Cross footbridge.

12.4 RIGHT at Youth Hostel.Continue into Alfriston, a show place village very well endowed with both pubs and tea places such as The Copper Kettle and Badgers.

At one time smugggling was as important to Alfriston as tourism is today. There is a 15th Century market cross and the large parish church is known as The Cathedral of the Downs. The medieval half-timbered and thatched clergy house was the first building to be acquired by the National Trust. It was purchased by them in 1896 for just ten pounds! There is an exhibition all season. Open April to end of October, daily, 10.30 to 17.00 or dusk if earlier.

13.2 RIGHT in the market square. Continue past Drusillas Park to roundabout on A27.

Drusillas, established over sixty years agao has the reputation of being 'The Best Small Zoo in the Country'. Numerous exhibitions such as a Meerkat Mound or Monkey Mountain Sanctuary. Open daily 10.00 to 17.00. Refreshments available for visitors.

14.6 STRAIGHT OVER at roundabout, signposted Dicker. After level crossing by Berwick station pass Arlington reservoir.

18.2 RIGHT, signposted Michelham Priory, Hailsham.

Michelham Priory lies within its original medieval moat and was founded in 1229. Some of the original buildings such as the gatehouse survived the dissolution to become part of a later Tudor dwelling. Much period furniture, tapestries as well as a collection of musical instruments. In the grounds are other attractions such as the Great Barn and working watermill. Refreshments available as well. Open daily from end March to October, 11.00 to 17.30 and Sundays only in March and November.

19.2   LEFT after Priory, signposted Wilmington/Arlington. Pass The Old Oak PH and the Abbots Wood picnic site, then LEFT again, signposted Wilmington/Polegate.

22.2   CROSS A27 again, signposted Wilmington Church/Long Man near The Giants Rest PH. Pass church and climb hill .

Like many chalk figures, the origins and meaning of the Long Man of Wilmington is lost in the mists of time. He could have been Hercules, Odin or a giant advertisment carved by the monks of Wilmington Priory. The South Downs at that time was used by pilgrims journeying between Winchester and Canterbury and in bad weather the sight of this giant chalk figure would be reassuring for those seeking overnight accommodation.
  There are still substantial remains of the 13th Century priory and a later farmhouse close by is now a museum of agricultural by-gones. Open daily except Tuesdays and Sunday mornings end of March to end of October. The parish church was intended for use by both monks and villagers. Some of the breeds depicted on the unusual stained glass Butterfly Window, such as the Camberwell Beauty, are now very rare or extinct.

24.4   LEFT on hill onto bridleway signposted Long Man. Continue upwards to the South Downs Way after passing turning to the Long Man. This is steep and an easier alternative would be is to carry on further up the road to join South Downs Way there.

24.6   RIGHT FORK onto South Downs Way. After gate follow directions on signposts carefully when the track becomes indistinct. It is easiest to keep close to the line of cultivated field. Generally easy cycling except for short, muddy stretch after another gate.

26.3   LEFT onto a firmer track before RIGHT again following South Downs Way signs. This is an awkward descent through the woods with many tree roots to contend with. After passing the church at Jevington, interesting with Saxon tower, join metalled section.

27.0   RIGHT at T-Junction by Hungry Monk Restaurant in Jevington village where the Banoffi Pie on offer sounds interesting. Immediately take the SECOND LEFT, again signposted South Downs Way. Follow another section of distinct bridleway as it regains the height lost before. The 659 feet reached here is the highest point of the whole ride. The track flattens out and there are very fine views in all directions, particularly to the left over Eastbourne. This section of track is rideable, though very slippery in places during wet weather.

29.6 CROSS A259. At trig point keep RIGHT and continue to car-park and B2103.

30.1 LEFT onto B2103, then RIGHT into Upper Dukes Drive. There is a long, though very twisting descent to the sea front.

Eastbourne has always been described as elegant and fashionable and that is the impression one gets today as when looking along the esplanade, designed by the 7th Duke of Devonshire in 1834, for there are no shops to interrupt the flow. The Wish Tower is number 73 of the 103 Martello Towers built during the Napoleonic Wars as protection against possible French invasion. The sheer scale of this operation can be realised in that it took over 2 years to build this example with half a million bricks being used. Inside there is an exhibition. Open daily March to October and weekends only at other times.

In Cornfield Terace, not far from the railway station, is a museum of shops, where over 50,000 items are displayed on three floors in authentic settings ranging from 1850 to 1950.

Being a popular seaside resort there is no shortage of refreshment places in Eastbourne.

32.0 LEFT into Devonshire Place opposite band stand. Continue to roundabout and follow ring road to station.

32.5 END

23 WHERE THE NORMANS CAME

This is an interesting ride of contrasts. Starting from Polegate, on the outermost fringe of Pevensey Levels, it follows the former railway line, now the Cuckoo Trail, northwards through Hailsham to Hellingly. From here it is into the Weald, a region of rolling hills, woodland and a sense of remoteness that is difficult to imagine in the South East. Relics of the old iron industry are found around Ashburnham and what a perfect setting for Penhurst. By Twelve Oaks the highest point is reached at 404 feet, before reaching Battle which grew up around the Abbey established by William the Conqueror. Continue on to the seaside at Cooden Beach, on the western fringes of Bexhill and on to The Levels and Pevensey Castle before once again The Cuckoo Trail and Polegate.

The first and last sections of this ride are easy but the middle section through the Weald can be most optimistically described as undulating. This is a small price to pay for such superb countryside.

Map	OS LR 199.
Distance	43.9 miles. Of this 7.3 miles is off-road, mostly very rideable with the exception of uncompleted sections of the Cuckoo Trail and near Catsfield Court.
Start/Finish	Polegate Station.

Railway access

Polegate is served half hourly to hourly by trains from London Victoria, Brighton, Hastings and Eastbourne.

Battle is on the line between London Charing Cross and Hastings could be used as an escape point.

Cooden Beach & Pevensey, on the line between Hastings and Eastbourne. *Normans Bay* and *Pevensey Bay* have a limited service.

Places to See

Penhurst.

Abbey & Battlefield (EH), Buckley's Yesterdays World - Battle.

Castle (EH), Mint House, Court House Museum & Jail - Pevensey.

Refreshments

Mill Coffee House - by Polegate Station.

Tea rooms - between Polegate and Hailsham on the Cuckoo Trail.

Tea-rooms & pubs - in the town and teas for visitors at Buckley's Yesterdays World, Battle.

Castle Cottage tea rooms - Pevensey.

Refreshments are scarce along the middle section through the Weald to Battle. A good idea to take your own provisions if you intend to linger there.

WHERE THE NORMANS CAME

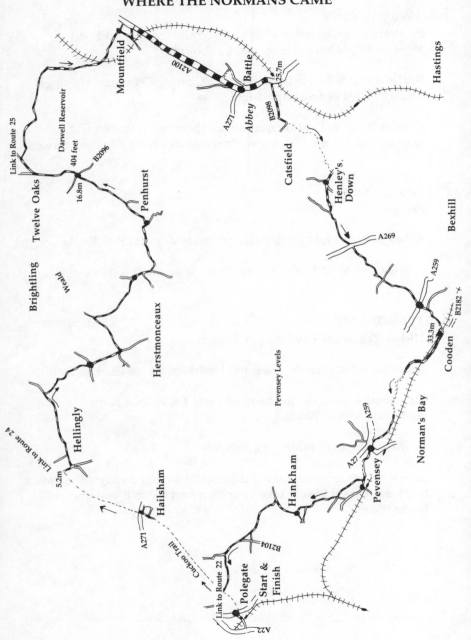

23 WHERE THE NORMANS CAME

0.0   LEFT from Polegate Station. **OS LR 199.** Close by is the Mill Coffee
       House which is open on Sundays. Following signs for the Cuckoo
       Trail, RIGHT at T-Junction by level crossing. Then RIGHT at next
       into Station Road.

0.3   LEFT into School Lane to join the Cuckoo Trail to Hailsham.

Polegate is one of those places that grew up around a railway junction. One
branch went northwards through Hailsham to Tunbridge Wells, and after it
closed the line reappeared as the Cuckoo Trail. Originally for walkers Sustrans
have recently converted it into a full blooded cycle path. At the time of writing
this has not been completed north of Hailsham, where it is very muddy, but
things could well be different now. Take great care with the many
inexperienced cyclists that are attracted to this trail and don't be too distracted
by the striking sculptures. Follow signposts around Hailsham where new
estates have been built over much of the old railway. Teas can also be obtained
en route.

2.9   CONTINUE into residential road then RIGHT and LEFT past pond.

3.1   LEFT again onto trail and pass the old station. After passing under
       the third bridge LEFT into housing estate and follow signs to
       Cuckoo Trail round to RIGHT to the stone pineapples.

3.9   LEFT onto the Cuckoo Trail once more. Cross over road at bridge,
       then over the A271. After the old station at Hellingly pass under
       bridge then LEFT up bank by stile into the car park of The Golden
       Martlet pub, a popular haunt with motorcyclists.

5.2   LEFT onto metalled road to cross bridge. At crossroads LEFT,
       signposted Horam.

7.0   RIGHT, signposted Cowbeech and at top of steep hill STRAIGHT
       ON over crossroads, signposted Herstmonceux. LEFT at staggered
       crossroads, signposted Bodle Street.

10.2   STRAIGHT on at Merryweather Farm Stables before RIGHT at T-
       Junction towards Bodle Street Green and LEFT at 40 sign.

11.0   LEFT at T-Junction. Continue up hill past the Herbal Medicine
       School before turning RIGHT, signposted Ponts Green. Follow this

beautiful though hilly lane.

13.4   RIGHT at T-Junction Then LEFT signposted Penhurst after the turning for Brownbread Street.

14.2   KEEP RIGHT down hill. Cross over mill leat at Ashburnham Forge.

The name Ashburnham Forge is an ample reminder of the iron industry carried on in this area. Half a mile north of the forge but not on the route are the ruins of the furnace and a series of hammer ponds. Cannon balls were made here and are still found from time to time. Iron working could have continued as late as 1828.

15.0   LEFT on hill to Penhurst.

What a perfect setting, the church and the small manor house, behind the pond where ducks swim. It is deep within rolling, wooded, remote countryside seemingly away from the pressures of the 1990s. The old iron industry has been put to sleep and the area slumbers on though even here change is evident, for farm buildings have been recently converted to studios. The church with its 14th Century oak screen is well worth visiting. The pulpit originated as far away as Long Melford in Suffolk.

16.8   CROSS B2096, signposted Brightling, then RIGHT, signposted Robertsbridge/Mountfield at Twelve Oaks.

By carrying straight on to Brightling it is possible to join Route 25 which runs north to Tunbridge Wells.

18.1   RIGHT, signposted Mountfield. Cross the conveyor belt used for the transportation of gypsum from mines in the area. Descend with distant views of Darwell Reservoir. Continue past the church to Mountfield. British Gypsum Ltd have a large plant here, surrounded by woods.

22.1   RIGHT, signposted Netherfield then LEFT before railway to A2100 where RIGHT and continue to Battle.

25.1   LEFT at roundabout, signposted A2100 Hastings. Follow through the town which is well endowed with eating places and cycle shops. Pass the Abbey (EH).

Battles might destroy but they can also create. William the Conqueror vowed to build a church on the site of the Battle of Hastings if he won. He kept his word and an altar was erected where Harold fell, though the spot is marked by a memorial stone today. The Abbey gatehouse still dominates the town and houses a museum depicting the history of the site from the Battle to its conversion to a country house. There is a mile long perimeter walk around the battlefield where relief models help to give an impression of what happened there. Run by English Heritage the Abbey is open all year round, 10.00 to 18.00 (or 16.00 in winter). Near the Abbey is Buckleys Yesterdays World, a museum dedicated to the ways our forefathers lived. Teas for visitors.

25.7   RIGHT onto B2098, signposted Catfield and continue past site of battle before LEFT.

26.7   RIGHT onto private road and bridleway, signposted Peppering Eye Farm. Continue through farm and along well surfaced stretch to Powder Mill Cottage.

27.4   RIGHT at the cottage. Shortly the surface gives out and the bridleway becomes a narrow path which can be muddy as it descends into the valley. Follow to concrete road.

28.2   LEFT past Catsfield Court, along gravelly unmade road, before joining metalled highway.

28.7   RIGHT, then LEFT, signposted Sidley/Bexhill.

29.0   LEFT at T-Junction, signposted Bexhill and immediately RIGHT into lane with width restriction then LEFT again at T-Junction.

30.4   CROSS A269 into Pear Tree Lane and follow OVER next crossroads, signposted Little Common/Cooden. Descend to the western fringes of Bexhill.

32.4   STRAIGHT ON at roundabout onto B2182, signposted Cooden Beach station.

33.3   RIGHT after passing under railway into Herbrand Walk After station continue to roundabout on outskirts of Pevensey.

This road runs very close to the coast at first, passing fishing boats hauled high up on the beach. In this direction the flatness of the area is broken by fine views towards the South Downs. After crossing the railway the road snakes inland across Pevensey Levels. This is a very flat, low lying area, at times no more than four feet above sea level, a product of the continuous process of coastal realignment where what is taken away from one place is given back somewhere else. With first the Saxons and then William the Conqueror setting examples, this area has always been considered dangerously open to invasion, with the result that a large concentration of Martello Towers was built to withstand possible French invasion. Now there are the holiday settlements of Norman's Bay and Pevensey Bay.

37.5   LEFT at roundabout, signposted A259 Eastbourne, then STRAIGHT ON at traffic lights into Pevensey High Street. Pass Pevensey Castle (EH). Teas can be obtained nearby at Castle Cottage.

Unlike the Martello Towers, Pevensey Castle has seen a great deal of active service from its origins as a Roman fortress. William the Conqueror built the first Norman castle. Attacked and besieged many times its massive walls have never been breached in warfare. It was even pressed into service again in 1940 and gun emplacements and pill boxes can be seen amongst the remains. Run by English Heritage open daily 10.00 to 18.00 (16.00 in Winter months).

Just as it has been by-passed by the A27, so Pevensey has been left high and dry as a port. At one time coins were minted here and the 14th Century Mint House is open to the public (all year, Monday to Saturday). In the High Street as well is the Court House Museum and Jail where old maps, seals, and other regalia of the former borough can be seen. This is claimed to be the smallest building of its type in England. Open daily, May to September.

38.5   RIGHT into Peelings Lane after Westham sign and church with tower, signposted car park then RIGHT again at crossroads, signposted Hankham. Cross A27 on bridge then CONTINUE straight on to T-Junction.

40.6   RIGHT, signposted Rickney/Hailsham then follow round to LEFT in order to reach the B2104.

41.8   RIGHT at T-Junction, signposted Hailsham then LEFT into Otteham Court Lane, signposted Little Friars Farm.

43.0   LEFT onto Cuckoo Trail and retrace to Polegate and station.

43.9   END

24 WEALD & FOREST

Southwards from Tunbridge Wells past High Rocks this route plunges into the High Weald - a countryside of ridges between which are deep wooded secluded valleys. Here the towns are built on the hill tops. What more perfect example could there be than Mayfield with its weather-boarded houses? Between here and Heathfield is the infant River Rother. Once Horam is reached it is time to turn back through Waldron and over Hadlow Down along deeply sunken lanes which appear to be held together by tree roots. But it is far more open through the forest itself where the trees have departed leaving a landscape clothed in various shades of brown, particularly in Autumn. After a high point of 715 feet near Duddleswell downhill is the predominant trend before returning once again by the rocky outcrops of High Rocks to Tunbridge Wells.

This is an extremely hilly route which crosses a succession of valleys. But balance the effort spent against the sheer quality of the scenery.

Maps	OS LR 188, 199.
Distance	47.7 miles from Tunbridge Wells or 38.2 from Eridge Station. 0.3 miles off-road at Groombridge.
Start/Finish	Tunbridge Wells or Eridge Stations.

Railway access

Tunbridge Wells has a frequent service from London Charing Cross on the Hastings line.

Eridge Station is on the line from Oxted to Uckfield and trains much less frequent.

Oxted connects with London Victoria via East Croydon and is also on the East Grinstead line.

Places to See

The Pantiles - and much more in Tunbridge Wells.

High Rocks - near Tunbridge Wells.

Mayfield.

Merrydown Cider, Countryside Exhibition & Farm Museum - Horam.

Wilderness Wood - Hadlow Down.

Refreshments

Cafes & pubs - Tunbridge Wells.

Bowers' Cafe - Mark Cross.

April Cottage - afternoons only, Mayfield.

Old Coach House Tea Rooms - on A265, Heathfield.

St Georges Vineyard - Waldron.

Tea rooms - for visitors to Wilderness Wood, Hadlow Down.

Tea rooms - Duddleswell.

No shortage of pubs on this route.

WEALD & FOREST

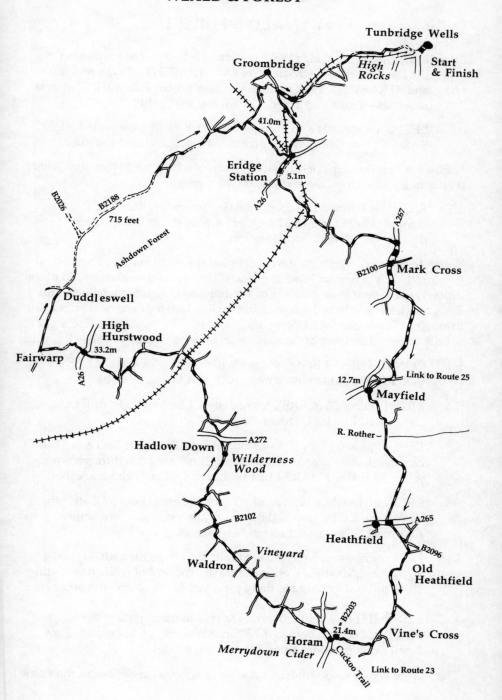

24 WEALD & FOREST

0.0   LEFT out of Tunbridge Wells Station via the London platform. **OS LR 188.** Continue past Safeways and STRAIGHT ON at junction, and STRAIGHT ON at roundabout, signposted A26. RIGHT at next roundabout into Major Yorks Road, and up the hill.

0.6   LEFT at crossroads into Hungershall Park Road, signposted High Rocks. Follow over railway and past High Rocks and the pub.

High Rocks are outcrops of sandstone, some of which are 40 feet high. There is an admission charge. Open daily 9.00 to sunset.

3.0   RIGHT at T-Junction, signposted Groombridge, then LEFT, signposted Eridge and STRAIGHT ON at top of hill for steep descent to pub and Eridge station.

This ride is also designed to start and finish at Eridge Station. This is on the very pretty line between Oxted and Uckfield and is still worked by old diesel units. There is definitely a feeling of a remote, forgotten branch line about it. Eridge station used to be known as Eridge Junction for there was once a line through to Tunbridge Wells. Now, after closure, it looks as if this line is going to be resurrected and part of the station is given over to the Spa Valley Railway.

5.1   CONTINUE past Eridge station which is now by-passed by the A26 then RIGHT onto marked cycle path and through lay-by.

5.4   RIGHT onto A26 (CARE). Immediately LEFT into Sandhill Lane, signposted Bowles Outdoor Centre.

6.8   LEFT to pass under railway. Continue past Redgate Mill and OVER crossroads, signposted Mark Cross. Climb long hill through woods. After Toad Hall SHARP LEFT to descend hill and climb another.

9.4   LEFT at T-Junction onto A267. Opposite here is Bowers Cafe, which, displaying a CTC sign and open daily, is a popular refreshment stop for cyclists. Continue through Mark Cross.

10.5   LEFT, signposted Tidebrook/Mayfield College then RIGHT, signposted Mayfield College, and pass the school while descending steep hill and getting mentally prepared for the climb the other side.

12.7   STRAIGHT ON at junction into Mayfield itself. Follow the High Street past church beforee LEFT into West Street, tea rooms. Pass April Cottage where afternoon teas are served.

The village sign shows children dancing in a grassy meadow as the name means virgins or 'maids' field. Perhaps its fitting that the old Archbishops Palace is now a Roman Catholic girls school. With its weather boarded and tile hung houses Mayfield must have one of the most attractive village streets to be found anywhere. Now much quieter it has been by-passed. The church is well worth a visit as well.

13.5   LEFT at T-Junction into Newick Lane (weight limit sign). Pass Piccadilly Lane which links up with Route 25 and could form an alternative route out of Tunbridge Wells. Continue down long fast descent, **OS LR 199,** into the Rother valley. This is paid for by a steep 10% climb through the woods, which although easier later on seems to go on for ever.

17.0   LEFT at top of the hill onto A265, signposted Hawkhurst/Battle (turning right leads to the welcome refreshment stop of the Old Coach House Tea Rooms on the outskirts of Heathfield). Immediately RIGHT onto B2096, signposted Battle.

17.4   FORK RIGHT, signposted Old Heathfiled/Vines Cross then RIGHT again at T-Junction and descend through Old Heathfield past church with The Star Inn behind it. After descent climb to Vines Cross.

Old Heathfield is separated from the new settlement which sprang up round the railway station by Heathfield Park. The area was a centre of the Sussex iron industry and was famous for its gun foundry. In 1895 natural gas was found and used to light the station and the street outside.

20.3   RIGHT, signposted Horsham/Heathfield into Vines Cross Road. Continue past vineyard into Horam where LEFT onto B2203, signposted Hailsham/Eastbourne. Continue to Horam Inn.

Pass over the Cuckoo Trail (see Route 23) linking Heathfield with Polegate along disused railway line. Horam Manor on the A267 just south of the town is home of Merrydown, makers of traditional and vintage ciders, as well as 1066 elderflower wines. Open throughout the year from Tuesdays to Fridays, but book in advance 0435 812254. There is also in the village a nature trail and picnic site along with a Countryside Interpretation Exhibition and Farm Museum housed in a 14th Century barn, open daily Easter to October.

21.4   RIGHT onto A267, Little London Road, then LEFT, signposted Lions Green/Waldron. Continue into Waldron where teas can be obtained at the restaurant belonging to St Georges Vineyard. Here LEFT by The Star Inn and OVER crossroads, signposted Blackboys.

25.4   CROSS B2102 at top of hill by staggered crossroads, signposted Hadlow Down/Buxted. Descend long hill past pottery. At T-

Junction not far from Blackboys Youth Hostel, RIGHT and immediately RIGHT again after bridge. Climb very long hill through woods to Hadlow Down.

Fork right just before Hadlow Down to reach Wilderness Wood. This is a working wood. There is a picnic area, a woodland trail and refreshments in the barn for visitors. Open all year round from 10.00 to dusk.

27.8   CONTINUE over A272, signposted Crowborough/Rotherfield. After long and very beautiful descent, especially in Autumn, LEFT up steep climb over railway bridge.

30.1   FORK LEFT and CONTINUE over crossroads, signposted High Hurstwood. Continue up and then down to T-Junction.

31.8   LEFT at T-Junction and RIGHT up Perrymans Lane. Continue up long climb to staggered crossroads with A26. **OS LR 188.**

33.2   RIGHT and immediately LEFT and continue with some downhill stretches through ford to Fairwarp.

34.3   RIGHT at crossroads onto B2026. Follow past entrance sign to Ashdown Forest and climbing through the open heathland and pass Duddleswell Tea Room before RIGHT onto B2088, signposted Groombridge/Tunbridge Wells. The highest point of the whole ride is soon reached at 715 feet. Pass The Half Moon pub and continue to Lye Green.

41.0   RIGHT at crossroads, signposted Motts Mill. Descend to mill where a sharp right hander leads to a short 20% climb. After left bend at top of hill RIGHT down Forge Road if using Eridge Station. Otherwise STRAIGHT ON, following sign to Groombridge to the church on the outskirts.

43.2   VERY SHARP RIGHT by Crossways. Continue over railway along bridleway which is narrow though reasonably firm.

Carrying straight on and not turning right leads to the main part of Groombridge. Half in Kent and half in Sussex it is very attractive around the triangular sloping green where tile-hung cottages line two sides and the moated manor house of Groombridge Place the opposite. A good place for pubs as well. Continue on the bridleway.

43.5   RIGHT onto metalled road and LEFT, signposted Tunbridge Wells/Frant. Then LEFT again, signposted High Rocks and retrace wheelmarks to Tunbridge Wells and station.

47.7   END

25 MAD JACK'S RIDE

Tunbridge Wells is again the start for a further adventure into the High Weald of Kent and East Sussex. It's up and down progress through the wooded green countryside to the outskirts of Mayfield, before s few miles following the course of the River Rother. Then up and over to Batemans(NT), by the River Dudwell, the former home of Rudyard Kipling. 'Mad Jack Fuller' built both the obelisk and the observatory that stand on Brightling Down, which at 646 feet is the highest point in East Sussex, and also the pyramid where he is buried in Brightling churchyard. Naturally it's a more downward than upward progress to Etchingham, then on to Stonegate and the pretty village of Wadhurst, past Bartley Mill, after a short retracing of the first part of the route. The return into Tunbridge Wells is entered a different way via Camden Park.

This is an extremely hilly route with long hills, particularly up to Brightling Down. Once again the superb scenery compensates for all the effort.

Maps	OS LR 188, 199.
Distance	41.8 miles. Of this 0.7 miles could be classified as off-road.
Start/Finish	Tunbridge Wells Station.

Railway access

Tunbridge Wells has a half hour to hourly service from London, Charing Cross and from Hastings.

Wadhurst, Stonegate, Etchingham & Robertsbridge are further down the line and could be used either for riding the whole route or for escaping from it.

Places to See

The Pantiles, Church of King Charles the Martyr - and much more, Tunbridge Wells.

Mount Farm - near Wadhurst Station.

Mayfield.

Batemans (NT) - Burwash.

Church, 'Mad Jack Fuller's Tomb', Bartley Mill - Brightling.

Bartley Mill - near Bells Yew Green.

Refreshments

Cafes & pubs - Tunbridge Wells.

Tea rooms - for visitors to Mount Farm, near Wadhurst Station.

April Cottage - afternoons only, Mayfield.

Tea rooms - for visitors to Batemans (NT).

Little SparrowsTea Rooms - at Sparrows Green, Wadhurst.

Tea rooms - for visitors to Bartley Mill.

No shortage of pubs on this route. *The Best Beech* near Tidebrook or *The Kicking Donkey* near Burwash Common are in useful positions.

MAD JACK'S RIDE

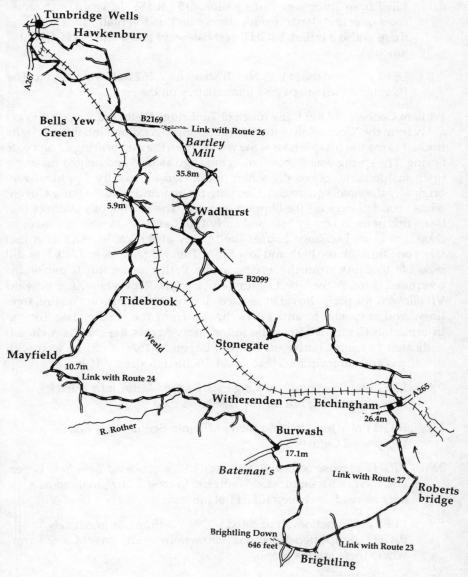

Start & Finish

Tunbridge Wells
Hawkenbury

A267

Bells Yew
Green

B2169
Link with Route 26

*Bartley
Mill*

35.8m

5.9m

Wadhurst

B2099

Tidebrook

Weald

Stonegate

Mayfield

10.7m
Link with Route 24

Witherenden **Etchingham**

A265

26.4m

R. Rother

Burwash

17.1m

Bateman's

Link with Route 27

**Roberts
bridge**

Brightling Down
646 feet

Link with Route 23

Brightling

25 MAD JACK'S RIDE

0.0 LEFT from Tunbridge Wells station. **OS LR 188.** To avoid confusion cross over and depart from entrance on London platform where there is also a buffet. RIGHT past Safeways and STRAIGHT ON at junction.

0.2 LEFT at roundabout into Nevill Street on A267 following sign to The Pantiles which are passed immediately on the right.

William Cobbett did not think much of Tunbridge Wells and was glad to get away from the 'Contagion of its Wen (London) engendered inhabitants' who flocked to the town to partake of the waters from the iron bearing Chalybeate Spring. The spring was discovered as long ago as 1606 and helped make the town fashionable, especially when patronised by royalty. Pantiles were originally the small square clay tiles paid for by Princess Anne (later Queen) whose son fell over on the slippery ground. The parade of buildings that bears this name is largely 18th and early 19th Century. As well as the coffee shop, the Corn Exchange houses the 'A Day at the Wells' exhibition that takes one through the high and low life in Tunbridge Wells in 1740. It is still possible to drink from the spring at the Bath House. Royal patronage continued through the 19th Century and into the 20th when King Edward VII allowed the prefix Royal to be used. Today The Pantiles are quaint, tree-lined and respectable and a true haven from the traffic. The Tourist Information Centre is also to be found here. Across the road is a church dedicated to King Charles the Martyr. Begun in 1676 it did so well with donations and subscriptions that it had doubled in size by 1696.

0.4 LEFT after the church of King Charles the Martyr into Warwick Park. Climb long hill up this tree-lined road.

1.3 RIGHT at T-Junction and then LEFT into Benhall Mill Road, signposted Cemetery.

2.9 RIGHT at crossroads at top of steep hill, signposted Bells Yew Green and then LEFT signposted Wadhurst to cross B2169, marked as a narrow road, and keep RIGHT at junction.

5.9 LEFT at T-Junction, signposted B2099 Wadhurst. Immediately RIGHT, signposted Tidebrook. Cross railway and pass Mount Farm where there is a tea room.

7.0 FORK LEFT onto disused road. Continue over subsided section, otherwise perfectly rideable. At Best Beech pub cross B2100, signposted Mayfield. Continue switchback progress through Tidebrook to the outskirts of Mayfield.

10.7　LEFT by Rose and Crown PH, signposted Broadoaks/Witherenden. A right turn here leads to the main part of Mayfield which is on Route 24 and an alternative way from Tunbridge Wells.

11.7　LEFT, and then STRAIGHT ON following signposts for Witherenden, mainly downhill and following the River Rother which is then crossed.

14.4　RIGHT, signposted Burwash Common. RIGHT at T-Junction by Kicking Donkey PH before LEFT into Spring Lane. and to the top of hill on outskirts of Burwash village. **OS LR 199.**

17.1　RIGHT onto A 265, signposted Heathfield/Lewes. Then LEFT, signposted Batemans and descend hill.

Batemans (NT) was the home of Rudyard Kipling from 1902 to 1936. Dating from 1634 the house was the home of a local iron-master. As well as his rooms and study, left much as they originally were, there are gardens and a watermill that still grinds the flour that is sold to help pay for further restoration, and which featured prominently in many of Kiplings Sussex stories like 'Puck of Pooks Hill'. Alongside, dating from 1903 is one of the earliest water turbines in the world, originally used to charge the batteries for the house lighting. Also on show in its original garage is Kiplings 1928 Rolls Royce. Refreshments available for visitors. Open April to end of October, daily, except Thursday and Friday, 11.00 to 17.30.

17.7　LEFT at Batemans then RIGHT at T-Junction, signposted Woods Green. Passing the entrance to the British Gypsum mine climb the very long hill to Brightling Down, which at 646 feet is the highest point in East Sussex.

The 65 foot high obelisk known as Brightling Needle was built by John Fuller, the local squire of Brightling, a loud mouthed but amiable eccentric, who after his outspoken attitude cost him his career as an MP in 1810, devoted his life to art and science. Follies were a way of decorating the landscape and 'Mad Jack' was well to the forefront, remarkable in a time of great economic hardship, but the building did provide employment for local people. Close to Brightling Needle is an observatory, built by Fuller and equipped with the latest equipment of the time including a camera-obscura. It is now a private residence.

20.3　LEFT at crossroads, then STRAIGHT ON to Brightling village.

The massive stone pyramid in Brightling churchyard is in fact the grave of John Fuller who caused it to be built 24 years before his death in 1834. He also gave the church a barrel organ - the largest in Britain in full working order and capable of playing 24 tunes.

21.2   LEFT after church, signposted Robertsbridge. Cross the conveyor belt from the mine (see Route 23) and the Jack Fuller Restaurant at the road junction. Going right here provides a link with Route 23 to Battle. CONTINUE mainly downhill until just before Robertsbridge sign where LEFT, signposted Etchingham. Follow this road with its steep switchbacks to T-Junction with A265 at Etchingham. **OS LR 188.** Straight on instead of left leads into Robertsbridge, the start of Route 27 and a possible starting point for this ride as well.

26.4   RIGHT at T-Junction with A265 (a cycle repairer is situated here) signposted Hurst Green, then LEFT into Church Lane. Cross the railway and the Rother and follow road round to left.

29.6   LEFT at T-Junction and continue to Stonegate where take FIRST RIGHT at crossroads, signposted Wadhurst.

32.6   LEFT at T-Junction onto B2099, signposted Wadhurst. Continue through this attractive village with its tile hung cottages.

34.4   RIGHT onto B2100, signposted Lamberhurst and continue into Sparrow Green where there are the Little Sparrow Tea Rooms combined with a childrens clothes shop. LEFT, signposted Woods Green and continue.

35.8   LEFT turn at T-Junction, signposted Bells Yew Green. Pass Bartley Mill before climbing to T-Junction with B2169.

Bartley Mill was once part of a hop farm and now mills organic wheat for the first time since the early 1900s. There is a small museum area, farm trail and shop. Also a tea room and picnic area. With the exception of Christmas and New Year open daily, 10.00 to 18.00.

37.3   LEFT at T-Junction onto B2169 then RIGHT and RIGHT at T-Junction, following signs to Hawkenbury.

40.6   RIGHT at T-Junction into Forest Road, on outskirts of Tunbridge Wells, then LEFT into Camden Park. Continue to end of private road before wheeling along footpath. RIGHT onto road then LEFT through gate into Camden Hill.

41.3   CONTINUE into Grove Hill Road at junction and descend to roundabout. Here LEFT and immediately RIGHT and RIGHT again at Safeways to station.

41.8   END

26 TO THE UNION

The first part of this ride from Hildenborough skirts Tonbridge by way of a bridlepath before being continuing onwards by Hadlow and its strange looking tower. The River Medway is crossed and later its tributary the Teise. The route twists through the hop fields before climbing into the hills at Horsmonden. Cranbrook has been called 'The Capital of the Weald' and the Union Mill dominates the town. After that it's into the woods gathered around the lake at Bedgbury Pinetum. There are more hills to be crossed through Lamburhurst towards Kippings Cross and the high point of 450 feet. Into Tonbridge and to the River Medway again following the towpath for a short stretch before crossing the bridge and heading north-west to Hildenborough.

Reasonably flat in the valley around the Medway and Tiese, but more hilly in the centre portion. The steepest climb is probably that up towards Kippings Cross.

Map	OS LR 188.
Distance	50.7 miles. Of this 4.6 miles are easy off-road.
Start/Finish	Hildenborough Station.

Railway access

Hildenborough has an hourly service from London, Charing Cross and from Tonbridge.

Beltring, Paddock Wood & Tonbridge offer alternatives or escape points.

Places to visit

Whitbread Hop Farm - Beltring.

Union Mill, church & museum - Cranbrook.

Bedgbury Pinetum.

Christ Church - Kilndown.

Bewl Water.

Scotney Castle Gardens (NT), Vineyard, Owl House Garden - Lamberhurst.

Badsell Farm Park - near Matfield.

Castle - Tonbridge.

Refreshments

Blue Bell Diner - Beltring.

Cafes & pubs - Cranbrook.

Tea rooms - for visitors to Bedgbury Pinetum.

Happy Eater - on A21, Kilndown.

Refreshment kiosk - Bewl Water.

Tea rooms & George & Dragon pub - for visitors to the vineyard, Lamberhurst.

Cherry Trees Tea Gallery - Matfield Green.

Cafe - for visitors to Badsell Farm Park.

Cafes & pubs - Tonbridge.

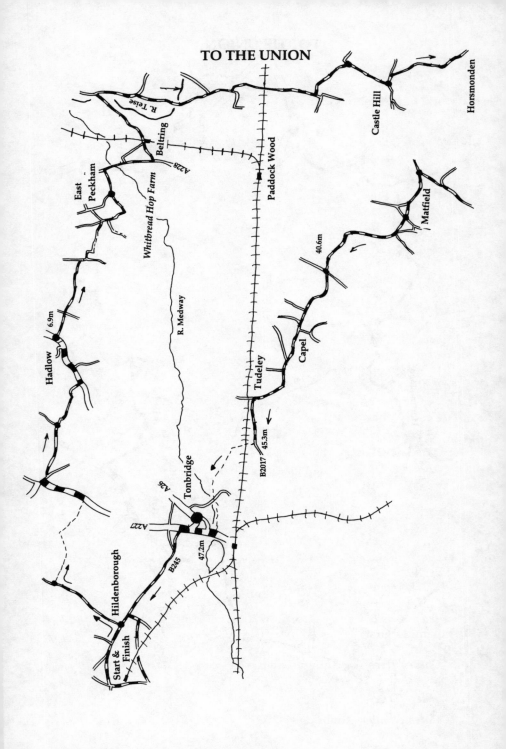

TO THE UNION

Horsmonden

Castle Hill

Matfield

40.6m

Capel

Tudeley

45.3m

B2017

Paddock Wood

Beltring

A228

East
Peckham

Whitbread Hop Farm

R. Teise

R. Medway

6.9m

Hadlow

Tonbridge

A26

A227

Hildenborough

B245

47.2m

Start &
Finish

TO THE UNION

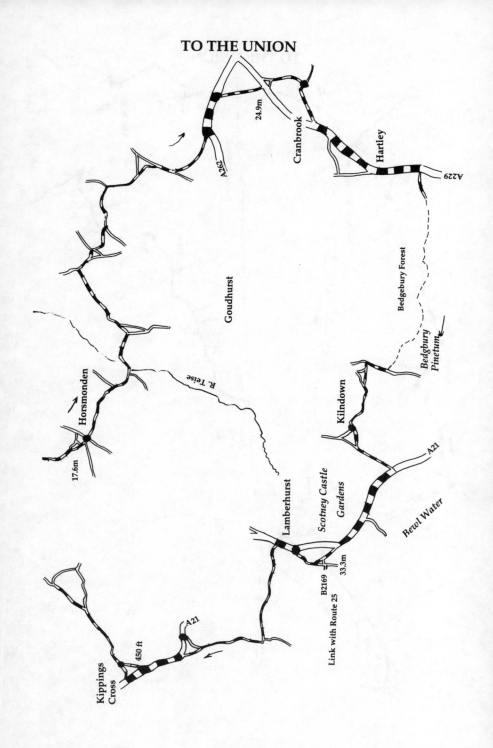

26 TO THE UNION

0.0 RIGHT from Hildenborough station. **OS LR 188**. Cross railway bridge. RIGHT, signposted Hildenborough along Noble Tree Road.

0.8 RIGHT at T-Junction onto B245. Pass The Half Moon PH then LEFT into Coldharbour Lane, signposted Nursery. Continue past Trench Farm.

2.3 RIGHT onto private road which is also a bridleway. It might be unmetalled but the surface is firm and rideable even in wet conditions. RIGHT again through the farmyard at Horns Lodge after which the road becomes metalled.

3.7 LEFT onto A227. Climb hill before RIGHT (CARE) then RIGHT into Ashes Lane, following signs for Hadlow. Pass The Three Squirrels PH to The Rose Revived PH.

6.0 LEFT at T-Junction onto A26. Continue into Hadlow on main street.

Hadlow is an attractive enough village in its own right but it is the 170 foot high Gothic tower that catches the eye. It is all that remains of Hadlow Castle, declared by William Cobbett as a building of 'the oddest appearance of anything I ever saw.' Ample imagination went into the crenellations and spires of this folly.

6.9 RIGHT into Court Lane and follow through to T-Junction after pub. LEFT here, signposted Beltring/Paddock Wood and continue into East Peckham. By The Merry Boys PH RIGHT at the T-Junction to The Rose & Crown PH.

9.9 RIGHT at T-Junction onto A228 (formerly B2015). After crossing the Medway, LEFT by The Blue Bell where there is a diner. Continue over level crossing and past station.

Straight on is the Whitbread Hop Farm with, it claims, the largest collection of Victorian oast houses in the world. Not simply a hop drying centre it also houses exhibitions, the Whitbread Shire Horse Centre, animals, birds, as well as refreshments. Open daily March to October from 10.00 to 18.00 (16.00 in winter).

11.9 RIGHT at T-Junction after narrow bridge over River Tiese signposted Laddingford/Horsmonden then LEFT, signposted Brenchley/Paddock Wood and continue past the pub.

13.7 LEFT, and following signs to Horsmonden, cross railway, then LEFT into Pearsons Green Road and RIGHT to climb up to Castle Hill. At The Castle Inn LEFT at T-Junction and RIGHT into Horsmonden.

17.6   LEFT at T-Junction, signposted Goudhurst/Cranbrook and continue through this attractive village. After crossing Tiese for the second time climb hill to B2079.

19.4   LEFT at T-junction, signposted Marden/Maidstone. On hill RIGHT, signposted Curtisden Green and RIGHT in this village of white weatherboarded houses, signposted Colliers Green/Cranbrook. Follow round past prison at Blantyre House.

22.8   RIGHT at T-Junction, signposted Goudhurst. By school LEFT and continue until A262.

23.8   LEFT and then RIGHT by lodge with archway. Follow to A229.

24.9   RIGHT and immediately LEFT into Quakers Lane which continues after turning immediately LEFT again.

25.1   RIGHT at T-Junction onto B2189 into Cranbrook where there are cafes and pubs. Follow through town to A229.

Cranbrook is known as the Capital of the Weald and found fame and fortune in the cloth trade when King Edward III, seeking to break the monopoly of the Flemish weaves, enticed some to come over here and so played them at their own game. Legend has it that so much was produced that Queen Elizabeth I walked from Cranbrook to a neighbouring manor on a pathway made from the local broadcloth. But now nothing is produced behind those white weatherboarded walls. Memories of former prosperity linger on in the large and airy church. An unusual feature is the font designed for total immersion - a move in the early 18th Century to counter the growing influence of the Baptists.

Perhaps to many the most dominating feature is the huge smock windmill, painted white to match the rest of the town. It was built in 1814 and got its name of Union Mill after it fell into the hands of a group of local creditors. Having been restored this mill is now open to the public from April to the end of September, grinding and selling wholemeal flour. Open 14.30 to 17.30 on Saturdays and the same time on Sundays and Bank Holiday Mondays during school holidays.

There is also a museum dedicated to local history and industries in an old timber framed farmhouse. Open March to November (0850 712696).

26.3   CONTINUE on A229. Pass through Hartley before RIGHT at staggered crossroads into Park Lane (No Through Road). This becomes an unmetalled forest road with a very firm surface. Pass house and follow main track through open forest and down to lake by Bedgbury Pinetum. Climb on road again to T-Junction.

It is an idyllic setting down by the lake where the slopes are graced by the Forestry Commissions superb collection of specimen conifers. There is a visitors centre and refreshments available during the summer months. Open daily all year round 10.00 to 20.00 or dusk if earlier.

29.7 RIGHT onto B2079 then LEFT by Tower Cottage. Follow the road through to Kilndown. LEFT at T-Junction by pub. Continue past the church to descend to A21.

Christ Church at Kilndown is a fine example of Victorian Gothic Revival architecture. Switching on the lights brings the vivid colours, the carvings, the reredos, and the figure of St George to life. But it was built of the wrong material, for the local sandstone is porous and damp caused paint to peel off the walls with the result that much has had to be abandoned.

32.2 RIGHT at T-junction onto A21, signposted Lamberhurst (to the left is a Happy Eater). Pass the entrance to Bewl Water.

This reservoir, the largest expanse of inland water in the South East, was created in the 1970s when several valleys were flooded to supply a Kent with water. There is a nature trail, information display and a kiosk serving hot and cold refreshments in the visitors centre. Open daily 9.00 to sunset.

33.3 LEFT onto B2169 signposted Frant by entrance to Scotney Castle (NT). Pass Lamberhurst sign after pub.

14th Century Scotney Castle, surrounded by its moat and luxuriant gardens, is perhaps one of the most romantic ruins to be found anywhere. It is at its very best in Autumn surrounded by the vivid colours of the many exotic plants. There is an ice-house in the grounds dating from the time when ice was cut in the winter months and preserved through the summer. How refrigeration is taken for granted nowadays! Gardens only open April to November, Wednesday to Friday 11.00 to 18.00 and 14.00 to 18.00 at weekends. Castle open same times May to September only.

33.6 STRAIGHT ON into Sands Road then at T-Junction RIGHT and down 10% hill into village proper.

Lamberhurst was once a centre for Weladen iron. Another old industry, wine making, originally carried out by monks, has been revived and the vineyards at Ridge Farm are the largest in Kent. There are guided tours form June to September and a shop. Refreshments also available. Open throughout year.

34.2 LEFT onto A21 again. Teas can be obtained at The George & Dragon PH. LEFT at the school on the hill, signposted Owl House Garden.

Owl House Gardens with its azaleas, lake and woodlands covers thirteen acres and is open daily except for Tuesday and Thursday. The half timbered cottage was once the home of wool smugglers but is not open to the public.

35.7 RIGHT at T-Junction, signposted Kippings Cross/Pembury. Climb steep hill before reaching A21. There LEFT onto A21. After further climbing RIGHT into Cryals Road (the turning before is shorter but very dangerous).

38.8 LEFT opposite Cryals Court. Continue past pub into Brenchley. Continue past Cherry Trees Tea Gallery to Standings Cross.

40.6 OVER crossroads, signposted Badsell Farm Park. Descend 10% hill past entrance.

Badsell Park Farm produces wheat and sweetcorn as well as fruit. Also breeds of rare farm animals and a nature trail. There is a cafe along with a picnic area. Open daily, end of March to end of November, 10.00 to 17.30.

42.3 OVER staggered crossroads, signposted Capel/Tonbridge. Continue through Capel before joining B2017. Follow through Tudeley, then swing round to left.

The 18th Century brick church has very distinctive stained glass windows by Marc Chagall, in memory of a tragic drowning.

45.3 RIGHT near top of hill into Postern Lane. This is a private road with a public footpath. Follow this potholed road through gate which might be locked, then past The Postern into Tonbridge.

46.7 CROSS Vale Road and walk along footpath by the side of The Medway. Then LEFT and RIGHT onto Medway Wharf Road by lock. Continue into the High Street.

Tonbridge is where the navigable section of The Medway starts and, standing guard over the bridge, are the massive towers of the Norman castle. Fine views of the town can be obtained from the battlements. There are also exhibitions and audio visual displays depicting what life was like 700 years ago. Open all year 9.00 to 17.00, 10.30 to 17.00 Sundays and Bank Holidays.

47.2 RIGHT at T-junction over bridge, then VEER LEFT at traffic lights onto B245, signposted Sevenoaks/ Hildenborough into suburbia.

49.2 LEFT onto B2027, signposted Edenbridge. Follow round to right to pass under railway and past The Old Barn where teas might be obtained. Before passing under A21 RIGHT, signposted Hildenborough Station then on hill after Gate pub RIGHT again.

50.7 END

27 BREDE & ROTHER RIDE

From Robertsbridge the hills beckon to the long climb to over 300 feet at Swaile's Green. Iron was once manufactured in this part of the Weald but now on its southward facing slopes there are vineyards. Through Three Oaks and Pett towards the sea which can be seen across the marshes of Pett Level. The 14th Century New Gate leads into Winchelsea, the ancient port now left high and dry. It is difficult to visualise that a battle was fought between English and Spanish fleets where the River Brede now flows. Through rolling, wooded hills to Northiam and then down to the River Rother. Bodiam Castle, which with it's moat is everything a castle ought to be, stands as a sentinel before the final hills are crossed back to Robertsbridge.

A hilly ride, but nothing too outrageous. The longest climb is that out of Robertsbridge. Leave plenty of time to view Winchelsea.

Maps	OS LR 199, 189.
Distance	36.7 miles.
Start/Finish	Robertsbridge Station.

Railway access

Robertsbridge is served by an hourly service from either London Charing Cross or Hastings.

Three Oaks or *Winchelsea*, from where there is an hourly service on the Hastings to Ashford line, could be alternative start or escape points. Tell the guard that you wish to get off or signal to driver if you wish to get on at either of these stations. Otherwise the train might not stop!

Places to see

Vineyards - Sedlescombe.

Church, museum, gateways, old town - Winchelsea.

Brickwall House, Great Dixter House - Northiam.

Kent & East Sussex Steam Railway - Northiam.

Quarry Farm Rural Experience, Castle (NT) - Bodiam.

Museum of Rural Life - Robertsbridge.

Refreshments

Cafes & pubs - Winchelsea.

Tea rooms - in Castle car park and for visitors to Quarry Farm Rural Experience - Bodiam.

Tea rooms - Sundays only at Rother Valley Railway Exhibition - Robertsbridge.

The Ostrich pub - Robertsbridge.

Good choice of pubs all the way round.

BREDE & ROTHER RIDE

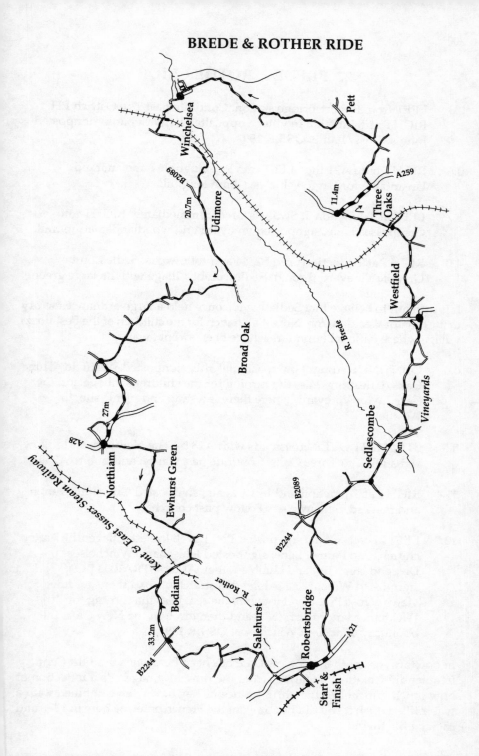

27 BREDE & ROTHER RIDE

0.0   LEFT from Robertsbridge station. Continue past The Ostrich PH. RIGHT at T-Junction in village opposite Nat West bank, signposted John's Cross/Battle. **OS LR 199.**

0.6   RIGHT onto A21 then LEFT into Poppinghole Lane, marked Unsuitable for Large Vehicles. Climb long hill.

3.7   LEFT at T-Junction at Swaile's Green. Immediately RIGHT into Compasses Lane, signposted vineyard and woodlands nature trail.

4.0   RIGHT at T-Junction onto B2244 and follow past Sedlescombe Organic Vineyard through Sedlescombe village with its large green.

It is difficult to believe that Sedlescombe once held a large ordnance factory in the days of Wealden iron. Now it's a haven for the children of the Pestalozzi village where national boundaries have been swept away.

6.0   CONTINUE straight on up Chapel Hill, signposted Westfield/Three Oaks/Guestling. Pass the turning for the childrens village and the Carr Taylor Vineyard, where there is a shop and picnic site, to Westfield.

8.5   STRAIGHT OVER crossroads with A28 by The New Inn, and follow signs LEFT to Three Oaks. Continue past station and pub to A259.

11.4   RIGHT at T-junction and LEFT again, signposted Guestling church and marked, narrow road. Follow past church.

13.0   LEFT at crossroads, signposted Pett Level. In Pett village LEFT after church, into Pannel Lane, signposted Icklesham/Winchelsea. Descend steep hill and climb another. At top STRAIGHT ON, signposted Winchelsea. Along this stretch of road there are fine views across Pett Level towards the sea. Pass the turning for Wickham Manor Farm (NT) and then through the New Gate, the boundary of ancient Winchesea. **OS LR 189.**

In one form or another, the New Gate has been here since the 14th Century. In splendid isolation, so far out from the present village, it's a reflection of how much Winchelsea has shrunk since its hey day. Even combined with a water filled ditch it still did not prevent the French entering here in 1380 and sacking the town.

17.2 RIGHT at T-Junction and continue into Winchelsea.

The sea, in the long term, proved to be a greater enemy to Winchelsea than the French. The original town was a prime contributor to the fleet of the Cinque Ports - a confederation that existed to provide mutual protection at sea to safeguard trade. Built on a sand spit it was swept away by two great storms in the 13th Century. King Edward I was responsible for building the new town, high up away from the sea and designed in a grid pattern. Its population would have been between 4000 and 6000 - very large for those times. But the sea intervened again. Just as it had destroyed the old it retreated from the new harbour leaving it high and dry, so that by the end of the 15th Century Winchelsea was no longer a port. It went through a period of terminal decline before the 19th Century saw a revival. An atmosphere of peace and beauty mixed with history made it a haunt of artists and writers. Turner and Millais painted, Thackeray and Conrad wrote here.

Nowadays Winchelsea has the atmosphere of the perfectly planned Georgian village, with well looked after houses and peaceful enough with main road traffic funnelled outside. The church is interesting and has fine decorated period architecture. The 13th Century Court Hall now houses a museum, though it also served as the towns goal. It is open mid-May to mid September, weekdays 10.30 to 12.30 and 14.30 to 17.30, and on afternoons on Sundays.

It is not far from Winchelsea to Rye - the start of Route 28.

17.5 CONTINUE straight on at The New Inn and past the coffee shop. At T-Junction LEFT and out through the Pipewell Gate. Here RIGHT onto A259 and descend steep hill to hairpin bend.

17.9 RIGHT, signposted Winchelsea station/Udimore. Cross the River Brede, over the level crossing and past the railway station before LEFT at Dumb Woman's Lane, signposted Float Lane, and marked, narrow road. This is flat at first before a steep climb.

20.7 LEFT onto B2089, signposted Broad Oak. Continue through Udimore on ridge road with fine views across the Brede valley, an area threatened, according to campaign posters, by a new road link. **OS LR 199**.

It was from this ridge that Queen Phillippa saw the English fleet under the command of Edward III and the Black Prince destroy a large contingent of Spanish pirates off Winchelsea in 1341. Difficult to imagine now with the sea so far away.

22.5 RIGHT, signposted Beckley/Peasmarsh. Descend hill, cross River Tillingham and ascend the other side.

23.9   LEFT, and following the signs to Northiam, STRAIGHT ON at crossroads then LEFT onto B2088 and continue past Frewin College and Brickwall House and Gardens.

Dating from 1490 the half timbered Brickwall House is partly used as a school. The garden has an 18th Century bowling alley. Open to the public from Easter to the end of September, Saturdays and Bank Holidays, 14.00 to 17.00.

27.0   RIGHT onto A28 at Northiam.

White weather boarded houses predominate in Northiam making it a very attractive village. Great Dixter House, a timber framed mansion dating from 1450, was bought by the Lloyd family in 1910 who used the services of Sir Edwin Lutyens to restore the house. One of the extensions was actually a medieval wooden framed building moved from elsewhere. House and gardens open from April to October, Tuesdays to Sundays plus Bank Holiday Mondays, 14.00 to 17.00.
    Northiam is also the current terminus of the Kent and East Sussex Railway. Steam operated it was recently used in the filming of 'The Darling Buds of May'. It runs 7 miles to Tenterden. Going the other way it is hoped to extend the line to Bodiam and eventually Robertsbridge. For details 05806 5155.

27.5   LEFT by The Plough & Sickle PH into Dixter Road, signposted Ewhurst/Bodiam, Great Dixter House. Immediately LEFT by veterinary surgery and, following signs to Bodiam, RIGHT past The White Dog PH through Ewhurst Green before RIGHT and RIGHT again at T-Junction. After the turning for Quarry Farm Rural Experience, cross the railway then The Rother before entering Bodiam. Pass entrance to Castle (NT) and climb long hill out of village.

The Quarry Farm Rural Experience contains a private collection of steam engines along with farm animals, rural bygones and an exhibition. Refreshments and a picnic site available. Open April to September. weekends and Bank Holidays, 10.00 to 17.00 and daily in school holiday periods.
    It is the castle that is Bodiam's chief attraction. Surrounded by a moat it is perhaps the most perfect example to be found anywhere in the country. Fear of possible French invasion that never came caused it to be built in 1385. It would not be here today but for the intervention of 'Mad Jack Fuller' who saved it from demolition. The castle is now remarkably intact, floors have been replaced in some towers where there are also audio-visual presentations. Open all year round, daily except Mondays, November to March, 10.00 to 18.00 or sunset in winter months. Tea room, accessible even if not visiting

castle, in car park. Also refreshments at Knollys and The Castle Inn.

33.2 STRAIGHT OVER crossroads by The Curlew Inn and Restaurant. Then LEFT to descend steep hill and climb another through the woods. At the top LEFT, signposted Robertsbridge. Continue through Salehurst and past pub to drop down to roundabout.

35.9 CROSS roundabout with A21 and continue into Robertsbridge. Pass Museum of Rural Life. RIGHT into Station Road to station.

36.7 END

Robertsbridge was once busy during the days of the Wealden iron industry and, like Sedlescombe, once had an ordnance factory. Now cricket bats are made here. The Museum of Rural Life is a blacksmiths and wheelwrights shop containing numerous countryside memorabilia. Open daily all year 10.00 to 16.00. At the station there is a Rother Valley Railway exhibition and tea and coffee is available when open, which is usually 10.00 to 18.00 on Sundays only.

28 THE MARSH RIDE

An old saying likened Romney Marsh to another continent, so far removed it is from the rest of the South East. Starting from the ancient port of Rye this route joins The Royal Military Canal and then on to Appledore and its wide street. From here it is up to slightly higher ground on the former Isle of Oxney before returning to the narrow twisting lanes of the Marsh. The direction is east to Ivychurch, Newchurch, and eventually Hythe via the towpath alongside the Royal Military Canal. Turning away from the coast it's again to the crooked lanes to St Mary in the Marsh, Old Romney and Lydd. From here on to Camber Sands and the sea, with Rye on its hill top drawing closer and closer.

This is a very easy flat ride though wind could make things difficult over this exposed terrain. Certainly the narrow twisting lanes in this area of spacious remoteness are like no others in the South East.

Rye is close to Winchelsea and Route 28 could be combined with 27 to make an enjoyable weekend.

Map	OS LR 189.
Distance	52.2 miles. Of this 2.0 miles into Hythe is easy off-road.
Start/Finish	Rye Station.

Railway access

Rye is served by an hourly service on the London Charing Cross to Hastings line, via Ashford.

Appledore, further down the line towards Hastings is an alternative.

Places to see

Royal Military Canal - Romney Marsh.

Village, church, bulb fields, Horne Place Chapel - Appledore .

Church - Ivychurch.

Romney, Hythe & Dymchurch Railway - Hythe.

Church - St Mary-in-the-Marsh.

Church - Old Romney.

Church & town - Lydd.

Lamb House, Mermaid Street, Heritage Centre, Ypres Tower, Lookout - Rye.

Refreshments

Cafes - at station, bakers nearby, and elsewhere in Rye.

Sentry Box Tea Rooms - Appledore.

Cafes - by railway station and elsewhere in Hythe.

Tea rooms - on Donkey Lane at the Lathe Farm Museum, Burmarsh.

Cafe - on A259, Old Romney.

Old Prospect Bakery - Lydd.

Cafes & pubs - especially in summer, Camber Sands.

THE MARSH RIDE

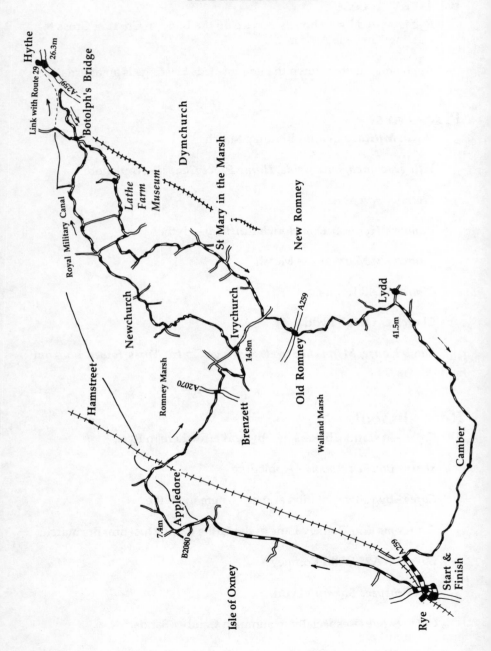

28 THE MARSH RIDE

0.0 STRAIGHT ON from Rye station where there is a cafe and a bakers combined with a coffee shop directly ahead. **OS LR 189.**

0.3 KEEP LEFT to join the one-way system, signposted A268 London. Cross railway.

0.4 RIGHT onto Military Road, signposted Appledore.

Running parallel to this road is The Royal Military Canal which, running from Rye to Hythe, makes the whole of the Romney Marsh area an island. The canal was built around 1804 for flooding the marshes in the event of French invasion. On the other side are the old cliffs, showing how recently this land was created. Towards Appledore the Isle of Oxney appears on the left. Surrounded by The Rother and various drainage ditches and channels it is still technically an island but now access is no problem.

6.3 LEFT at T-Junction into Appledore. The Sentry Box Tea Rooms are opposite The Red Lion PH. Carry on through village.

Appledore has wide streets with Tudor houses and it's difficult to believe that it was once a port which stood on a projection of higher ground on the Isle of Oxney, overlooking a sea creek. Nowadays it is noted for its bulb fields to the south.

7.4 RIGHT, signposted Hamstreet. Pass Hornes Place Chapel (EH).

This 14th Century domestic chapel was once attached to the manor house. After use as a barn it has been carefully restored. Open Wednesdays only 10.00 to 17.00.

8.1 RIGHT, marked Weight Limit 13 tons. Cross the Royal Military Canal, which between here and Appledore is owned by the National Trust, and over the railway at the level crossing.

10.7 RIGHT at T-Junction and then immediately LEFT, signposted Snargate. At crossroads, STRAIGHT ON, signposted Brenzett then follow to A2070.

The A2070 runs from Ashford through to Brenzett and is undergoing dramatic 'improvement', causing a great deal of controversy. Romney Marsh with its mass of twisting water courses and miles of narrow twisting flat lanes is a perfect place for cycling and so far unspoilt. However it is by no means a wilderness for the soil is rich and William Cobbett noted the sheer quality of the corn grown in the area. The land was used for fattening cattle but now sheep are more prevalent - the Romney Marsh breed is world famous.

12.3   RIGHT at T-Junction onto A2070 then LEFT following twisting course through fields. RIGHT at T-junction then LEFT at next and continue to Ivychurch.

Although the 70 foot tower of St Georges church might not seem very high it was sufficient to provide a look out for invaders. Anyone wanting to know what a 'hudd' is will see a very fine example here. Before the days of umbrellas, when priests wore long wigs, these contraptions, like portable sentry boxes, were used at funerals on rainy days.

14.8   LEFT at T-Junction near The Bell PH, signposted Hamstreet/Appledore then RIGHT along twisting Melon Lane past Little Appledore.

17.2   RIGHT at crossroads, signposted Newchurch. RIGHT at T-Junction, signposted St Mary-in-the-Marsh then immediately LEFT at Newchurch, signposted Hythe. Follow past the church and The Black Bull pub.

20.3   CONTINUE over staggered crossroads, signposted Hythe/Lympne through to Botolph's Bridge to West Hythe. Cross Royal Military Canal to the base of a steep hill.

24.3   RIGHT onto track through No Entry sign and follow canal. The track, or bridleway, runs at the bottom of the banking but a better view and surface is to be obtained by following the path at the top. The last part of the track is surfaced into Hythe.

26.3   RIGHT at traffic lights to cross canal once again.

This ride meets Route 29 from and back to Canterbury here. On the other side of the canal is the terminus for the Romney, Hythe & Dymchurch Railway. Opened in 1927 it claims to be 'The worlds smallest public railway' and operates steam and diesel locomotives one third of normal size on a 15 inch gauge. Despite their size, trains are capable of speeds up to 25 mph as they travel the 14 miles up the coast to Dungeness. Operates late February to end of October. For information 0679 62353. There is a cafe by the station.

Following one-way system to RIGHT at traffic lights continue on the A259 until The Prince of Wales PH.

27.4 RIGHT and follow through to Botolph's Bridge once again. After the pub LEFT into Donkey Lane, signposted Burmarsh. Along here pass Lathe Farm Museum where teas are served.

29.8 RIGHT at T-Junction into Burmarsh, then at next, RIGHT signposted Aldington/Ashford.

32.0 LEFT past the ruined church then LEFT at T-Junction and LEFT at next on reaching Blackmanstone Bridge.

35.0 RIGHT, signposted St Mary-in-the-Marsh and continue through the village past the church and the 15th Century Star Inn.

With new development springing up it looks as if this village is starting to be 'discovered'. The church is built on a mound to protect it from floods and nearby, marked by a simple wooden gate, is the grave of E. Nesbit who wrote 'The Railway Children'.

37.7 OVER crossroads with B2070, signposted Old Romney then CROSS A259, where there is a cafe up the road to the left, into the village.

The River Rother used to flow where the main road is now. Old Romney was an important port but suffered from silting. So New Romney was established closer to the river mouth. However a tremendous storm in 1287 altered the course altogether until now The Rother reaches the sea at Rye.

Keep LEFT by The Rose & Crown PH and cross goods railway line that leads to Dungeness at Swamp Crossing, before reaching Lydd with the church dominating the scene on the approach to the town.

Lydd is another former port. It was a centre for smuggling at one time as the buried remains of a customs officer will testify. To the south is Dungeness Nuclear Power Station and also close by is a large artillery range. The church narrowly escaped destruction from a bomb in the last war. In fact the chancel was demolished while air raid wardens were on duty in the tower. Teas can be obtained at The Old Prospect Bakery in Skinner Road, south of Coronation Square in the centre of the town. The old fire station is now a museum.

41.5 RIGHT at T-Junction in front of church, signposted Camber/Rye. Follow through area of desolate marshland on one side and artillery range the other. Continue through the seaside resort of Camber where refreshments are available, particularly in high season.

50.9   LEFT, at T-Junction, signposted A259 Rye. LEFT at roundabout, signposted Town Centre. RIGHT at roundabout, signposted B2089 Battle and then follow round to station.

52.2   END

Rye is a crowded place at holiday times and the reason is apparent enough when walking along the cobbled Mermaid Street with its mixture of half timbered and brick houses. This is Old England as it should be, especially from the point of view of the film maker. The 1287 storm that diverted the Rother made Rye the only fully functioning port for miles around but it later fell into decay after repeated French raids and silting, though it revived to some extent later on.

At the top of Mermaid Street is Lamb House (NT) the home of the Lamb Family who were mayors of Rye on no less than 78 occasions! Later, Henry James the novelist resided there, followed later by E.F Benson of Mapp and Lucia fame. The television series was filmed close by. Open April to end of October, Wednesdays and Saturdays only, 2-6.

The 13th Century Ypres Tower houses a museum devoted to the history and social life of Rye. Open daily Easter to mid-October. From the Lookout one can see across the quay and the old port but the whole lot can be seen in miniature at the Rye Heritage Centre. Open daily Easter to end of October and weekends only at other times.

29 THE FRENCH CONNECTION

The ancient city of Canterbury is soon left for the North Downs. At Petham orchards have given way to the woods and fields as the small lane gradually ascends the long chalk valley. At 597 feet the crest is gained then a steep descent to the Pilgrims Way. From Brabourne, it's across the valley to the final ridge and Lympne, high above Romney Marsh before the seaside at Hythe and a bracing ride along the promenade. But it's back onto the hills at Newington. Who cannot fail to notice the Channel Tunnel and the Exhibition Centre. But that is forgotten as the steep side of the North Downs is tackled before descending to Elham. Then it's up the long valley this village has given its name to, along which flows the Nail Bourne. Then the gabled and half timbered village of Patrixbourne before taking the North Downs Way through orchards to return to Canterbury.

A fairly hilly ride but the climbs tend to be long and gradual. The exception to the rule is the ascent from Newington.

Maps	OS LR 179.
Distance	44.7 miles. Of this approximately 1.5 miles easy off-road.
Start/Finish	Canterbury East Station.

Railway access

Canterbury East is served by an hourly service from London Victoria and Dover.

Canterbury West, served by trains from either London Charing Cross or Victoria, can be used instead.

Westernhanger, Sandling & Folkestone are the best escape points.

Places to see

Cathedral - and much more in Canterbury.

Village & church - Brabourne.

Zoo Park, Mansion & Gardens - Port Lympne.

Lympne Castle.

Romney, Hythe & Dymchurch Railway, church and town - Hythe.

Eurotunnel Exhibition Centre - Cheriton.

Village & church - Elham.

Parsonage Farm Rural Heritage Centre - North Elham.

Village & church - Patrixbourne.

Refreshments

Cafes & pubs - Canterbury.

Cafe - for visitors to Port Lympne.

Cafe - by station in Hythe.

Little Chef - Seabrook.

Cafe - for visitors to Eurotunnel Exhibition Centre, Cheriton.

Tea rooms - for visitors to Parsonage Farm Rural Heritage Centre, North Elham.

THE FRENCH CONNECTION

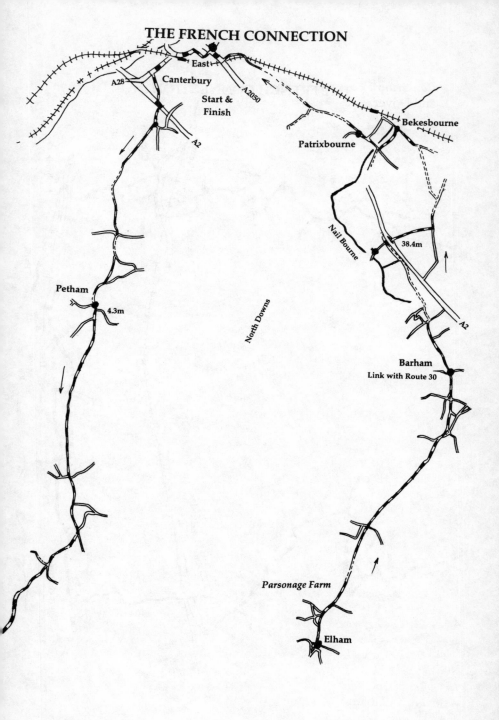

THE FRENCH CONNECTION

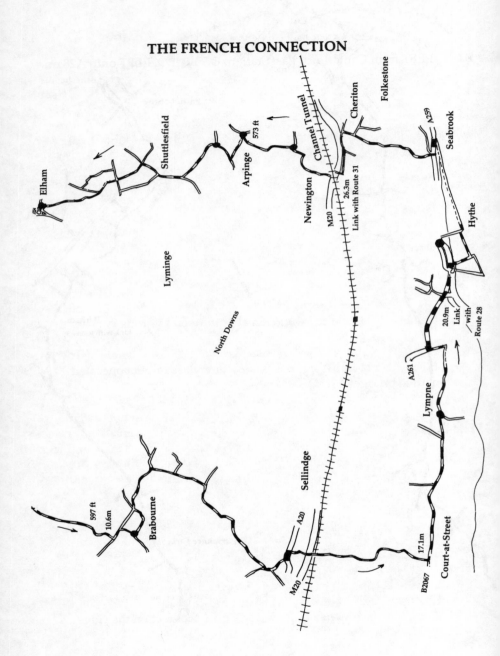

29 THE FRENCH CONNECTION

0.0   LEFT from Canterbury East Station. **OS LR 179.** LEFT onto A28 on roundabout by Man of Kent pub. Pass under railway bridge and past Kings Head PH.

0.4   LEFT into Hollow Lane. Pass under A2 then LEFT into Newhouse Lane by telephone box, signposted Chartham. After long gradual climb through orchards descend to crossroads.

3.0   OVER crossroads, signposted Petham/Waltham then RIGHT at T-Junction to continue past The Duke PH.

4.3   STRAIGHT on into Duckpit Road, signposted Elmsted/Evington. Follow this delightful lane up the valley into the North Downs.

7.4   RIGHT at T-Junction, signposted Elmsted then STRAIGHT ON at crossroads, signposted Brabourne. A gradual climb which becomes steeper towards the top of the North Downs and a high point of 597 feet. Steep descent to T-Junction at bottom on Pilgrims Way.

10.6   LEFT onto Pilgrims Way then RIGHT to Brabourne where at The Five Bells PH LEFT, signposted Sowting. Pass rather concealed church on right.

Brabourne is one of those villages that is attractive without being pretentious. The church is worth investigating. Much is of Norman origin and one window still has its original 12th Century stained glass. No less than eighteen generations of the Scott family are buried here including Sir John Scott, Lord Warden of the Cinque ports and Reginald Scott, regarded as the father figure of the Magic Circle in England.

12.1   RIGHT by telephone box signposted Sellindge then RIGHT at T-Junction by The Black Horse PH, LEFT at junction and continue to Stone Hill.

15.0   LEFT at T-Junction onto very quiet A20. Immediately RIGHT up Harringe Lane. Cross both M20 and railway, gradually climbing along this narrow twisting road to Court-at-Street on the ridge overlooking Romney Marsh. Meet Route 31 here.

17.1   LEFT at T-Junction on B2067, signposted Lympne/Hythe. Follow past Port Lympne Zoo Park, Mansion and Gardens, entrance to

Lympne Castle and village itself.

Both Zoo Park and Mansion at Port Lympne are closely linked together. The park itself specialises in the breeding of rare animals while there are exhibits and a wild life picture gallery in the 20th Century House where Rex Whistler had a hand in the design of the ostentatious interior. Open daily all year 10.00 to 19.00 (17.00 in winter months). Refreshments for visitors.

Lympne was very important in Roman times as a port. On the site of a Roman watch-tower a castle was built in 1360, dramatically situated looking over Romney Marsh. Exhibitions inside. Open daily April to early October, 10.30 to 18.00.

20.4   RIGHT onto A261 for fast descent to Hythe.

20.9   LEFT at traffic lights, signposted Town Centre. Meet Route 28 from Rye here. This point is close to the terminus of the Romney Hythe & Dymchurch Railway. Cafe near station.

21.1   RIGHT to cross Royal Military Canal at Stade Street, and LEFT into South Road, following signs for swimming pool.

Hythe is a remarkably undeveloped old fashioned type of seaside resort, but with a long pedigree, for it was one of the Cinque Ports until it became silted up. A sign of turbulent times is that buried beneath the crypt inside the imposing Norman church of St Leonards are over 1,000 skulls and 8,000 thigh bones.

22.6   RIGHT at T-Junction and follow very uncluttered sea front. Swing to left to T-Junction with A259 by Little Chef at Seabrook.

23.9   LEFT and immediately SECOND RIGHT by The Fountain PH into Horn Street. Pass under old railway, climb hill and cross bridge.

25.4   LEFT at T-Junction by Tescos. Follow past Eurotunnel Information Centre and Exhibition, Continue through car-park and footpath by side of M20.

The Exhibition Centre is very informative and describes the projects history. Along with a model railway of the terminals and tunnel there are mock-ups and computer terminals designed to answer any questions that might be asked. Refreshments for visitors. Open all year, 10.00 to 17.00 (18.00 in summer months).

RIGHT onto footbridge over motorway and continue to A20 LEFT through bridge beneath new railway.

26.3 RIGHT, signposted Newington/Peene. Meet route 31 from Dover here again. Continue through Newington into Peene, passing the museum of railway memorabilia connected with the Elham Valley Line. Climb steep hill on narrow lane with grass growing in the middle. Such a rural idyll far from the Channel Tunnel workings, until one looks behind.

27.2 LEFT at T-Junction and continue to top of hill up to 573 feet. LEFT at T-Junction at Home Farm, Arpinge.

28.4 RIGHT at T-Junction, signposted Shuttlesfield/Hawkinge. LEFT, signposted Shuttlesfield then RIGHT at next T-Junction, signposted Shuttlesfield/Acrise. Pass through the tiny hamlet of Shuttlesfield.

29.8 LEFT then RIGHT at T-Junction before LEFT again, signposted Elham. Keep STRAIGHT ON to descend steep 17% hill into the valley. Take care here. Follow into Elham village.

Elham is a large village with a church that is worth visiting for its furnishings alone. It has given its name to the valley which bears the Nail Bourne river northwards to the River Stour. Its green pasture lands set amongst the chalk hills make this a very attractive area. The route passes Parsonage Farm Rural Heritage Centre just to the north. There are traditional and rare breeds of livestock including an exhibition, tea room and shop. Open Easter to September, Tuesday to Sunday, and on Bank Holidays, 10.30 to 17.00.

31.8 RIGHT at T-Junction and continue through village and up the valley past The Dolls House, Rural Heritage Centre and the Elham Valley Vineyard. Route 30 joins at Barham providing an alternative route to Canterbury.

38.4 RIGHT under the A2, signposted Highland Court Farm. After the farm entrance this becomes a beautiful narrow road as it passes through orchards. At crossroads LEFT, signposted Patrixbourne/ Bekesbourne then again LEFT across open downland.

39.5 RIGHT, then at T-Junction LEFT and descend past hop farm.

40.7 LEFT, signposted Bekesbourne Church, away on the left, and follow narrow lane into Patrixbourne. The map shows two fords but the Nail Bourne only flows here when the underlying chalk bed has become saturated and can hold no more water. It can stay dry for years at a time.

41.2   RIGHT at T-Junction at Patrixbourne and continue through village or left to visit the church.

The half timbered houses are infilled with hand made bricks and with the Dutch gables and oast houses make Patrixbourne worth stopping for. However it is the church that is the crowning glory. There is the elaborately carved Norman doorway and the Swiss glass windows, enamelled rather than stained, dating from around 1538 to 1670. A depiction of a man walking on the St Gothard Pass is a scene far removed from this Kent village.

41.4   STRAIGHT ON at roundabout. Immediately VEER RIGHT down Hode Lane and follow the North Downs Way past Hode Farm, and through orchards drawing ever closer to Canterbury with its cathedral on the skyline.

42.9   STRAIGHT ON at crossroads and continue past locked gate into residential part of Canterbury. LEFT into Pilgrims Way immediately after crossing railway. RIGHT at T-Junction onto main road A2050.

44.1   LEFT at traffic lights into Upper Chantry Lane then RIGHT at traffic lights at church into Old Dover Road. LEFT at roundabout onto A28 ring road, signposted Ashford. FORK LEFT for Canterbury East station.

44.7   END

30 TIMEBALL & CASTLES RIDE

From Canterbury the Great Stour is followed to Fordwich, from where narrow lanes thread their way through the numerous orchards in this area to Richborough Castle which was once on an island in the Wantsum Channel between the mainland and the Isle of Thanet. On to Sandwich where the Stour finally reaches the sea. Then on to Sandwich Bay before reaching Deal and Walmer with a long trip along the seafront past the Timeball Tower and two castles to the white cliffs at St Margaret's. Up to the North Downs before Dover, reached by a serpentine road with yet another castle in the distance. This town is left by a narrow valley. While the railway goes through the tunnel, the road climbs to its highest point of 420 feet at Coldred. Then the Elham Valley and return to Canterbury through the city walls.

The first part of the ride along to Walmer is very flat before the North Downs intervene. The steepest climb is from Kingsdown to St Margaret's.

Map	OS LR 179.
Distance	50.3 miles. Of this 1.9 miles is off-road but rideable.
Start/Finish	Canterbury West Station.

Railway access

Canterbury West has an hourly service between London Charing Cross and Margate. Some trains from London Victoria via Maidstone terminate here but are rather slow.

Canterbury East has a faster hourly service from Victoria on the line to Dover.

Sandwich, Deal, Walmer, Dover & Shepherdswell can be used as escape points.

Places to see

Cathedral - and much more in Canterbury.

Old Town Hall - Fordwich.

Richborough Castle (EH).

Barbican, quay & town - Sandwich.

Timeball Tower, Castle (EH), museum - Deal.

Castle (EH) - Walmer.

Bleriot Memorial, Castle,Crabble Mill - and much more in Dover.

Refreshments

Cafes & pubs - Canterbury.

Little Cottage Tea Rooms - Sandwich.

Cafe on the Green - by the lifeboat station in Deal.

Cafes & pubs - Dover.

Willowbeck Restaurant & Tea Rooms - Bridge.

TIMEBALL & CASTLES

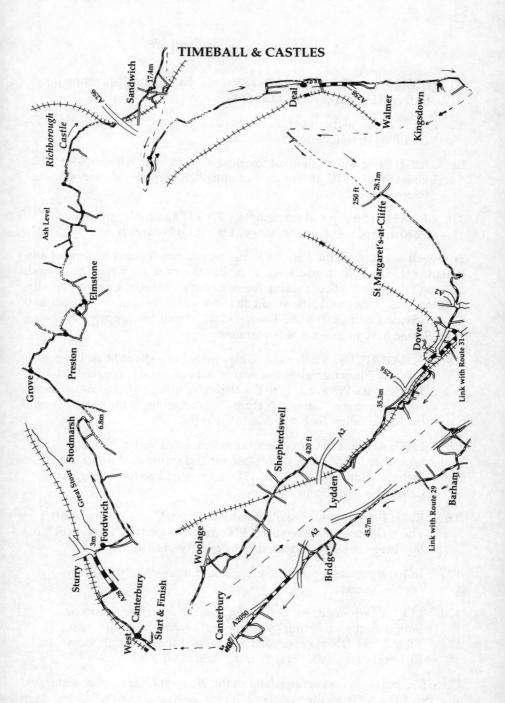

30 TIMEBALL & CASTLES

0.0   RIGHT from Canterbury West Station then LEFT at T-Junction into
      St Dunstans Street A290. **OS LR 179.**

0.2   LEFT at roundabout before West Gate into North Lane. STRAIGHT
      OVER next, signposted Broad Oak.

1.8   RIGHT into Vauxhall Road, marked weak bridge. After crossing the
      Great Stour LEFT at roundabout onto A28, signposted Margate.
      Recross river.

3.0   RIGHT at Sturry and immediately RIGHT again, signposted
      Fordwich. Cross Great Stour yet again into Fordwich.

Fordwich was one of the Cinque Ports, an alliance formed to protect and
enhance trade in the Middle Ages. It was the port for Canterbury and,
although there was talk of making the river navigable all the way to the city,
nothing was done, with the result that Fordwich became silted up and
Sandwich used instead. The Old Town Hall still stands and is open for viewing
from Easter, May to the end of September.

3.4   STRAIGHT ON when road swings round to right at Moat Lane
      LEFT at T-Junction at end of narrow lane. Follow through
      Trenleypark Wood along to the attractive village of Stodmarsh, near
      where there is a National Nature Reserve amongst the reedbeds of
      the Stour Valley. Swing round to the right.

6.8   LEFT, signposted Grove Ferry/Preston. LEFT at T-Junction,
      signposted Grove/Preston/Upstreet and continue through the
      orchards until, at Grove, RIGHT, signposted Preston/Wingham.
      Cross The Little Stour.

9.6   RIGHT at T-Junction, signposted Wingham/Canterbury and after
      The Half Moon & Seven Stars PH enter Preston. LEFT into Mill Lane
      by village stores, signposted Elmstone/West Marsh.

10.7 LEFT, signposted public telephone and immediately LEFT by
      telephone box.

11.1 LEFT at crossroads by interesting looking church at Elmstone.
      Follow narrow twisting lanes through orchards to Ware then
      STRAIGHT ON at crossroads, signposted Richborough. Pass
      Richborough Castle (EH) over the fields to the left.

Once Richborough was on an island in the Watsum Channel that separated
the isle of Thanet from the mainland. It was from here in AD43, in the reign

of Claudius, that the Romans set out to invade the rest of Britain. As William built Battle Abbey so the Romans built a huge triumphal arch, the foundations of which can still be seen. In its heyday there was a bustling township of shops, storehouses and granaries, now there are just the remains of the massive fortifications. Nothing endures for ever except for the wind that blows through. Open daily April to October, 10.00 to 18.00..

CONTINUE over level crossing and pass under A256.

16.9   LEFT at T-Junction by fire station into Sandwich and STRAIGHT ON at The Barbican that guards the bridge onto the quay.

The Barbican dates from 1539 and protected the entrance to the town by the Stour. The bridge came two hundred years later and levied tolls until 1977. The tariffs displayed under the timber arch are for 1905 and make interesting reading. As a port, Sandwich suffered the universal problem of silting up but enjoyed great prosperity as a cloth making centre in the 16th Century with the result that there are many fine buildings dating from that period. Certainly a place to wander around. The Little Cottage Tea Rooms on the quay are open seven days a week and there are other places in the town.

17.4   CONTINUE along quay and then follow road to RIGHT and then LEFT past church. along Sandown Road. After the golf course enter a toll road and pass the bird observatory.

The saltings, mudflats and freshwater marshes of the area around Sandwich Bay attract a wide variety of birds. It is owned by the National Trust and forms part of a Site of Special Scientific Interest.

CONTINUE on ancient road between Sandwich and Deal and follow across this very exposed country towards Deal.

22.1   LEFT into Godwyn Road on the outskirts of Deal then RIGHT onto the sea front. CONTINUE onto A258 and follow past Timeball Tower and castle.

William Cobbett called Deal 'a most villainous place' and said it 'was full of filthy looking people'. But then it was a run-down military town and not the quiet seaside resort it is today. The Timeball Tower began life in 1795 as a semaphore station before being converted to tell the time to shipping out at sea. The time-ball still drops every hour on the hour. Inside are displays on satellite communication and time. Open end of May to beginning of September, Tuesday and Sunday, plus Bank Holidays 10.00 to 17.00.
  Deal Castle (EH) was built by Henry VIII after his excommunication by the pope when he feared invasion. Low and menacing and built in the shape of a Tudor Rose it once had 119 guns. In the basement there is an exhibition on

the nations defences. Open all year except Mondays and Tuesdays in Winter.

23.6   VEER LEFT by lifeboat station, signposted Kingsdown/Walmer Castle. There is the Cafe on the Green close by. Continue past Walmer Castle to Kingsdown.

Walmer Castle (EH) was another coastal fort built by Henry VIII but has been upgraded into more of a stately home with fine gardens as the residence of Lord Warden of the Cinque Ports. Open all year except for January and February, 10.00 to 18.00 (16.00 in winter).

25.5   VEER LEFT when road swings up hill. Keep on towards the white cliffs before turning inland on the unadopted Oldstairs Road.

26.1   STRAIGHT ON (No Through Road) and immediately FORK RIGHT, signposted Kingsdown Riding Centre. Follow unmetalled but rideable track as it climbs Otty Bottom to T-Junction at St Margarets.

28.2   LEFT at T-Junction at The Red Lion PH and RIGHT by The Hope Inn. Pass the holiday camp and the aerials before the road twists to give spectacular views of Dover East Docks and across the valley to the castle. Cross A2 on bridge and pass the Bleriot Memorial into the top part of Dover.

This outline of a simple monoplane marks the spot where Louis Bleriot landed in 1909 after the first powered flight across the Channel.

31.9   LEFT at T-Junction and immediately RIGHT down Connaught Rd.

32.4   LEFT into one-way system and immediately RIGHT into Avenue Road. LEFT into Beaconsfield Road.

32.6   RIGHT into London Road. Follow and keep to LEFT signposted, River /Temple Ewell. LEFT at traffic lights, signposted River/ Crabble Corn Mill.

33.7   RIGHT into Lower Road, passing the mill. Follow up Valley Road.

Built in 1812 this watermill is a remarkable example of how automation could be achieved without the aid of modern day high technology. Open all year from weekends only in winter months up to every day in August, 10.00 to 17.00 (12.00 on Sundays). Restaurant for visitors.

34.3   RIGHT at T-Junction and immediately LEFT into River Street followed by RIGHT at T-Junction by church.

34.5   LEFT at T-Junction by Dublin Man of War PH and LEFT at next, before bridge, into Alkham Road, signposted Kearsney Abbey.

34.9 RIGHT by park, signposted Temple Ewell and under bridge.

The church at Temple Ewell contains some more fine examples of the Swiss glass seen at Patrixbourne on Route 29.

35.3 LEFT at T-Junction by The George & Dragon PH, signposted Canterbury. After passing under railway RIGHT at Lydden into Stonehall Road, signposted Eythorne. After descent and ascent RIGHT at T-junction, signposted Shepherdswell/Coldred. Cross railway which goes easy way through tunnel and climb hill to A2 at top of hill.

37,2 LEFT onto A2 then immediately RIGHT, signposted Coldred/ Eythorne. CONTINUE through Coldred to Shepherdswell and pass the railway station.

38.9 STRAIGHT OVER crossroads by Circle K and STRAIGHT OVER next, following signs to Woolage Green then Woolage Village on the edge of the now defunct Kent coal mining district.

41.0 CONTINUE over crossroads, signposted Snowdown/Nonington and at next turn LEFT, signposted Barham/Canterbury. LEFT at T-Junction. Pass Woodpecker Country Hotel.

42.2 LEFT at T-Junction onto B2046, signposted Barham/Canterbury. STRAIGHT ON at roundabout before bridge over A2, then RIGHT at T-Junction and immediately LEFT, signposted Barham.

43.1 RIGHT at crossroads, signposted Barham Church, into village. RIGHT at T-Junction into Valley Road. Join Route 29 here for an alternative route to Canterbury.

45.7 VEER LEFT, signposted Bridge/Canterbury. Continue along old A2 past Willowbeck Restaurant and Tea Room in Bridge. CROSS A2 and follow A2050 towards Canterbury. LEFT into Old Dover Road by pub. CONTINUE over traffic lights to A28 ring road.

49.5 STRAIGHT OVER roundabout through city walls into Watling Street, signposted Town Centre. CONTINUE into Beer Cart Street then RIGHT into Stour Street marked No Through Road. LEFT at T-Junction into St Peters Street. This is marked as a cycle way to West Gate though cycling is not permitted at busier times. At West Gate continue into St Dunstans Street before RIGHT into Station Road for Canterbury West.

50.3 END

31 FROM THE WHITE CLIFFS

The White Cliffs of Dover is where the North Downs jump into the English Channel. These hills need to be climbed before the much flatter terrain where the lanes twist in a complex arrangement to Wateringbury on the banks of the River Medway. The switchbacks of the Greensand Ridge are tackled before they are left at Seal, then up to the North Downs and along the Pilgrims Way to Otford before the hills are scaled to a height of over 700 feet. From the top it is not all downhill for there are deep dips around Cudham before the long gradual descent to Bromley.

This ride starts and ends with hard climbs. The middle section from Lympne to Yalding is much easier and it would be easy to split this ride into sections.

Maps	OS LR 179, 189, 188, 187, 177.
Distance	81.1 miles from Dover; 72.1 from Folkestone; 56.4 from Ashford.
Start	Dover Eastern Docks, Folkestone or Ashford Stations.
Finish	Bromley South Station.

Railway access

Dover Priory, Folkestone & Ashford all have frequent services from London Victoria or Charing Cross.

Bromley South has frequent trains into Victoria.

Pluckley, Wateringbury, or Otford useful for splitting the route.

Places to see

Castle, White Cliffs Experience, Museum - Dover.

Castle, Port Lympne Zoo Park - Lympne.

Swanton Mill - South Stour.

Village & church - West Peckham.

Ightam Mote (NT).

Downe House.

Refreshments

Cafes & pubs - Dover.

Tea rooms - Capel le Ferne.

Little Chef - Cheriton.

Tea rooms - Grafty Green Garden Centre.

Riverside Restaurant - Wateringbury.

Willow Tree Tea Rooms, Gossips - Otford.

Tea rooms - Christmas Tree Farm, parish hall, and delicatessen - Downe.

FROM THE WHITE CLIFFS

FROM THE WHITE CLIFFS

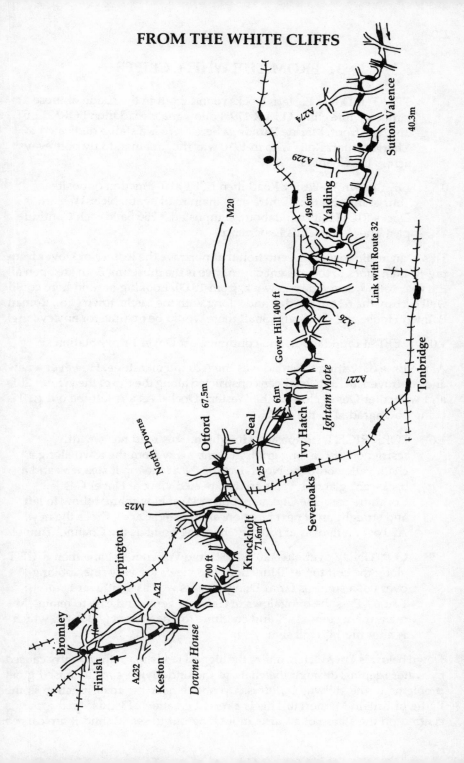

31 FROM THE WHITE CLIFFS

0.0 START at Dover Eastern Docks roundabout in the shade of those famous white cliffs. **OS LR 179.** Follow main road then FORK LEFT onto sea front, Marine Parade, where there is a statue dedicated to Charles Stuart Rolls who in 1910 was the first man to fly both ways across the Channel.

0.5 LEFT down Wellesley Road then LEFT at T-Junction opposite Tourist Information Centre onto main road again. Near Western Docks RIGHT at roundabout, signposted A256 Sandwich Continue past The White Cliffs Experience.

This is an audio-visual presentation that portrays the history of Dover from pre-Roman times to the present day. Above is the museum. Both are open all the year round, seven days a week, from 10.00. Looking around here could well occupy the rest of the day and, along with the castle, town gaol, Roman Painted House and the Grand Shaft there would be no time for any cycling!

1.0 LEFT at roundabout, and continue past Dover Priory Station.

At the time of writing this road was the A20 to Folkestone. However a new and controversial route has been constructed along the top of the White Cliffs and will enter Dover close to the Western Docks. As a result the old A20 is being downgraded to the B2011.

1.6 FORK RIGHT, signposted Hougham. This road has a width restriction. It is a long gradual climb away from the town along a chalk valley onto the North Downs. Near the top it steepens and a backward glance reveals an unexpected view of Dover Castle. Continue past The Chequers pub at West Hougham, follow to left and straight on at next junction, signposted Capel. Cross the new A20 over a flyover at roughly the same point as the Channel Tunnel.

5.9 CONTINUE over old A20 (B2011) into Winehouse Lane then RIGHT along the cliff top at T-Junction. The views are very fine, looking over Folkestone as far as Dungeness as well as southwards to France. Pass the bungalows of Capel-le-Ferne and cafe to rejoin old main road. Here LEFT and continue to The Valiant Sailor PH which is after the 14% hill sign.

Down below is The Warren, one of the biggest landslips in the country caused by water seeping through the chalk to the underlying clay. It caused great problems to the railway builders. Up above near the road junction is the Battle of Britain Memorial. This is a recent creation of landscaped grounds centred on the statue of an airman looking out to sea. Round it are carved badges of various RAF squadrons. It is unfinished at the moment and was set up by the Battle of Britain Memorial Trust.

FORK RIGHT after The Valiant Sailor and in company with the North Downs Way follow the small road along Creteway Down. From a height of 559 feet there are fine views across Folkestone. Descend to the A260.

8.5 CONTINUE OVER staggered crossroads, into Crete Road West. Once again cross the A20,down below in a tunnel and continue past houses, still remaining close to North Downs Way. From here there are panoramic views of the Channel Tunnel complex, in fact far better than those obtained from the Eurotunnel Exhibition Centre on Route 29.

10.8 FORK LEFT down hill into Newington. There is certainly a stark contrast between the old village and the Channel Tunnel workings landscaped behind a large earthbank. Meet Route 29 at this junction.

11.7 RIGHT at T-Junction onto A20.

A dog-leg route from Folkestone joins here and is described below. The town has the reputation for being rather a staid seaside resort, its growth from a fishing village helped by the railway and the establishment of a cross-channel ferry service as an alternative to Dover. H.G.Wells was a famous resident and much of 'Kipps' is set here.

0.0 RIGHT from Folkestone Station. Immediately LEFT and LEFT again at roundabout, signposted A20 Ashford. Follow through three sets of traffic lights and past Little Chef to roundabout over M20 at Cheriton.

2.0 CONTINUE straight over, signposted A20 Newington. After passing under railway REJOIN DOVER ROUTE.

Follow the,now very quiet A20 over railway and M20 to junction with A261 at Newingreen.

15.8 STRAIGHT ON at staggered crossroads, signposted Lympne. Continue into village before RIGHT at crossroads at top of the hill. Meet Route 29 from Canterbury here. CONTINUE past Lympne Castle and Port Lympne Zoo Park (see Route 29) through Court-at-Street along road with fine views across Romney Marsh to the sea beyond.

19.5 FORK RIGHT, onto Roman Road, signposted Aldington/Merson/ Ashford. Follow through the rather non-descript village of

Aldington Corner, Clapp Hill and along way marked on map as a Roman road. In the distance can be seen the distant towers of Ashford.

22.2 CONTINUE over crossroads, signposted Swanton Mill. Continue to Cheeseman Green.

Swanton Mill is a weather boarded water mill on the East Stour, dating from the 17th Century. There is a large water garden and flour is ground on the site. Teas available for visitors. Open weekends, April to September, 14.00 to 18.00.

23.2 LEFT at T-Junction, signposted Kingsnorth/Bilsington. **OS LR 189.** STRAIGHT ON over bridge crossing both railway and the new controversial A2070 between Ashford and Brenzett in Romney Marsh. Pass Finn Farm before turning SECOND LEFT and at T-Junction RIGHT, signposted Great Chart/Hothfield.

25.8 CROSS old A2070, into Magpie Hall Road, and continue through Stubbs Cross to the A28. At T-Junction RIGHT, signposted Great Chart /Ashford.

28.5 LEFT, signposted Great Chart/Hothfield and immediately LEFT again and continue past Purchase Farm. After descent through woods LEFT at T-Junction, signposted Hothfield. Join the dog-leg route from Ashford here, the route is described below.

In a strategic crossroads position where the Great Stour and East Stour rivers meet, Ashford was once known as a cattle market town. In the 19th Century it became an important railway junction. New has almost entirely replaced old and the town has mushroomed ever outwards with the arrival of large overspill populations from London. Now it is entering a new railway age as the terminal for the Channel Tunnel. An International Station is being built alongside the old along with parking for 6,000 vehicles.

0.0 CONTINUE from station car-park - the right hand side overlooked by the discount furniture warehouse. **OS LR 189.** Immediately LEFT at roundabout and cross railway. VEER RIGHT at next roundabout, signposted Trading Estate.

0.7 RIGHT at roundabout, signposted B2229, South Ashford and RIGHT at traffic lights, signposted Brookfield/Cobbs Wood. STRAIGHT ACROSS next roundabout by Roman Catholic church and follow through to the A28.

2.2 STRAIGHT ACROSS roundabout, signposted Great Chart and RIGHT in village signposted Hothfield.

4.3   JOIN DOVER ROUTE. CONTINUE past Bridge Farm, golf driving range and under railway.

30.5   LEFT at T-Junction at Rippers Cross, signposted Pluckley, then LEFT at next signposted Chambers Green/Bethersden and FORK RIGHT by Dowle Street Farm.

33.2   CONTINUE over staggered crossroads, signposted Smarden/ Egerton. Pluckley Station is to the left. By garage RIGHT at T-Junction, signposted Pluckley/Charing and immediately LEFT by chapel, signposted Egerton.

34.2   LEFT at T-Junction, signposted Smarden Bell/Headcorn. Immediately RIGHT, signposted Mundy Bois/Egerton Forstal. Continue past The Rose & Crown PH before turning RIGHT, signposted Boughton Malherbe.

36.5   LEFT at T-Junction, signposted Headcorn. At Broadstone pass Grafty Garden Centre where a coffee sign is displayed. There RIGHT, signposted East Sutton. **OS LR 188.**

38.1   CONTINUE over staggered crossroads, signposted East Sutton/ Sutton Valence and then CONTINUE to left, signposted Sutton Valence/Maidstone before RIGHT at T-Junction by Park Wood, signposted East Sutton,then LEFT.

39.2   LEFT at T-Junction then at farm LEFT to A274 near Brook House.

40.3   RIGHT at T-Junction onto A274. Continue past Sutton Valence sign and cafe on the right Then LEFT, signposted Forsham Lane.

41.9   RIGHT and FORK RIGHT before RIGHT at T-Junction at Lambs Cross, signposted Chart Sutton/Sutton Valence.

43.1   LEFT, signposted Wierton. After Red House STRAIGHT ON at junction with East Hall Hill, then LEFT at T-Junction down Long Lane before RIGHT at next, signposted Linton/Maidstone. Join Route 32 from Maidstone here.

46.0   RIGHT at T-Junction onto A229 then LEFT just before Linton sign, signposted Hunton/Yalding down Redwall Lane. After hop fields and orchards, RIGHT at T-Junction then CROSS staggered crossroads into Lughorse Lane, signposted Farleigh Green/West Farleigh. Follow into Yalding.

49.6   LEFT at T-Junction onto B2010, before RIGHT into Kenward Road, signposted Wateringbury. (Yalding is covered in Route 32). Follow past hop fields and up hill followed by descent to the Medway.

Cross bridge and level crossing by Wateringbury Station. To the left is the Riverside Restaurant which serves Sunday teas.

51.9 LEFT onto the B2015 opposite The Railway Inn. Continue through Nettlestead before RIGHT into Gibbs Hill. On descent LEFT into Park Road then climb before descending steep hill after ruined gatehouse on the edge of Mereworth Park. This is a very attractive stretch of wooded narrow lane. RIGHT after isolated church, No Through Road. Descend to the A228 (formerly B2016). Walk across (CARE) to turn RIGHT. Descend to roundabout.

55.1 STRAIGHT ON signposted B2016 Wrotham then LEFT at crossroads, signposted West Peckham/Plaxtol. Climb Gover Hill and enjoy the fine views.

West Peckham is only a short distance from this route. An idyllic spot with church and pub facing a large village green. The church is interesting and contains a giant family pew with its own separate entrance so that the local gentry would not have to mix with the villagers.

57.4 LEFT into Roughway Lane, signposted Crouch/Borough Green. Descend long hill. By The Kentish Rifleman PH RIGHT at T-Junction. Follow signposts through Dunks Green to Plaxtol. At Plaxtol Spout LEFT at T-Junction and climb past The Papermakers Arms PH into the main part of the village.

60.0 RIGHT at T-Junction by The Rorty Crankle Inn. In Anglo-Saxon this means Inglenook Follow round to left past the church to A229. There RIGHT at T-Junction and climb hill.

61.0 LEFT, signposted Ivy Hatch/Seale/Sevenoaks/Ightham Mote. Follow into Ivy Hatch. After the left turning for Ightham Mote and passing The Plough Inn, FORK LEFT signposted Stone Street.

Ightham Mote (NT) is reached down a steep hill. This is a beautiful medieval moated manor house with later additions. To appreciate it, at its serene best, view away from the Sunday afternoon crowds. Teas for visitors. Open April to end of October, daily except for Tuesdays and Saturdays, 12.00 to 17.00.

CONTINUE into Stone Street past The Rose & Crown PH to enjoy mostly downhill run past The Padwell Arms.

64.3 RIGHT at T-Junction, signposted Seal. Continue into village. LEFT onto A25 then by library RIGHT into School Lane, signposted Kemsing. LEFT at T-Junction to descend hill, cross railway and motorway and, after the Kemsing sign, climb the other side drawing ever closer to the North Downs.

66.1 LEFT at T-Junction onto Pilgrims Way until reaching A225. LEFT at bend and descend past railway station into Otford.

67.5 RIGHT at roundabout around pond, width limit.

Situated where The Darent breaks through the barrier of the North Downs, Otford was once a place of considerable importance as the ruins of the early 16th Century Archbishops Palace will testify. Refreshments at the Willow Tree Tea Rooms by the roundabout and also Gossips antique establishment on the way out of the village.

68.4 RIGHT into Twitton Lane. Climb past The Rising Sun PH before LEFT and immediately RIGHT after crossing railway, No Through Road. Where road ends in large circle continue straight on along bridleway. Pass through tunnel under the M25 and climb steeply around two very sharp hairpin bends to regain the old road. Ascend through the woods to reach the crest of the North Downs at The Polhill Arms PH.

69.5 CROSS A224 into Otford Lane, following sign for Polhill Riding Centre into Halstead. After The Rose & Crown PH LEFT at crossroads into Knockholt Road, signposted Knockholt/Cudham. Follow into Knockholt Pound where RIGHT at T-Junction and climb gradually to the high point of the ride at 700 feet, passing the church and The Crown PH.

71.6 RIGHT into narrow lane for 1 in 5 descent (CARE) followed by similar the other side. Follow switchback progress to Cudham. OS LR 187. Enter the London Borough of Bromley which has a great deal of countryside within its boundaries. RIGHT at The Forge and continue through village past Cudham Place and the pub.

74.9 LEFT down 25% hill where GREAT CARE is needed. At bottom there is another steep climb through the woods to Downe passing Christmas Tree Farm where teas can be obtained at the garden centre.

Charles Darwin the naturalist, whose theories of evolution caused so much controversy in the 19th Century, resided at Down House just outside the village. It is now a museum, open March to January, daily except Monday/ Tuesday, 13.00 to 18.00. Teas are served at the parish hall on Sunday afternoons between April and October, also at the delicatessen and cafe at No 7 on the way out towards Bromley.

76.3 STRAIGHT ON by George & Dragon and Queens Head pubs. Follow road down then up to main road where RIGHT at mini roundabout onto A233. Follow through narrow twisting section.

78.3 LEFT onto B265, signposted Keston Village. Follow past picnic area and windmill into village. At first mini roundabout STRAIGHT ON and at second FORK RIGHT into Baston Road, signposted B265 Hayes. **OS LR 177.**

79.3 CROSS A232 at traffic lights and STRAIGHT OVER roundabout, signposted B265 Bromley into the front ranks of suburbia through Hayes. Pass Norman Park.

81.1 FORK LEFT, signposted alternative route, along Hayes Road B2212. At Westmoreland Road RIGHT at T-Junction, signposted B228 Bromley. Immediately LEFT at traffic lights to pass station on right.

81.8 END

32 THE LOOSE LOOP

From the tight congestion of Maidstone down by the River Medway it is uphill to the twisting jumbled streets and streams of Loose and higher still to Boughton Monchelsea. There gaze upon the Weald and contemplate the steep descent to the orchard and hop country by the River Beult, which, like this route, is on its way to Yalding. The Medway is crossed at Wateringbury then on to the hills and Mereworth with its domed castle, Georgian church and the woods where the highest point of the ride at 468 feet is reached. Knights 'Tipped the Quintain' at Ofham, bishops built a castle at West Malling. Then twisting narrow lanes through the orchards to the outskirts of Maidstone at Ditton. Aylesford is entered by another crossing of The Medway, perhaps the best of all.

This is not a particularly hard ride apart from the climb to Loose and around Mereworth. There is much to see in Maidstone, despite the traffic, and in the Spring the orchard blossom is an outstanding sight.

Map	OS LR 188.
Distance	32 miles.
Start/Finish	Maidstone East Station.

Railway access

Maidstone East has a frequent service on the line between London Victoria and Ashford. Also from Charing Cross but not on Sundays.

Maidstone West & Maidstone Barracks could be used from Victoria by changing at Strood.

Yalding, Wateringbury, West Malling & Aylesford are escape points.

Places to see

Archbishop's Palace, Tyrwhitt-Drake Museum of Carriages - and other attractions, Maidstone.

Village & Wool House (NT) - Loose.

Boughton Monchelsea Place & church.

Village & medieval bridges - Yalding.

Georgian church - Mereworth.

Great Comp Garden - Platt.

Quintain - on village green, Offham.

Village, St Leonard's Tower - West Malling.

Priory & village - Aylesford.

Museum of Kent Rural Life - Sandling.

Refreshments

Cafes & pubs - at the station and elsewhere in Maidstone.

Riverside Restaurant - Wateringbury.

Cafe - Mill Yard Craft Centre, but not Sundays, West Malling.

Cafe - the Priory, Aylesford.

Cafe - Tyland Barn, Sandling.

THE LOOSE LOOP

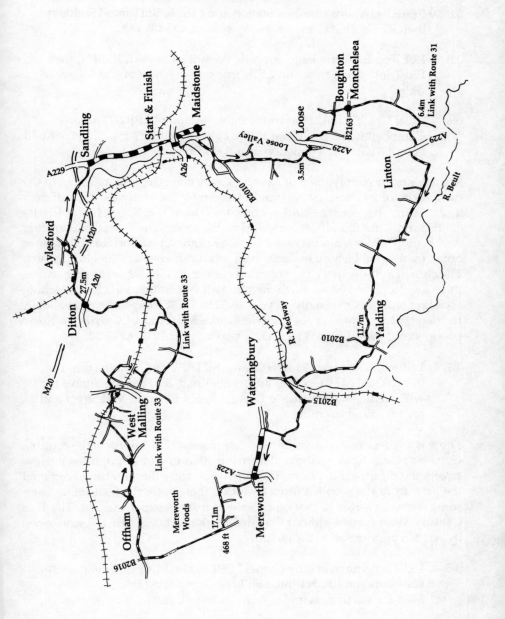

32 THE LOOSE LOOP

0.0   START at Maidstone East Station and turn RIGHT into Week Street then KEEP RIGHT into one-way system. **OS LR 188.**

0.3   LEFT up Pudding Lane opposite Fremlins Brewery, RIGHT, then LEFT into Mill Street and LEFT into on-way system and follow to right.

0.6   CONTINUE on A229 at traffic lights and on hill RIGHT into Campbell Road. RIGHT at traffic lights then LEFT into College Road before RIGHT at T-Junction into Tovil Road.

Maidstone, the county town of Kent, is a busy enough place, reflected in the complexity of its one-way system. But down by the Medway. it is different and within the gardens and waterfalls where the River Len adds its contribution, are the oldest buildings in the town. The recently renovated Archbishop's Palace has become a heritage centre. It was originally a manor house for the Archbishops of Canterbury who ungraded it in the 14th Century. The church in those days had enormous power so it is not surprising to find there are dungeons beneath where John Ball was imprisoned for preaching social revolution. Open daily all year 10.30 to 17.30. Refreshments available. In the stables is housed the Tyrwitt-Drake Museum of Carriages, horse powered but including old bicycles. Open all year 10.00 to 17.00.

1.7   LEFT by The Rose PH into Straw Mill Hill Road. Climb steep hill then STRAIGHT ON into Busbridge Road, marked unsuitable for wide vehicles. Continue to Loose where LEFT into Mill Street and follow round to church.

Loose is a village that one would associate more with the north of the country. Cottages rise in terraces above the streams that thread through the narrow streets and disappear in places. The pure water and fuller's earth encouraged the growth of the woollen industry. Once there were thirteen mills. Later some were converted to that other Kent industry - paper-making. The 15th Century Wool House, although owned by the National Trust, is only open by written application to the tenant.

3.5   LEFT by church and by chapel LEFT again. Immediately after The Chequers Inn RIGHT into Salt Lane, signposted Boughton Monchelsea to pass under A220 and climb steep hill.

Loose was by-passed as early as the Napoleonic Wars when this bridge was built to speed the passage of troops.

4.2   LEFT into Haste Hill Road, signposted Boughton Green then RIGHT at the crossroads by The Albion Inn and STRAIGHT ACROSS, signposted Boughton Monchelsea church. Pass entrance to house and church before steep hill.

The still inhabited Boughton Monchelsea Place was built in the 15th Century and overlooks a deer park. Teas available for visitors. Open April to October Sundays and Bank Holidays, 14.15 to 18.00. The view from the churchyard across the Weald of Kent is splendid, especially in the spring or autumn.

6.4   RIGHT at crossroads at bottom of hill, signposted Linton. Join Route 31 from Dover, Folkestone, Ashford here.

7.0   RIGHT at T-Junction on A229 and before Linton sign, LEFT, signposted Hunton/Yalding down Redwall Lane. RIGHT at T-Junction, signposted Yalding and STRAIGHT ON at staggered crossroads, signposted Farleigh Green/West Farleigh into Lughorse Lane and Yalding.

11.5   LEFT at T-Junction with B2010 into village proper.

Yalding is one of the centres for the Kent hop growing industry. It is quite a river junction with the Medway, Tiese and Beult all joining forces. One of the three medieval bridges is believed to be the longest of its kind in Kent and has a shop and house half way along. With its cobbled walks and timbered fronts Yalding set the scene for much of the work of the poet Edmund Blunden.

11.7   RIGHT into Kenward Road, signposted Wateringbury. Pass hop fields before climbing hill and descending to bridge over the Medway. Cross the railway and enter Wateringbury. Sunday teas can be obtained at the Riverside Restaurant.

13.6   LEFT at T-Junction by The Railway PH onto B2015. Continue through Nettlested before RIGHT up Gibbs Hill. Climb hill then descend to A26.

15.4   LEFT at T-Junction. Pass Mereworth Castle with its distinctive domed roof before turning RIGHT, signposted Mereworth. CROSS A228 and immediately RIGHT up Butchers Lane. Climb past The Queens Head PH.

Mereworth has a distinctive Georgian church built by the 7th Earl of Westmoreland to replace the one he knocked down along with a large part of the village when he built Mereworth Castle.

17.1   LEFT at T-Junction into Beech Road and RIGHT at next by Beech Restaurant onto B2016. Continue through Mereworth Woods, one of the largest surviving tracts of ancient woodland in Kent.

19.2   RIGHT at crossroads at bottom of hill, signposted Offham/West Malling.

A left instead of right here leads to Great Comp Gardens, stretching over seven acres and containing trees and shrubs amongst its walls and terraces. Shop and tea room for visitors. Open daily April to October, 11.00 to 18.00.

20.4   RIGHT at T-Junction at Offham.

Offham has the last surviving example of a quintain in England. The art was for knights on horseback to 'tilt' one end with a lance and avoid being knocked off by the heavy weight at the other.

21.3   LEFT into Offham Lane then RIGHT at T-Junction into Norman Lane at West Malling LEFT at T-Junction into the High Street.

22.2   RIGHT into Swan Street, signposted East Malling.

West Malling is a large up and coming village, a convenient dormitory settlement for London or Maidstone but its attractive enough with its Georgian and Elizabethan houses. St Leonards Tower (EH), an example of a Norman tower keep, was built in 1080 by Gundalf, Bishop of Rochester. It can be viewed at any reasonable time. The Manor Park is a good place for picnics while there is a tea room at the Mill Yard Craft Centre, not Sundays, passed on the right. Route 33, also from Maidstone, crosses here, and the two itineraries can be swapped.

Pass station and under A228.

23.1   RIGHT into Broadwater Road. Cross railway then LEFT after Broadwater Farm and continue through orchards. STRAIGHT ON at junction and OVER crossroads into Sweets Lane, signposted Ditton. RIGHT into Easterfields and carry on past the Horticultural Research Station into Ditton.

27.5 CROSS A20 at traffic lights, signposted Aylesford. Continue through non-descript built up area over M20, past station, over railway before entering Aylesford on the graceful medieval stone bridge.

It is hoped to ban motor traffic from this bridge so making it much easier to photograph the classic view looking across to the steep gabled houses and old timbered buildings that step up the hill. Carmelite Friars came here in 1242 . Its original owners, evicted by the dissolution, returned in 1949. They built a new church exactly where the original was. The Priory is open to the public each day. There is a cafeteria as well.

29.0 RIGHT at traffic lights in Aylesford. Cross M20 and pass the Museum of Kent Life at Cobtree.

This exhibits various aspects of Kent rural life in the setting of a working farm. There is oast house, a collection of farm implements as well as a 'Darling Buds of May' exhibition recreating life in the 1950s. Tea rooms for visitors. Open daily Easter to end of October, 10.30 to 17.30.

30.7 RIGHT at roundabout onto A229 into Maidstone. At the time of writing there were extensive road works due to the widening of the M20. New cycle lanes are being provided. Follow past Springfield Roundabout to where one-way system starts and road swings to left. Here it is easiest to push along the pavement past the post office buildings to reach the station.

32.0 END

33 OVER BLUE BELL HILL

For the first few miles out of Maidstone we follow the Medway Valley, so admired by William Cobbett. The river itself is crossed at East Farleigh and Teston then it's uphill to 'The North Pole' and down amongst the twisting lanes that thread their way through the orchards. Continue to West Malling but from here on the ride takes on a different texture as it heads towards the North Downs. At Holly Hill 643 feet is reached, then it's down a woodland track to Great Buckland and the long gradual drop to Cuxton. Here the Medway has grown very much bigger and is crossed by a motorway bridge. It is not long before the North Downs are climbed and followed to the viewpoint of Blue Bell Hil at 610 feetl. Then down to the Pilgrims Way as far as Detling before, once more, Maidstone beckons.

A hilly route, especially around the North Downs, but with a tremendous variety of scenery and fine views.

Maps	OS LR 188, 178.
Distance	36.5 miles. Of this 2.9 miles is off-road.
Start/Finish	Maidstone East Station.

Railway access

Maidstone East has a frequent sevice on the line from London Victoria to Ashford. Also from London Charing Cross but not on Sundays.

Maidstone West & Maidstone Barracks is an alternative but slower service and from Victoria necessitates changing at Strood onto the line that runs through to Paddock Wood.

West Malling, Strood & Cuxton are well placed escape points.

Places to see

Archbishop's Palace, Tyrwhitt-Drake Museum of Carriages - and other attractions, Maidstone.

Medieval bridge, churchyard memorial - East Farleigh.

Bridge & picnic site - Teston.

St Leonard's Tower, Abbey, Manor Park, Mill Yard Craft Centre - West Malling.

View point - Holly Hill, Blue Bell Hill.

Tyland Barn & Museum of Kent Rural Life - Sandling.

Refreshments

Cafes & pubs - at the station and elsewhere in Maidstone.

Cafe - Mill Yard Craft Centre, not Sundays, West Malling.

Cafe - Tyland Barn, Sandling.

OVER BLUE BELL HILL

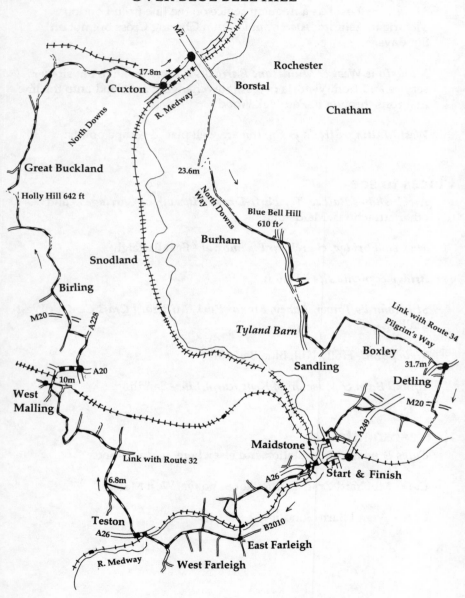

33 OVER BLUE BELL HILL

0.0 RIGHT from Maidstone East Station into Week Street. **OS LR 188.**
Join the one-way system through the traffic lights following signs
for A26, Tonbridge. Cross bridge over Medway and pass Safeway
and Maidstone West Station.

0.9 LEFT into Bower Place, marked Unsuitable for Large Vehicles. LEFT
into Bower Lane.

1.1 STRAIGHT ON into Lower Fant Road. Follow round to The Fox PH
and LEFT at T-Junction into Upper Fant Road before right swing
into Hackney Road and left to Gatland Road. Then LEFT into
Farleigh Lane out of town. Descend hill before crossing railway by
old fashioned station, and then over the river and up the hill the
other side to East Farleigh.

Near a group of oasts this five arched medieval bridge spans the Medway
and is reckoned to be one of the finest in Southern England. There is a weir
to add to the peaceful scene. Yet in the Civil War across marched the
Roundheads under General Fairfax to capture Maidstone. With hop fields
and orchards William Cobbett claimed the seven miles from Maidstone to
Merryworth to be the 'finest seven miles I have seen in England or anywhere
else.'
  Hop-picking was regarded as a holiday by many Londoners. But conditions
were squalid enough in 1849 for 43 to die of cholera. A simple monument
stands to them in the churchyard.

3.5 RIGHT at T-Junction by The Bull PH onto B2010. Pass the church
and continue to West Farleigh where RIGHT, signposted B2163
Teston. Descend the hill to cross the river by another medieval
bridge near a picnic site. Recross the railway.

5.5 LEFT at T-Junction onto A26, then LEFT signposted Teston/East
Malling. Climb the hill through the village.

An error by a signwriter at the former railway station resulted in Teeson
becoming Teston. On the way up on the left is a factory dedicated to the
traditional manufacture of cricket and hockey balls.

6.8 RIGHT at staggered crossroads by The North Pole PH. Descend hill.

7.5 LEFT at crossroads, signposted Well Street. Meet Route 32 here for a quick return to Maidstone by going right.

8.0 STRAIGHT ON into Pickey Lane then LEFT at T-Junction and climb hill before swinging round to the right. There are fine views across the orchards. Cross bridge over A228.

9.7 LEFT at Lavenders into West Malling. On the way pass St Marys Abbey where the tower and gatehouse of the original nunnery are adjacent to the new buildings, home to Anglican monks and nuns.

10.0 RIGHT in West Malling (see Route 32 for more details of the village) into the High Street. Exit to roundabout where RIGHT onto A20 and LEFT at next onto A228, signposted Birling, towards the M20. Unfortunately the shorter and much quieter route is one-way.

11.3 LEFT and following signs RIGHT at crossroads by Grange Park College entrance, before crossing M20 and reaching Birling.

12.5 RIGHT at T-Junction past church then LEFT into Stangate Road, signposted Harvel/Meopham/Holly Hill for a frontal assault on the North Downs. This is a long climb through open fields at first before becoming more enclosed and steeper after crossing the Pilgrims Way.

14.3 RIGHT, signposted Holly Hill where, at 643 feet, there is an open space and a fine place for picnics. Follow past car-park and Holly Hill House onto unmetalled by-way. FORK LEFT and descend through woods. This section can be muddy after wet weather, though there is nothing impassable.

15.3 RIGHT at T-Junction onto metalled road past Great Buckland.

Close by is the tiny isolated Norman church of Dode. This village will not be found on the map for it disappeared in the 14th Century, its population wiped out by the Black Death. The house of God was built of more enduring materials than those of its congregation.

15.7 STRAIGHT ON at junction down long gradual descent along beautiful tree lined lane. OS LR 178. At next junction STRAIGHT ON again before turning RIGHT, signposted Cuxton and continue down long hill.

17.8 LEFT at crossroads by The White Hart PH at Cuxton onto A228,

LEFT onto cycle path which rejoins main road later on. After crossing the railway, cross M2 before turning RIGHT, signposted Rochester/Borstal Cycle Way over the Medway on the left side of the motorway bridge.

The Medway always presented an obstacle to pilgrims heading to Canterbury and various crossing points have been suggested including Cuxton and Aylesford. Now the river can be crossed in style on this modern concrete bridge, with fine views down to Rochester.

21.1   RIGHT at T-Junction and pass under the motorway then LEFT towards Burham across open country.

23.6   LEFT again at crossroads into by-way, Hill Road. Follow unmetalled climb through woods before RIGHT onto the North Downs Way. This is level and rideable enough apart from very large puddles after heavy rain. From Burham Hill Farm it becomes metalled. Pass the entrance to the isolated Robin Hood Inn and Blue Bell Hill where there is a picnic site and an opportunity to enjoy the fine views from a height of 610 feet. Then cross the bridge over the A229.

26.3   CROSS over the old road by The Upper Bell Inn. Swing round to the right before descending steep twisting hill to Lower Warren Road. Here RIGHT at T-Junction and follow to A229.

27.5   LEFT, signposted Maidstone. Join dual carriageway very briefly.

Going straight on through the underpass leads eventually to Kit's Coty House (EH), a prehistoric dolmen - two massive upright stones supporting a horizontal one. Not far away is Little Kit's Coty or the Countless Stones (EH) - supposedly because no two people can count them and arrive at the same answer. The Lower Bell Inn is here as well with an adjacent transport cafe which looked permanently shut at the time of writing.

27.9   LEFT, signposted Boxley then at T-Junction LEFT into Tylands Lane.

A left turn by the garage past rows of parked cars leads to the Pilgrims Way. This can be followed to link up with the route later on near Boarley. However at the time of writing it was a quagmire and impassable. Along here will be seen The White Horse Stone, another prehistoric megalith.
 Right into Tylands Lane leads to Tylands Barn, a restored 17th Century barn which is now a visitors centre with information on Kent's wildlife. It also has a cafe and shop and is open Tuesday to Sunday plus Bank Holidays, 10.00 to

17.00 all year except Christmas and January.

28.9   LEFT at crossroads, signposted Boarley, road closed.

On private land straight ahead are the remains of Boxley Abbey, an enormous stone-built tithe barn together with surrounding walls. At one time it was the most important monastic settlement in Kent and pilgrims flocked there to see the Boxley 'Rood'. This was a life sized model of Christ on the cross, and secretly operated by the monks, it could be made to pull faces of divine displeasure if an offering was not enough and display corresponding grace if satisfactory. Eventually, along with the abbey, it was ruthlessly destroyed by Henry VIII.

Continue up road which becomes a steep metalled path after Boarley Farm to reach The Pilgrims Way.

29.7   RIGHT and at bend RIGHT again before continuing STRAIGHT ON at junction, again onto The Pilgrims Way. This is a beautiful undulating road with views to Maidstone on one side and woods the other.

31.7   CROSS A249 with care at Detling and follow to the right. At The Cock Horse PH RIGHT again to continue down hill.

32.0   STRAIGHT ON at Hockers Lane and cross M20. RIGHT at crossroads then at roundabout RIGHT again, signposted crematorium.

33.7   STRAIGHT ON an next roundabout onto A249 - a recent road alteration, and at next STRAIGHT ON by The Chiltern Hundreds Inn into Penenden Heath Road on the outskirts of Maidstone. LEFT immediately into Heathfield Road.

35.5   LEFT at crossroads into Boxley Road and at prison RIGHT at T-Junction into Lower Boxley Road before LEFT at roundabout, signposted Town Centre.

36.3   LEFT following one-way at The Hare & Hounds PH again signposted Town Centre. RIGHT, signposted Chatham. Push across pedestrian crossing to station to avoid being swept past by the one way system.

36.5   END

34   ACROSS TO CHARING

From the large village green at Bearsted it is not long before the North Downs and Pilgrims Way. From Hollingbourne the steep scarp face is tackled to the high point of 628 feet. It is then a gently descending lane for several miles before Doddington and Newnham. Then the balance switches the other way with a long gradually ascending wooded lane up a dry valley. Down into Charing, with its half-timbered houses and along the foot of the hills to Lenham and Harrietsham. Leeds Castle is close to the lane to Broomfield and can be seen from the ridge. Then into the midst of the Kent orchards near Otham and past 14th Century Stoneacre before Bearsted is reached.

Hilly except for the portion between Charing and Harrietsham. The steepest climb is from Hollingbourne The lanes in this part of the North Downs are very quiet and make for excellent cycling.

Maps	OS LR 178, 189, 188.
Distance	37.4 miles with 0.7 miles off-road some of which is metalled.
Start/Finish	Bearsted Station.

Railway access

Bearsted has a half hourly service on slow and fast trains between London Victoria, Maidstone East and Ashford.

Hollingbourne, Harrietsham, Lenham & Charing are all on the same line and served by services which are are usually hourly.

Places to see

Village green - Bearsted.

Village, church & Eyhorne Manor - Hollingbourne.

Doddington Place Gardens.

Village, Archbishop's Palace - Charing.

Lenham village.

Leeds Castle - Broomfield.

Stoneacre (NT) - Otham.

Refreshments

Cafe - for visitors to Doddington Place Gardens.

Happy Eater - on by-pass, Charing.

Armada Tea Rooms - Charing.

Cafe - for visitors to Leeds Castle.

ACROSS TO CHARING

34 ACROSS TO CHARING

0.0   LEFT from Bearsted Station then LEFT under railway towards the North Downs. **OS LR 178.**

Bearsted is now a suburb of Maidstone. But the old houses and oasts around the village green manage to give it a rural atmosphere. Cricket has been played here for over 250 years, before that the less peaceful pursuit of warfare with skirmishes between Roundheads and Cavaliers and an even earlier fixture between Wat Tylers peasant army and the local gentry.

Continue up hill to The Black Horse PH at Thurnham.

1.4   RIGHT onto The Pilgrims Way, following sign to Hollingbourne.

4.4   LEFT at T-Junction by The Dirty Habit PH, signposted B2163 Bredgar/Sittingbourne and 1 in 8 climb to the crest of the Downs.

Hollingbourne certainly has its share of old houses. Inside the church is a replica of the altar cloth made by the four daughters of Lady Elizabeth Culpepper in the 17th Century. Right down at the bottom of the village near the A20 is Eyhorne Manor, a 15th Century half timbered house. The garden and collection of historic laundry implements is open to the public, afternoons from Easter to September, weekends and Bank Holidays as well as Monday to Friday in August.

5.4   RIGHT at top of hill and follow signs to Ringlestone and Doddington. Pass the isolated Ringlestone pub and enjoy a long gradual descent.

10.3 STRAIGHT ON through Doddington and still gradually downhill past Doddington Place Gardens to Newnham.

These Edwardian gardens cover over ten acres. There is a gift shop and tea rooms. Open April to September, Wednesdays and Bank Holiday Mondays, 11.00 to 18.00 and on Sundays as well in May.

12.1 SECOND RIGHT after church at Newnham, signposted Eastling and climb hill along narrow and very attractive lane. RIGHT at T-Junction, signposted Otterden into Eastling with its good crop of half timbered houses.

13.1 LEFT at The Carpenters Arms, signposted Throwley. Climb hill. Pass Yew hedges then descend hill.

14.8 RIGHT at T-Junction at Hockley, signposted Throwley Forstal/ Stalisfield church. **OS LR 189.** Join Route 35 from Faversham here.

Follow up long gradual downland climb along road lined with small trees and across common land In some places hedges have been grubbed up to create a very exposed landscape, particularly when cycling against the wind. Pass the isolated Stalisfield Church.

17.9   RIGHT at T-Junction, before LEFT at Hawk's Nest and after Crowshole Farm, LEFT, signposted Charing before RIGHT down The Wynd. This is a very steep twisting descent.

19.1   RIGHT at T-Junction onto main road A252 (CARE). LEFT while descending hill, signposted Village Centre, into Charing. Straight on along the main road is a Happy Eater.

Well worth lingering here. Once an important staging post close to the Pilgrims Way, heavy traffic no longer thunders past the half timbered houses and Georgian frontages of Charing. Henry VIII, on his way to the famous summit with Emperor Charles V at The Field of the Cloth of Gold, stayed at the Archbishop's Palace, the remains of which stand next to the parish church. In the main street are The Armada Tea Rooms.

19.8   CROSS A20, signposted Smarden/Pluckley and the railway by the station. Then RIGHT by the shop and follow the sign to Charing Heath.

21.6   SECOND RIGHT after the pub, signposted Lenham then LEFT, signposted Lenham Heath and, after the village, cycle along a lane which still enjoys a measure of rural tranquillity despite only being a stones throw from the M20. The noise of the traffic signifies a different and restless world not so far away. This area is an important transport corridor to be joined in a few years by the Channel Tunnel rail link.

24.4   RIGHT near The White Horse Inn, signposted Lenham then RIGHT again at T-Junction into Headcorn Road. Continue into village.

Lenham is another very attractive village. Around the cobbled square are grouped many timbered houses. Remove the parked cars and the modern shop frontages and one could well be back in another age.

25.5   LEFT into Maidstone Road by The Red Lion PH then LEFT at T-Junction on A20. Follow to garage then RIGHT into Dickley Lane, past the Marley Floors establishment into Harrietsham where STRAIGHT ON at junction after church. Pass under railway.

27.5   RIGHT at crossroads onto A20, then RIGHT, signposted West Street Harrietsham to continue along the old main road out of the village. Practically rejoining A20 keep straight on onto other slip road.

28.3   RIGHT into Goddington Lane then LEFT at T-Junction into Holm
        Mill Lane. Again just before A20 RIGHT into Forstal Lane and LEFT
        at T-Junction. **OS LR 188** . Continue to A20 and pass under M20.

29.8   SECOND LEFT, signposted Broomfield.

By carrying straight on the entrance to Leeds Castle can be reached. Dubbed
'The loveliest castle in the world' it stands on two islands in a lake formed
from the River Len. From a stone fortress Henry VIII transformed it into a
palace. From the interior tapestries through to the gardens there is a lot to
see including a most unusual museum of antique dog collars. Refreshments
for visitors. Open every day 10.00 to 17.00 (15.00 in winter).

> Follow lane from which distant views of the castle can be obtained,
> past a private entrance, before descending steep hill (beware of wild
> fowl) to cross the River Len. Climb through Broomfield to ridge top.

30.8   RIGHT at top of hill. The castle can again be seen in the distance.
        RIGHT at T-Junction then at crossroads LEFT where there is another
        private entrance to the castle grounds. Continue into Leeds.

32.1   LEFT at T-junction in village onto B2163 by The George Inn then
        RIGHT, and following signs for Otham LEFT at T-Junction then
        RIGHT into Avery Lane where a fine row of poplars helps to shield
        the orchards from the elements.

34.1   STRAIGHT ON at junction then RIGHT at T-Junction into Otham
        and RIGHT onto public bridleway before the village proper. This
        rather bumpy but rideable track leads past Stoneacre (NT). The view
        is magnificent from up here. With Autumn colours its more
        reminiscent of the Lake District than Kent.

Stoneacre is a small half-timbered 15th Century Yeomans house. Falling into
disuse it was restored to something like its original state in the 1920s and
later presented to the National Trust. Much material used in the fittings was
actually recycled from other old houses but this original dwelling is
nevertheless well worth a visit. Open April to end of October, Wednesdays
and Saturdays, 14.00 to 18.00.

> Follow, now metalled, road to T-Junction.

35.2   RIGHT to descend hill past waterfall and climb the other side. LEFT
        at T-Junction onto A20 and follow into the new part of Bearsted
        where, by The Kentish Yeoman PH RIGHT into Yeoman Lane. LEFT
        at the T-Junction at The Harvester pub by village green and follow
        sign to station.

37.4   END

35 THE WYE RIDE

F aversham is an ancient port lying at the head of a sheltered creek. But it is into the North Downs that this route heads, through Ospringe and gradually up those long wooded valleys that are such a feature of this area. From a height of 556 feet it does not take long to descend to Westwell and the valley of the Great Stour. It is then through Wye and over the river before another excursion into the North Downs. It is steep and rolling through Crundale and up to Sole Street then mainly down through Denge Wood. Chilham follows before cycling into orchard country to Boughton Hill and eventually back to Faversham.

A hilly ride but the trend is long and gradual, the steepest bits being around Crundale. Very quiet roads over the North Downs. Difficult to believe that this is part of the crowded South East.

Maps	OS LR 178, 189, 179.
Distance	36.2 miles. Of this 0.5 mile is off road.
Start/Finish	Faversham Station.

Railway access

Faversham is an important junction so is served by trains from London Victoria to Dover via Canterbury East or to Ramsgate. It is normally a half hourly service.

Wye & Chilham are not on the Faversham line but could be used as alternative start/finish points. As escape points it is best to disembark at Canterbury West and ride across to the East station to get back to Faversham.

Places to see

Maison Dieu (EH) - Ospringe.

Village & church - Westwell.

Town & church - Wye.

Castle Gardens, church, village - Chilham.

Mount Ephraim Gardens - Boughton Street.

Fleur de Lis Heritage Centre, Shepherd Neame Brewery, Chart Gunpowder Mill - and much more in Faversham.

Refreshments

Cafes & pubs - at the station and elsewhere in Faversham.

Cafes & pubs - wide choice in Wye.

Cafe & Copper Kettle - at the Castle for visitors and in the village square - Chilham.

Cafe - Mount Ephraim Gardens.

THE WYE RIDE

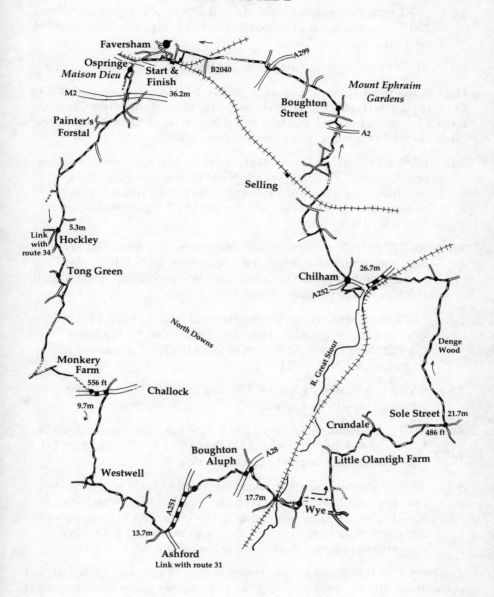

35 THE WYE RIDE

0.0   LEFT from Faversham Station. **OS LR 178.** RIGHT into Briton Road, LEFT at T-Junction into School Road/Cambridge Road and LEFT at next into Ospringe Road.

0.8   RIGHT at T-Junction onto A2 by The Ship Inn. LEFT into Water Lane.

Here in the main street of Ospringe stands the Maison Dieu (EH) a 13th Century pilgrims hostel where royalty once stayed on its way to the Continent. Later it became a hospital. Inside is an exhibition about Ospringe in Roman times. To view telephone the key keeper 0634 842852.

1.1   LEFT into Vicarage Lane before church by fine half timbered house and climb hill. The vineyard/hopfield on the right gives the view to the church something of a European flavour. RIGHT at staggered crossroads and before Painter's Forstal LEFT, signposted Belmont/ Throwley/Stalisfield.

2.8   RIGHT past Churchman's Farm, signposted Stalisfield. Road climbs long and gradually through the woods onto the North Downs passing a house on the left known as New York. Keep straight on at Hockley where you meet Route 34.

5.3   LEFT, signposted Throwley Forstal at this junction. **OS LR 189** . Continue on long gradual climb between wooded hedgerows through Tong Green. At bottom of short hill RIGHT across open downland. CONTINUE to right.

6.9   OVER crossroads, signposted Charing then LEFT at next after coppiced wood and immediately LEFT at T-Junction.

8.5   RIGHT by Monkery Cottages and follow this beautiful narrow tree-lined lane to T-Junction with A252 then LEFT by Challock sign. At 556 feet this is the highest point of the ride.

9.7   RIGHT, at crossroads signposted Westwell and it is mostly downhill crossing both North Downs Way and Pilgrims Way. After sign, RIGHT then LEFT by crossroads at The Wheel Inn, signposted Kennington/Boughton Lees/Wye. Pass church and old mill now converted to a house. Follow along foot of Downs.

The church of this pretty village seems to be full of columns, round and octagonal with two more stopping the rare vaulted Early English chancel from falling down.

13.7   LEFT at T-Junction, signposted Ashford then LEFT at next onto

A251, signposted Challock, by the entrance to Eastwell Park.

14.6   RIGHT on green after Boughton Aulph sign, not Boughton Lees as shown on map, for North Downs Way. CONTINUE over staggered crossroads onto Pilgrims Way. Follow narrow twisting road then RIGHT at T-junction, signposted Wye and at next LEFT onto A28.

16.1   RIGHT at staggered crossroads, and follow sign past station, over level crossing and over the Great Stour into Wye. LEFT into Church Street then RIGHT into High Street by church and continue past college buildings.

Streets like Church Street where the houses are of various sizes, yet all in harmony, are never boring The church is unusual with a classical style chancel in complete contrast to the rest of the medieval building. This was due to the spire falling down on top of it in 1696 and a replacement was built in the reign of Queen Anne. The college was founded by a former Archbishop of Canterbury, John Kempe, as a school for priests, After the dissolution it became a grammar school and today it is Wye College of Agriculture, part of the University of London. There are pubs and restaurants in the town.

17.7   LEFT, signposted Crundale then RIGHT onto bridleway, signposted North Downs Way. Follow through college grounds.

18.3   LEFT at T-Junction then RIGHT at Little Olantigh Farm and follow sign to Crundale. Quite a steep climb over a shoulder of the North Downs with an even steeper drop the other side.

20.5   STRAIGHT on at junction, signposted Crundale Church from which there is a fine view. Drop into a valley bottom with a steep climb the other side but it is worth lingering on this beautiful wooded road.

21.7   RIGHT at T-Junction and continue past The Compasses Inn at Sole Street. Then next LEFT at T-Junction, signposted Penny Pot. Follow through Denge Wood and down long hill past Upper Mystole Park Farm.

25.3   LEFT at T-Junction, signposted Chilham. Follow very quiet lane due to level crossing over railway being permanently locked. Bicycles can be pushed through the side gates. But TAKE GREAT CARE.

28.7   LEFT onto A28 then RIGHT onto A252, signposted Charing/ Maidstone then LEFT into Chilham.

Villages like Chilham just seem to be too perfect. The square is lined with half timbered Tudor and Jacobean houses and also fills up with visitors at weekends. Little remains of the original castle, the name being transferred to the house built in 1616. Only the gardens are open to the public and on summer weekends knights in armour can be seen jousting, along with falconry displays. Tea room for visitors. Open April to October daily 11.00 to 17.00. On the other side of the square is the airy spacious church. Also in the centre of the village is The Copper Kettle restaurant where teas can be had.

27.6   CONTINUE down Church Hill, Pilgrims Way, by The White Horse Inn. CROSS over A252, signposted. Selling Continue up long gradual hill through orchards. **OS LR 179.**

29.4   LEFT at T-junction, signposted Selling then RIGHT, signposted Winterbourne. After more orchards LEFT at T-Junction.

30.8   RIGHT at T-Junction, signposted Boughton/Dunkirk then RIGHT, marked as No Through Road. Follow to A2 which is on high embankment. Climb to subway either up steps or on zig-zag path. Reverse procedure the other side. There CONTINUE on road and follow to crossroads where RIGHT to Boughton Hill.

32.1   LEFT by The Woodmans Hall on old A2 and immediately RIGHT, signposted Staplestreet. Pass Mount Ephraim Gardens.

This is a seven acre hillside garden featuring daffodils and rhododendrons along with a lake and woodland walks. There is a craft centre as well as a cafeteria for visitors. Open April to September, daily 13.00 to 18.00 and from 11.00 on Bank Holiday weekends.

33.8   LEFT before A299, signposted Faversham and cross this busy road by bridge then LEFT at crossroads, signposted Faversham.

35.3   LEFT at T-Junction over railway, signposted B2040, Faversham. **OS LR 178.** LEFT by The Market Inn then RIGHT into William Street . LEFT into St Mary Road by The Royal William pub. Follow into Station Road.

36.2   END

If there is time it is worth looking round Faversham which has over 400 listed buildings and a cared for appearance. It was a port, ships were built here and powder made for the guns aboard those ships. Close to the railway station is the Fleur de Lis Heritage Centre which is an audio-visual and museum display of the towns history. It is open daily Monday to Saturday and on summer Sundays, 10.00 to 16.00. The Shepherds Neame brewery can be visited by appointment (0795 532206) while the restored Chart Gunpowder mills are supposed to be unique now in this country. Open April to October, weekends and Bank Holidays, 14.00 to 17.00.

36 TWO ISLANDS TOUR

From Newington in orchard country this route runs along the foreshore for a while before crossing the tidal River Swale to reach the Isle of Sheppey by Kingsferry Bridge. It then does a clockwise circuit of the island, visiting Queenborough and Sheerness in the west before climbing to its highest point at just under 250 feet at Minster Abbey. From here it is a gradual easterly run downhill to Warden before a southward dog-leg onto the low lying Isle of Harty to reach the 'Ferry Inn' on the Swale where marshland and mudflats predominate. With a short detour to St Thomas' church it is back the same way until reaching the road to Eastchurch and completing the circle by crossing Kingsferry Bridge.

This is an easy route with long flat stretches and no major hills. The route is somewhat exposed and could be more difficult in windy conditions.

Map	OS LR 178.
Distance	41.8 miles. 1.9 miles, in two sections, off-road and rideable.
Start/Finish	Newington Station.

Railway access

Newington is served half hourly from London Victoria or Faversham from Monday - Saturday and hourly on Sundays.

Sittingbourne provides a service to Sherness on which line Swale is a request stop. This service is again half hourly Monday to Saturday and hourly on Sundays.

Places to see

Church - Queenborough.

Minster Abbey & local museum in the gatehouse.

St Thomas' Church - Harty.

Aviation Memorial Wall - Eastchurch.

National Nature Reserve - Swale.

RSPB reserve - Elmley marshes.

Refreshments

Cafes & pubs - Sheerness and Minster.

Ferry Inn - serves food and teas, Harty.

Cafe - at Iwade just off A259 at right turn to Lower Halstow, not open Sundays.

TWO ISLANDS TOUR

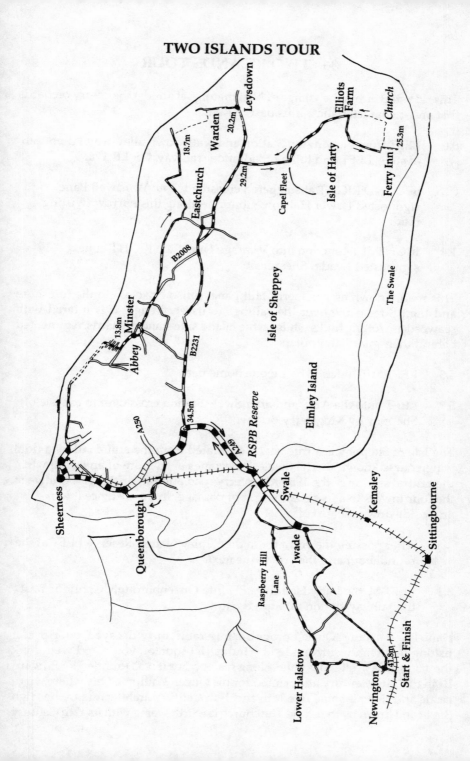

36 TWO ISLANDS TOUR

This ride starts from the village of Newington, set amidst the cherry orchards that are so characteristic of this part of Kent.

0.0   LEFT from Newington Station and walk down alley-way. At bottom of steps LEFT and follow road under railway. **OS LR 178.**

0.3   SECOND RIGHT at staggered crossroads into Wardwell Lane, signposted Lower Halstow. Continue along this narrow twisting road.

1.4   RIGHT at T-Junction into Vicarage Lane then RIGHT at next, signposted Iwade/Sheerness.

This road, known as Raspberry Hill Lane, runs very close to the foreshore and high tides come over the saltings to its very edge. It is littered with seaweed are rotting hulks while on the inland side stand orchards, regimented behind their guardian poplars

4.5   LEFT at T-Junction by mobile home park.

5.3   LEFT onto the A249 and after Swale Station cross over to the Isle of Sheppey by Kingsferry Bridge.

The Isle of Sheppey is a true island separated from the mainland by a tidal watercourse known as The Swale. It becomes even more of an island when the central section of the 1959 Kingsferry road and rail bridge rises between the four towers to allow a ship right of passage. In the distance it looks like an upside down table.

After passing the entrance to the Elmley Nature Reserve LEFT at the roundabout and then on to the next.

8.1   LEFT by the Lady Hamilton PH into Queenborough. Continue past the railway station through the town.

Daniel Defoe found Queenborough a 'miserable, dirty, decayed, poor, pitiful fishing town' and, surrounded by industrial squalor, you could well think the same today. Yet looks belie a long history. For it was founded by Edward III in the 14th Century and named for his Queen Philippa. Once there was a castle and there is some fine 18th and 19th Century architecture in the High Street and down by the creek. The church is worth seeing with its 17th Century painted ceiling (0795 663553 for opening times).

9.4   LEFT at roundabout for Sheerness Docks. Follow road round through industrial area. Beware the ungated level crossing with its awkwardly placed railway lines.

Surveyed by Samuel Pepys the port of Sheerness dates from the reign of Charles II and became an important naval base. In 1797 the Nore Mutiny took place here, a protest against the savage conditions on board ship. It was ruthlessly put down. Preserved in alcohol, Nelsons body was landed here after Trafalgar. After years of decay Sheerness has been revitalised by the vehicle ferry to Vlissingen and a large number of lorries trundle in and out of the docks.

10.8   RIGHT at mini-roundabout and continue along High Street and Bridge Street to Sheerness-on-Sea, the holiday resort part of the town. A good choice of cafes can be found here, particularly in high season. KEEP LEFT at the clock tower and follow the signs to Minster along a road that runs very close to the shore beneath a high sea- wall. However this service is due to cease in 1994, putting the ports future under strain.

12.9   CONTINUE straight on at corner by restaurant along a road which affords reasonable views of the sea. Follow it inland past the Beach Hotel.

13.8   LEFT at T-Junction to the High Street and Minster Abbey.

Minster Abbey stands on the highest point of the Isle of Sheppey with fine views across the flat lands to the estuary and North Downs. Founded in 664 it is one of the oldest churches of England. Amongst the monuments inside is that of Robert de Shurland, Lord Warden of the Cinque Ports in the 14th Century, and his horse, Grey Dolphin. Legend has it that de Shurland died from an infection received by kicking the skull of his faithful steed who he had previously slain on the beach to get round the prophecy of a witch. The Abbey is usually open on weekdays from mid-May to early September (0795 873185).

In the gatehouse is housed a small museum devoted to the Isle of Sheppey which with the exception of Thursdays is open afternoons from mid-July to mid September.

From Abbey continue round one-way system past Highlander and Bethnel Congregational Church.

15.2 LEFT into Plough Road before water tower, signposted Plough Inn and continue along open road which again gives fine views.

16.7 LEFT, signposted Warden Road/caravan parks. Continue past caravan sites and pub to pass monastery and chapel.

18.7 RIGHT onto bridleway past Warden Springs Caravan Park and continue along bumpy track into housing development.

19.4 LEFT at T-Junction and RIGHT at the next in Warden. Continue past pub and holiday village.

20.2 RIGHT at T-Junction onto Leysdown Road (B2231).

21.2 LEFT signposted Ferry Inn. Continue along delightful open lane over the narrow Capel Fleet onto the Isle of Harty and follow to the Ferry Inn.

Harty is really a separate island. Until recently the whole area was known as the Isles of Sheppey, to include the main island and the smaller ones of Harty and Elmley. With the wide open skies and feeling of spaciousness there is a remarkable feeling of remoteness about the area. The ferry to the mainland near Faversham no longer runs and with its closure the three miles of travelling involved has increased to almost thirty. Such is progress! Meals including afternoon teas can be obtained at the Ferry Inn.

Eastwards stretches The Swale National Nature Reserve. The large areas of salt marshes, mudflats and creeks provide feeding and roosting areas for large numbers of wildfowl and waders and a total of 216 different species of bird have been recorded here. There are marsh frogs and some unusual jet black rabbits at mid-summer. A unique aspect of Sheppeys wildlife is that it is the only place in the country where scorpions can be found in the wild. They are a harmless variety introduced over one hundred years ago.

25.3 RETRACE your wheel-marks from the Ferry Inn and at next T-Junction RIGHT to Sayes Court and the church of St Thomas.

Unsignposted and only shown as a small cross on the map, this must be one of the remotest churches in Britain. No electricity, lit by oil lamps or just plain natural light and no sound except for wind or the cries of sea-birds - a place to get away from the hustle and bustle of city life. At one time the small barrel organ played three hymns and the knights still joust amongst the carvings of the 14th Century wooden chest.

CONTINUE from church along unmade track to Elliotts Farm and back along the road you came in on.

29.2   LEFT at T-Junction onto B2231 signposted Eastchurch.

This road now by-passes Eastchurch. On the wall opposite All Saints Church are carved replicas of early flying machines, for much of the pioneering work in aviation took place here. Charles Rolls was killed nearby in 1910 and Lord Brabazon succeeded in the first powered flight over a mile. Short Brothers also built the first aircraft factory in England.

After Eastchurch continue past the Elm Tree Inn until reaching roundabout.

34.5   LEFT at roundabout onto A259 and recross Kingsferry Bridge.

Before leaving Sheppey, the road passes the entrance to Elmley Marshes, a nature reserve run by the Royal Society for the Protection of Birds. Important as a wildfowl refuge and as many as 30,000 birds may be seen at a time. Restricted opening times.

36.5   RIGHT after bridge and Swale Station, signposted Ridham Dock
       You can either return by the way you came or follow this road to Iwade.

37.7   RIGHT at T-Junction onto A249 again and continue into Iwade, then RIGHT after church, signposted Lower Halstow. There is a cafe here but is not open Sundays. Continue to Newington.

41.4   LEFT at T-Junction signposted Rainham/Sittingbourne then RIGHT after railway bridge into alleyway to station.

41.8   END

USEFUL ADDRESSES

BIKE 1
P O Box 105, Fleet, Hampshire, GU13 8YR (0252) 624022.
Bike 1 organise one day cycle rides each month in a different county. Routes to suit all abilities are waymarked, route sheets are provided, along with refreshments, first-aid and mechanical back-up. All you have to do is to ride your bike.

CYCLISTS TOURING CLUB
Cotterell House, 69 Meadrow, Godalming, Surey, GU7 3HS (0383) 417217.
The CTC is the main national organisation promoting cycling as a means of transport and travel. It campaigns on behalf of cyclists, gives expert legal aid, assistance on technical problems, specialist insurance including free third party, as well as a magazine, handbook and touring information. There are holidays abroad for members as well as 200 local groups.

ENGLISH HERITAGE
Membership Department, PO Box 1BB, London, W1A 1BB 071 973 3400.
English Heritage, sponsored by the Department of National Heritage, is responsible for the maintainance and up-keep of many of our historic buildings. Membership entitles you to free admission, along with a handbook and quarterly magazine.

LONDON CYCLING CAMPAIGN
3 Stamford Street, London, SE1 9NT 071 928 7220.
The LCC is concerned with the needs of cyclists in and around London. It provides a cycling lobby in Parliament, free third party insurance and legal aid, access to good insurance for you and your bicycle, discounts at many bike shops, cycle maintenance classes, a bikemate scheme to improve cycling skills, advice on all aspects of cycling, weekend and evening rides, and a magazine to go with it.

NATIONAL TRUST
PO Box 39, Bromley, Kent, BR1 1NH (for membership).
The National Trust is a charity and the largest private landowner and conservation society in Britain. By joining you get free admission to the many properties they run as well as a handbook and magazine.

SUSTRANS
35 King Street, Bristol, BS1 4DZ (0272) 268893.
Sustrans is a charity which designs and builds cycle paths, often on disused railways and alongside rivers. The Cuckoo Trail in this book is one of their achievements and if you want to see more of the same, then they are worth supporting.

TWO WHEELS

BREATHING SPACES - Bike Rides Within Easy Reach of London - Patrick Field.
24 bike rides, easily reached from London by car or by train. A great mix of on and off-road routes, all day rides for mountain bikers and tourers, leisurely country lanes and family rides. With route maps, details of places to see and refreshment stops. *Pbk, 170pp, £7.99.*

COUNTY RIDES - Thirty Rides in Thirteen Counties - Simon Shaw & Anna Pond, Bike 1 Bicycle Tours.
This collection of 30 rides will allow all cyclists to explore the glory of the English countryside - from beginners looking for a leisurely ride in the countryside to dedicated enthusiasts searching for mileage. With detailed maps and easy to follow directions. *Pbk, 168pp, £8.99.*

Haute-Savoie & Mont Blanc - Mountain Bike Guide - Cassani & Lamory.
Discover one of the best kept mountain biking secrets in Europe - from the southern shore of Lake Geneva to the Mont Blanc area. A selection of 50 routes from challenging high level rides, to superb forest tracks and gentle low level excursions. *Pbk, 192pp, £8.99.*

GET LOST - Off-Road Adventures With A Bicycle Within Easy Reach Of London - Patrick Field.
An off-road follow up to Breathing Spaces, packed with great escapes from London and the suburbs to the countryside. *Pbk, 192pp, £7.99.*

Available from all good bookshops or direct from the publisher plus £1 postage & packing per copy. Two Heads Publishing, 12A Franklyn Suite, The Priory, Haywards Heath, West Sussex, RH16 3LB.